CO-DEPENDENCE

Healing The Human Condition

The New Paradigm For
Helping Professionals
And People In Recovery

Charles L. Whitfield, M.D.

Health Communications, Inc.
Deerfield Beach, Florida

Charles L. Whitfield, M.D.
Box 420487
Atlanta, GA 30342
404-843-4300

Library of Congress Cataloging-in-Publication Data

Whitfield, Charles L.
Co-dependence: healing the human condition: the new paradigm for helping professionals and people in recovery / by Charles L. Whitfield.
p. cm.
Includes bibliographical references.
ISBN 1-55874-150-X
1. Co-dependence (Psychology) 2. Rehabilitation I. Title.
RC569.5.C63W469 1991 91-8606
158'.1—dc20 CIP

ISBN 1-55874-150-X

Publisher: Health Communications, Inc.
3201 S.W. 15th Street
Deerfield Beach, FL 33442-8190

Special Thanks and Acknowledgments

I give special thanks to the following people who read drafts of this manuscript and who gave me constructive feedback: Barbara Harris, John White, Sally Merchant, Rebecca Peres, Ralph Raphael, Stanislav Grof, Christina Grof, Jed Diamond, Ken Richardson, Mary Richardson, Annie Dykins, Ed Green, Micky Whitfield, Judith Flanders, Herb Gravitz, David Berenson, Steven Wolin, Garrett O'Connor, Marie Stilkind, Lisa Moro, Eliana Gill, Martin Smith, Ray Giles, Pam Levin, and Mary Jackson. And to Mary Johnston for her excellent typing. Also thanks to the authors of the various definitions of co-dependence that are reproduced in Table 1.

Grateful acknowledgment to the following for permission to reprint some of their writing: To Timmen L. Cermak and the Johnson Institute for permission to reprint his diagnostic criteria for co-dependence; and to the fellowship of Co-Dependents Anonymous to reprint their list of characteristics of co-dependence. To Wayne Kritsberg for permission to reprint the Co-dependent Relationship Questionnaire from Wayne Kritsberg, Family Integration Systems. To Kenneth Ring and Christopher Rosing and the *Journal of Near Death Studies* for their permission to quote from their article, "The Omega Project: an empirical study of the NDE-prone personality" in vol. 8, no. 4, 1990, of the *Journal of Near Death Studies.* To the self-help fellowship of Alcoholics Anonymous for permission to reprint their Twelve Steps, as modified in the text.

And to all the writers, speakers and other recovering people in the movement for sharing their observations, strength and hope.

(The Twelve Steps are reprinted and adapted with permission of Alcoholics Anonymous World Services, Inc. Permission to reprint and adapt the Twelve Steps does not mean that AA has reviewed or approved the content of this publication, nor that AA agrees with the views expressed herein. AA is a program of recovery from alcoholism — use of the Twelve Steps in connection with programs and activities which are patterned after AA, but which address other problems, does not imply otherwise.)

The Twelve Steps of Alcoholics Anonymous

1. We admitted we were powerless over alcohol — that our lives had become unmanageable. 2. Came to believe that a Power greater than ourselves could restore us to sanity. 3. Made a decision to turn our will and our lives over to the care of God *as we understood Him.* 4. Made a searching and fearless moral inventory of ourselves. 5. Admitted to God, to ourselves and to another human being the exact nature of our wrongs. 6. Were entirely ready to have God remove all these defects of character. 7. Humbly asked Him to remove our shortcomings. 8. Made a list of all persons we had harmed, and became willing to make amends to them all. 9. Made direct amends to such people wherever possible, except when to do so would injure them or others. 10. Continued to take personal inventory and when we were wrong promptly admitted it. 11. Sought through prayer and meditation to improve our conscious contact with God, *as we understood Him,* praying only for knowledge of His will for us and the power to carry that out. 12. Having had a spiritual awakening as the result of these steps, we tried to carry this message to alcoholics, and to practice these principles in all our affairs.

Contents

List Of Tables And Figures

Tables

Figures

Part I

What Is Co-dependence?

1

Co-dependence: A Disease Of Lost Selfhood

Co-dependence is a disease of lost selfhood. It can mimic, be associated with, aggravate and even lead to many of the physical, mental, emotional or spiritual conditions that befall us in daily life.

We become co-dependent when we turn our responsibility for our life and happiness over to our ego (our false self) and to other people.

Co-dependents become so preoccupied with others that they neglect their True Self — who they really are.

In Table 1.1, I list 23 definitions of co-dependence at the end of this chapter. Clearly, co-dependence is not easily encapsulated. However, we can define it briefly as any suffering or dysfunction that is associated with or results from focusing on the needs and behavior of others.

When we focus so much outside of ourselves we lose touch with what is inside of us: our beliefs, thoughts, feelings, decisions, choices, experiences, wants, needs, sensations, intuitions, unconscious experiences, and even indicators of our physical functioning, such as heart rate and respiratory rate. These and more are part of an exquisite feedback system that we can call our *inner life.* (See Figure 1.1) Our inner life is a major part of our consciousness. And our consciousness is who we are: our True Self.

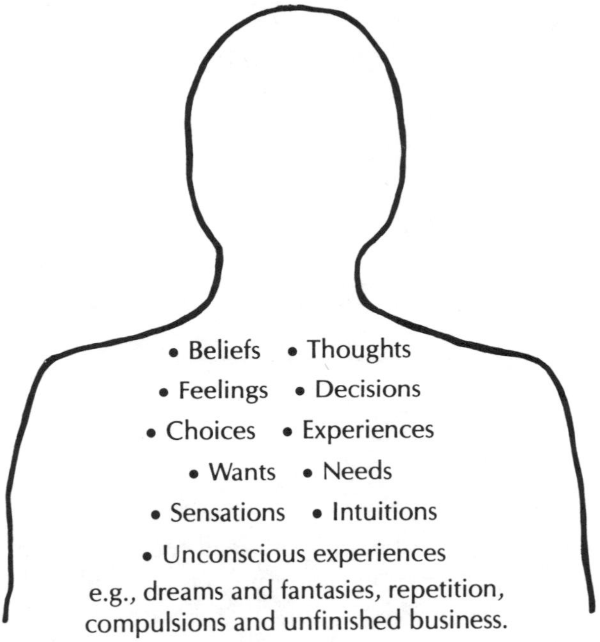

Figure 1.1. My Inner Life

Addiction To Looking Elsewhere

Co-dependence is the most common of all addictions: the addiction to looking elsewhere. We believe that something outside of ourselves — that is, outside of our True Self — can give us happiness and fulfillment. The "elsewhere" may be people, places, things, behaviors or experiences. Whatever it is, we may neglect our own selves for it.

Self-neglect alone is no fun, so we must get a payoff of some sort from focusing outward. The payoff is usually a reduction in painful feelings or a temporary increase in joyful feelings. But this feeling or mood alteration is predicated principally upon something or someone else, and not on our own authentic wants and needs.

The remedy sounds simple: We need a healthy balance of awareness of our inner life and our outer life. But such a healthy balance does not come automatically, especially in a world where nearly everyone is acting co-dependently most of the time.

In fact, we learn to be co-dependent from others around us. It is in this sense not only an addiction but a contagious or acquired illness. From the time we are born, we see co-dependent behavior modeled and taught by a seemingly endless string of important people: parents, teachers, siblings, friends, heroes and heroines. Co-dependence is reinforced by the media, government, organized religion and the helping professions. Co-dependence is fundamentally about disordered relationships. Those relationships include our relationship with our self, others and, if we choose, our Higher Power. One of our reasons for being is to get to know ourselves in a deeper, richer, and more profound way. We can do that only if we are truly in relationship with our selves, with others and with the God of our understanding.

In *Healing the Child Within* I said that co-dependence comes from trying to protect our delicate True Self (Child Within) from what may appear to be insurmountable forces outside ourselves[645]. But our True Self is a paradox. Not only is it sensitive, delicate and vulnerable, but it is also powerful. It is so powerful that, in a full recovery program for co-dependence, it heals through a process of self-responsibility and creativity that is often awesome to behold.

When our alive True Self goes into hiding, in order to please its parent figures and to survive, a false, co-dependent self emerges to take its place. We thus lose our awareness of our True Self to such an extent that we actually lose awareness of its existence. We lose contact with who we really are. Gradually, we begin to think we *are* that false self — so that it becomes a habit, and finally an addiction.

Co-dependence is not only the most common addiction, it is the base out of which all our other addictions and compulsions emerge. Underneath nearly every addiction and compulsion lies co-dependence. And what runs them is twofold: a sense of shame that our True Self is somehow defective or inadequate, combined with the innate and healthy drive of our True Self to realize and express itself. The addiction, compulsion or disorder becomes the manifestation of the erroneous notion that something outside ourself can make us happy and fulfilled.

Like other addictions and other disorders, co-dependence has been viewed as being an escape from the pain of everyday life. But on another level co-dependence and the adult child condition is a search for ourself and for the God of our understanding. When we find our True Self and experientially connect it to God, we are then free to relate to others in a healthy way, and thus to have fulfilling relationships with all three: self, others and God.

The Advantage Of Multiple Definitions And Dimensions

Some people — both inside and outside of the co-dependence and adult child field — have expressed concern that there is no single unified or widely accepted definition of co-dependence [428,707]. This is certainly understandable. But there are several clear advantages to having these multiple definitions.

Perhaps the strongest advantage is that having many definitions gives us a broader and deeper understanding of our lives on multiple levels. They also clarify our view of the human condition in all its dimensions.

The terms *co-dependence* and *adult child* have to do with our True Self and its interactions with its assistant the false self, and — more importantly — our True Self's relationship with its Higher Power. In this context, it is clear that these terms cannot be limited by simple boundaries of a single definition or set of diagnostic criteria. When we absolutize anything we use it inefficiently and run the risk of becoming addicted to it.

These terms teach us what we are *not* (a false self), what we can get free of (co-dependence and its unnecessary pain and suffering) and who we really are: our True Self in healthy relationship with itself, others and our Higher Power. Co-dependence is not a trivial or even glib reframing of the truths that we have discovered. Rather, as concept and movement it helps us identify, clarify, define, link and expand all that we have experienced and known from our past and present in our relationships.

Nearly all ideas that come from our inner life can be like a double-edged sword: They can be important or unimportant, helpful or harmful. They can be understood, grasped and used constructively, or misunderstood, discarded prematurely or used destructively. It is in this delicate balance where we may sometimes find ourselves, and in which we can comprehend the many dimensions of these ideas.

Pushing away or even reacting to such feelings as fear, shame and anger can block both our cognitive and experiential comprehension and understanding of words and ideas like co-dependence and adult child[611]. If we grew up in a dysfunctional family or have been in an unhealthy relationship or if we are hurting in any way now, it can be useful to allow ourselves to find out what might have happened, what went wrong, what darkness might be underneath. The way to the light is through the darkness. The way to get free is to work constructively through the pain. These concepts and this approach can give us a constructive way to do that work.

Using The Multiple Dimensions Of Co-dependence

Let's explore co-dependence further, its potential and actual meanings in some of its multiple dimensions (Figure 1.2). The terms *co-dependence* and *adult child* may be all of these: a disease and dis-ease, a condition, an educational tool, a psychological concept, a common dynamic, a metaphor, a movement and most important, a vehicle for healing.

Co-dependence is also a mode of surviving what may feel like an overwhelming situation — trying to grow up in an unsafe and mistreating family and environment. Finally, co-dependence is not who we really are, it is not our permanent identity. It is only an interim label, a temporary identification, a term that we can use to help us describe the truth of what really happened, what we really experienced and what we may still be experiencing.

We will explore these multiple dimensions throughout this book. Co-dependence provides us all — helping professionals and people in recovery — with a clearer and expanded way of describing the dynamic that underlies most neuroses, addictions and other disorders. It is the human condition.

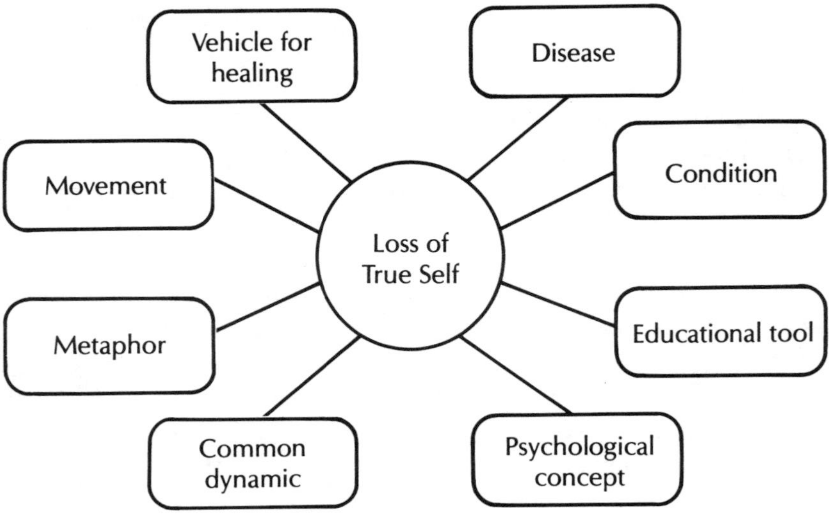

Figure 1.2. The Multiple Dimensions of Co-dependence.

Table 1.1. Some Definitions of Co-Dependence

1. A multidimensional (physical, mental, emotional and spiritual) condition manifested by any suffering and dysfunction that is associated with or due to focusing on the needs and behavior of others. It may be mild to severe and most people have it. It can mimic, be associated with and aggravate many physical, psychological and spiritual conditions. It develops from turning the responsibility for our life and happiness over to our ego (false self) and to others. It is treatable and recovery is possible. (Whitfield 1987, 1990). This is my expanded and current definition.

   The following definitions are in approximate order of year of publication:

2. An exaggerated dependent pattern of learned behaviors, beliefs and feelings that make life painful. It is a dependence on people and things outside the self, along with neglect of the self to the point of having little self-identity (Smalley, S., cited in Wegscheider-Cruse 1985).
3. Preoccupation and extreme dependence (emotionally, socially and sometimes physically) on a person or object. Eventually, this

dependence on another person becomes a pathological condition that affects the co-dependent in all other relationships. This may include . . . [people] who (1) are in a love or marriage relationship with an alcoholic; (2) have one or more alcoholic parents or grandparents; or (3) grew up in an emotionally repressive family. . . . It is a primary disease and a disease within every member of an alcoholic family (Wegscheider-Cruse 1985).

4. Ill health, maladaptive or problematic behavior that is associated with living with, working with or otherwise being close to a person with alcoholism (other chemical dependence or other chronic impairment). If affects not only individuals, but families, communities, businesses and other institutions, and even whole societies (Whitfield 1984, 1986). My early definition.
5. An emotional, psychological and behavioral pattern of coping that develops as a result of an individual's prolonged exposure to, and practice of, a set of oppressive rules — rules that prevent the open expression of feeling, as well as the direct discussion of personal and interpersonal problems (Subby 1984, 1987).
6. A personality disorder based on: a need to control in the face of serious adverse consequences; neglecting one's own needs; boundary distortions around intimacy and separation; enmeshment with certain dysfunctional people; and other manifestations such as denial, constricted feelings, depression and stress-related medical illness (paraphrased from Cermak 1986).
7. A disease that has many forms and expressions and that grows out of a disease process that . . . I call the addictive process . . . the addictive process is an unhealthy and abnormal awareness that leads to a process of nonliving which is progressive (Schaef 1986).
8. A stress-induced preoccupation with another's life, leading to maladaptive behavior (Mendenhall 1987).
9. Those self-defeating learned behaviors or character defects that result in a diminished capacity to initiate, or participate in, loving relationships (Larson 1987).
10. A set of maladaptive, compulsive behaviors learned by family members to survive in a family experiencing great emotional pain and stress . . . behaviors . . . passed on from generation to generation (Johnson Institute prior to 1987, quoted in Beattie 1987).
11. A person who has let someone else's behavior affect him or her, and is obsessed with controlling other people's behavior (Beattie 1987).

12. Individuals who organize their lives — decision-making, perceptions, beliefs, values — around someone or something else (Brown 1988).
13. A dysfunctional pattern of symptoms of adult children (see text and core issues) of living which emerges from our family of origin as well as our culture, producing arrested identity development, and resulting in an over-reaction to things outside of us and an under-reaction to things inside of us. Left untreated, it can deteriorate into an addiction (Friel and Friel 1988).
14. [A disease wherein a person has difficulty]: (1) experiencing appropriate levels of self-esteem; (2) setting functional boundaries; (3) owning and expressing their own reality; (4) taking care of their adult needs and wants; (5) experiencing and expressing their reality moderately (Mellody 1989).
15. A disease induced by child abuse, that leads to self-defeating relationships with the self and others. [It is primary, progressive, chronic, fatal and treatable.] (Snow and Willard 1989).
16. A psychological disorder caused by a failure to complete psychological autonomy . . . necessary for the development of the self, separate from parents (Weinhold and Weinhold 1989).
17. A pattern of painful dependence on compulsive behaviors and on approval from others in an attempt to find safety, self-worth and a sense of identity. Recovery is possible (*U.S. Journal* pre-conference forum 1989).
18. A stressful learned behavior associated with an unhealthy focus on the needs of others and/or attempting to take responsibility for or control the thoughts, feelings or behavior of others . . . motivated by a need for safety, acceptance and self-worth (Des Roches 1990).
19. A learned behavior, expressed by dependencies on people and things outside the self; these dependencies include neglecting and diminishing of one's own identity. The false self that emerges is often expressed through compulsive habits, addictions, and other disorders that further increase alienation from the person's true identity, fostering a sense of shame (National Council on Codependence 1990).
20. A maladaptive bonding within a family system. To survive psychologically and socially in this dysfunctional family, the child adopts patterns of thinking, acting and feeling that at first dull the pain but finally are self-negating in themselves. These patterns become

internalized and form an essential part of the personality and world view of the individual. The child continues to practice these self-destructive patterns of thinking, behaving and feeling in adulthood and in so doing recreates over and over again the bonding in which the destructive patterns originated (Kitchens 1990).

21. A particular form of unconscious loving . . . an agreement between people to stay locked in unconscious patterns. . . . an unconscious conspiracy between two or more people to feel bad and limit each other's potential, (wherein) the freedom of each is limited. Inequality is a hallmark (Hendricks 1990).

22. . . . an often-fatal disease of emotional confusion, marked by severe alienation from one's own feelings. Living for and through others, due to the inadequate development of self-love as a true basis for loving others. Variously defined as: (1) the addiction to living for others at the expense of one's own development; (2) the substitution of adaptation for honest self-expression; (3) the vicious cycle of using and blaming that arises when we make others responsible for what we feel and do; (4) the mechanism of control/controlling that locks people into futile dependencies and impossible demands; (5) abuse and discounting disguised in the attitudes and gestures of love, loyalty, devotion, caretaking, people pleasing. Any combination of the above. (Lash 1990).

23. A spiritual condition, the shadow side of our love nature. . . . a "dis-ease" of unequal relationships being acted out, of giving our power away (Small 1991).

2

A Brief History Of Co-dependence

The principles of co-dependence and the adult child syndrome are still evolving. Yet they are neither flimsy, weak nor arbitrary. Indeed, they are built on sound principles and a strong and increasingly solid legacy.

No one knows for sure exactly where, when and from whom the term co-dependence first emerged. But the idea and dynamics of how family members and close friends of alcoholics, other chemical dependents and other dysfunctional people may affect one another seems to have emerged around the end of the nineteenth century. Since then clinicians, theorists, writers and groups have built on the contributions of their predecessors. And each person or group has contributed another part of the puzzle of the human condition and relationships.

On the next two pages I summarize the recent history of the adult child and co-dependence concepts as they have evolved over time (Table 2.1). Following this table, I discuss some of these historical events.

Table 2.1. Recent Historical Overview of the Family, Adult Child and Co-dependence Continuum

Approximate Year	Theoretical And Clinical Events	Formation of Self-Help Group
1896	Groddeck and others: Unconscious Freud: Unconscious forces from personal/historical experience Jung: Relationships and collective unconscious; letter to Bill W. (in 1930s) Adler: Birth order, sibling relationships and rivalry Sullivan: Interpersonal and intrapsychic dynamics Moreno: Psychodrama Horney: Importance of Real Self in relationships; the "neurosis of our time" Klein: Importance of relationships and projective identification	
1935	Mahler: Early childhood development Object Relations theorists, e.g., Winicott (True Self in relationships) and self psychologists Miscellaneous observations of spouses of alcoholics (e.g., Rado, etc.) Cork: *The Forgotten Children* Studies of loss and post-traumatic stress begin	Alcoholics Anonymous
1950	Satir and others: Begin generic family therapy movement	Al-Anon
1960	Bateson; Jackson; Haley: Double bind, etc. Bowen: Systems theory; reciprocal relationship, etc.	
1970	Johnson: Family dynamics and intervention; co-alcoholism	

1975	Minuchin: Structural family therapy; Philadelphia Child Guidance Clinic	
	Booz-Allen study (NIAAA): Children of alcoholics	
	Berenson: Integration of family therapy with mainstream recovery	
	Wegscheider: Adapts and expands Satir's family roles and dynamics to alcoholic families	
	Steinglass, et al: Research, theory	ACoA
1978	First CoA conference (NIAAA)	
	First AC therapy group (Brown et al)	
1980	Residential programs add family treatment	
	Miller and Masson: Clarify child mistreatment and abuse, expanding trauma theory	
1983	Many conferences begin	(NACoA)
	First Adult Child focused intensive residential treatment	ACA
	Co-dependence theory and recovery intensifies	ACoDF
1987	Child Within (True Self) healing techniques expanding	CoDA
	Books proliferate	
	Spirituality importance expands	
	Co-dependence and Adult Child recovery importance in relapse prevention, therapy and serenity	
	Criticisms aired more often	
1989	Co-dependence and Adult Child approaches begin to be integrated into general mental health treatment	
1990	The decade of psychological and spiritual growth for increasing numbers of people	
1991—	Continued spread to other specialties and disciplines	

Early History: Creativity Versus Active Co-dependence

In the late 1800s George Groddeck, and then Sigmund Freud, Carl Jung and others, began to name and explore the human unconscious: This is where we store our adult child unfinished business — also called unresolved childhood memories — until we work it through. They also began to look at some family dynamics from an individual perspective. While Freud (who like most people appears to have been an unrecovered co-dependent and adult child of a dysfunctional family) facilitated our understanding, he also slowed it down. For example, Miller and Masson independently describe how Freud dropped his crucial trauma theory — probably due to unconscious fears of being rejected by his peers (could it be called active co-dependence?) — in favor of the less useful oedipal theory[410,437,438]. Unfortunately, most of his followers did the same for almost a century.

In 1896 Freud had presented his findings that many of his patients had been sexually abused as children[221,410]. Although his peers urged him never to publish this information, he did so as "The Aetiology of Hysteria." Over the next few years the external and internal pressure grew, and Freud eventually announced that he had made a mistake in believing his patients. He explained that their traumatic memories were only fantasies[410]. This must have been a comforting view for the society of that time, although it has unfortunately been perpetuated by psychology theory and practice ever since. Only recently, as the adult child and child abuse movement has gained momentum, some clinicians have begun to correct this grave mistake. Freud's error is in striking contrast to many authentic and useful discoveries that he and his followers made: the reality of the unconscious, the nature of transference and resistance, repression, unconscious fantasies, the power of unconscious emotions and the dynamics of the repetition compulsion[410,411,736].

Carl Jung, like most of those in Freud's inner circle, eventually went his own way. He made numerous contributions to our understanding of the psyche, including the importance of the collective unconscious, the dual masculine and feminine nature in each person, working through life's other dualities and the importance of spirituality in the recovery process[330a]. He and William James later contributed scientific support to the founding of the Twelve-Step self-help fellowships [368].

In the early twentieth century Alfred Adler described birth order and sibling relationships and rivalry [33], and Sullivan described more dynamics of interpersonal relationships. Moreno then created the healing technique of psychodrama, from which have evolved Gestalt therapy, reconstruction and family sculpture, all of which we now use in many of our recovery programs [228,652].

The Middle Years: Relationships, The Twelve Steps And Family Therapy

Karen Horney was one of the first to break away from describing our true identity by the confusing and inaccurate term "ego." She preferred to call it our real self, and was one of the first self psychologists [303,304]. Melanie Klein then described the importance of early child development and of relationships, as did her contemporary Mahler, and the defense of projective identification, which her followers later refined [451].

Object relations and self psychology theory and practice began to clarify further our true identity as true self rather than ego. Over the years they made other substantial contributions: the importance of early childhood development, the importance of the dynamics in relationships and the dynamics of projection and projective identification [137]. They helped move the individual into the systemic, which addresses relationships. Also during this time psychiatrists such as Rado, psychologists and others were beginning to describe their observations of the spouses of alcoholics, giving us some preliminary ideas about these relationships.

In 1935 the fellowship of Alcoholics Anonymous was founded, and over the next four years its early members created the Twelve Steps [368]. These Steps and the Twelve Traditions have now been used worldwide by over 100 self-help groups, including Co-Dependents Anonymous.

Although one brief article on children of alcoholics was published in the 1930s [289], the first literature to get any publicity was Margaret Cork's *The Forgotten Children* [164]. Even this remained mostly unnoticed until the early 1980s, when the adult child movement began to blossom. The 1940s also saw increasing attention to the dynamics of loss and trauma, spurred by returning World War II veterans. This, with the help of motivation from the pain of more recent war veterans, has enabled us to recognize and treat what we now call post-traumatic stress disorder (PTSD) and dissociative disorders[175,422,504].

In the early 1950s Virginia Satir and others created the practice of family therapy, and thus began the generic family therapy movement. The fellowship of Al-Anon also was founded around this time[19,20]. And it was also during this decade that humanistic psychologist Abraham Maslow was exploring the dimensions of mentally healthy people[299,408,409]. He observed that the definition of mental health during the 1950s was related to conformity to community standards, a viewpoint that we might describe today as being potentially dangerous and co-dependent.

During the 1950s and into the 1960s, more people contributed to the theories of human interaction, including Ackerman, Bateson, Bell, Jackson, Haley, Lida, Weakland and Watzlawick[265]. For example, building upon the work of these and others, Bowen developed a theory of family systems, including such concepts as undifferentiated ego mass (fusion), triangulation, and what he and Kerr described as a "reciprocal relationship," which helped explain co-dependence among family members[354].

The Later Years: Developing Terms And Groups

In 1973 Vernon Johnson described the dynamics that operate in an alcoholic family[324]. He introduced the term *co-alcoholism* and the process of family intervention to help the alcoholic get into treatment and recovery. In the following few years the word "dependent" was often used for the alcoholic or drug-dependent person in a family. By the early 1980s the term co-dependent began to be used to describe anyone close to the chemically dependent person, and shortly it began to be used to describe what we now know as the condition of co-dependence. Salvador Minuchin and other family therapists and theorists were also making contributions to the slowly growing field of family therapy, including beginning to describe the importance of boundaries.

About 1974 the National Institute of Alcoholism and Alcohol Abuse (NIAAA) commissioned a study on the children of alcoholics, conducted by the research organization Booz-Allen and Hamilton. In 1976 Berenson integrated family therapy principles with mainstream chemical dependence recovery[67]. And around 1977 Sharon Wegscheider adapted and expanded Satir's family roles and dynamics to those of alcoholic families[631].

In the mid to late 1970s the field began to broaden. In 1979 NIAAA sponsored the first national conference on children of alcoholics[473]. In this year Brown and colleagues began the first therapy group for adult children of alcoholics, in Palo Alto, California[146]. From 1977 to 1980 the first ACoA self-help meetings began[5,17,615]. In about 1980 residential chemical dependence treatment facilities began to add a family treatment component as part of their total treatment of the individual.

In 1983 the National Association for Children of Alcoholics (NACoA) was founded by many of the pioneers who are now still active in the field. Many conferences and workshops on children of alcoholics and other dysfunctional families began, and thereafter increased in numbers and popularity in many cities over North America. From this time on, the clinical term *co-dependence* and its more popular variant "co-dependency" began to be used with progressively more frequency.

Recent Developments

The first intensive residential treatment for adult children and co-dependent people was offered in 1984. This recovery experience is now more widely available and, beginning in about 1989, is being incorporated in many innovative psychiatric units and hospitals. This addition has contributed to an increased recovery success for many of their patients.

Adult child self-help fellowship groups continued to expand into Adult Children of Dysfunctional Families, so that anyone from a dysfunctional family could benefit from this remarkable and effective program of recovery.

As I attended workshops and conferences on these topics during the early 1980s, I began to notice the terms *child within* and *inner child* being used with increasing frequency. In 1984 I realized that the Child Within *was* the True Self, and wrote *Healing the Child Within*. Since then, this principle has been applied successfully in the recovery process of countless people.

My view is that while there are many references to "child," none of the examples that follow is the True Self/Child Within:

- adaptive wounded child
- broken child
- free child
- magical child
- child ego state
- adult ego state
- toddler child (and other developmental stages)
- vulnerable child
- precious child
- "little professor," etc.

However, terms such as these may help us in exploring the dimensions of the True Self and are thus useful representations, symbols or archetypes. According to their "map" of the psyche, what some people may call the "child" is actually levels 1, 2, and the first part of level 3 of a seven level Being. While some may tend to divide and split the Child Within into parts, I find it more helpful to thus unify what appears to be who we really are — our True Self, in its connection to its Higher Power (see Table 15 on page 130 of *HCW* for a further description of these levels).

As books on these topics proliferated, so did the importance of spirituality in recovery. The 1990s promise to be a decade of great psychological and spiritual change. For this change to happen I believe that we are now right on time, because the Child Within — our True Self — is the only part of us that can connect to God and thus realize a fulfilling spirituality.

In the late 1980s we realized the importance of untreated co-dependence and adult child issues as major factors in the relapse of addictions and compulsions. In the 1990s we may make a similar discovery about the relapse of other disorders. In 1986 the self-help fellowship of Co-Dependents Anonymous (CoDA) was founded and has now grown to more than 3,000 groups worldwide. In 1990 the National Council on Co-dependence (NCC) was founded. Its mission is to disseminate information and resources on co-dependence and recovery.

Not unexpectedly, a few people began to express criticisms toward the adult child and co-dependence movement (I address these criticisms in Chapter 21). Even so, the movement continues to evolve and grow at a rapid pace.

Brief Summary Of Recent Developments In The Adult Child/Co-dependence Field

Of all the important concepts discovered and developed throughout the twentieth century, co-dependence appears to offer perhaps the most practical and effective solution to helping people recover in a more complete way from a variety of disorders. The following sequence of events, principles and dynamics summarize and clarify some of these recent developments in the continuing emergence of the concept of co-dependence.

1. Observers who deliver therapy for, and who research, write and teach about the adult child condition and co-dependence come from diverse backgrounds and professions, including medicine, psychiatry, psychology, counseling, social work, nursing, clergy and the recovering community.
2. For practical purposes of therapy and recovery, the adult child condition and co-dependence can be viewed as being one condition, and can be called by either name, some other name or can simply be called a major part of "the human condition." Perhaps most accurately, co-dependence is *a major manifestation of the adult child syndrome.*
3. Many of its characteristics and dynamics were partially described long before it was given these names. These descriptions come from many sources, including:
   - Ancient legends and myths [85,86]
   - Freud's and others' trauma theory [410]
   - Theory and practice of working with the human unconscious
   - Jung's and others' expanded psychology
   - Object relations and self psychology's differentiation of the true and false self and developmental stages [137,414]
   - Study of traumatic stress and dissociative disorders [422,504]
   - Family therapy dynamics [265]
   - Humanistic and transpersonal psychology
   - Addictions dynamics and recovery experience
   - Twelve-Step self-help groups [368]
4. Johnson described co-alcoholism about 1973. In around 1980 several observers began to expand and describe it as

co-dependence. At first it was associated with living with or being close (co-) to an active alcoholic or other chemical dependent. Then it was shown also to be associated with living with or being close to any dysfunctional person.

5. The origin of co-dependence is primarily due to having grown up in a troubled, unhealthy or dysfunctional family. It is clinically useful then to describe many of its features as being part of a condition that can be called co-dependence, or the adult child syndrome.
6. Throughout the 1980s and into the 1990s its characteristics and dynamics were clarified and described in more detail.
7. Central to this concept was the observation in the mid-1980s that what many writers, teachers and Twelve-Step groups called the "Child Within" was the True Self that others had begun to describe decades earlier[645].
8. The cause of co-dependence is a wounding of the True Self to such an extent that to survive, it had to go into hiding most of the time, with the subsequent running of its life by the false or co-dependent self. It is thus a disease of lost self-hood. (I explore this wounding process further in Chapters 4 and 6.)
9. The above developments and realizations gave many people with various disorders (physical, mental, emotional and spiritual ones, which are either *manifestations of* or *aggravated by* this wounding) certain advantages in their healing:
   - The term *Child Within* gave them an easier understanding of their True Self and how they might begin to access it.
   - The term *co-dependent self* gave them an easier understanding of their false self or "negative ego" and how they might begin to disidentify with it.
   - The terms *co-dependence* and *adult child* gave them a clearer description of the dynamics and manifestations of their woundedness and its relationship to any Stage Zero conditions (see Table 4.1) and to everyday life. They have spoken to the deep malaise in our society today[260].
10. This approach frees people from the stifling and self-esteem damaging idea that they are somehow inferior or defective — bad, sick, crazy or stupid — or even untreat-

able. Rather, in recovery they learn that they are none of these. They are simply wounded.

11. This wounding is learned — mostly experientially and to some degree cognitively. And what is learned can be unlearned. Unlearning happens slowly during the healing and recovery process[145].
12. Other diagnoses, that is, of what can be called Stage Zero disorders or conditions, are useful mostly in Stage One recovery. These diagnoses are less useful in Stage Two recovery, where the woundedness, adult child condition and co-dependence are addressed in more detail (See Table 4.1 on page 36).

I continue to be grateful to be able to play a part in this rapidly evolving movement, which is helping so many people in their recoveries from all sorts of conditions. I believe that the phenomenon of co-dependence is a major part of a new paradigm in the helping professions and in human well-being, as I describe in Part III.

3

How To Identify Co-dependence, Part I

How can we recognize co-dependence? How does it present itself to us? And what are some of the many variations and guises that it may take?

Recognition, Diagnosis And Dynamics

Co-dependence may be present in any one or a combination of the following ways: (1) persistent stress-related or functional illness or complaints, (2) stress-related illness that is unresponsive or only partially responsive to conventional therapy; (3) relapse of addictions or compulsions; (4) most medical or psychological conditions and many problems in living, including (5) difficulties in relationships with self, others, and our Higher Power. While it is not the only causal factor for each of these categories or conditions, it can be helpful therapeutically to view co-dependence as a major underlying condition and dynamic in them.

Making The Diagnosis

To help make the diagnosis, one may use the various definitions of co-dependence given in Table 1. I know of no precise equivalent diagnostic survey instruments for co-dependence similar to the Michigan Alcoholism Screening Test for the diagnosis of alcoholism. However, there are several survey tests that the clinician may consider using, which I list in Appendix B.

The clinician who needs further assistance in making the diagnosis should consider the manifestations and cardinal characteristics described below. While making the diagnosis of co-dependence is useful at any time, it appears to be *most* useful in late Stage One recovery and in *relapses* or exacerbations of *any* disorders (Stage Zero conditions) and in Stage Two recovery (the Stages are summarized in Table 4-2 on page 37).

Cardinal Characteristics

Co-dependence has at least 12 cardinal characteristics:

1. It is **learned** and **acquired.**
2. It is **developmental.**
3. It is **outer focused.**
4. It is a disease of **lost selfhood.**
5. It has personal **boundary distortions.**
6. It is **a feeling disorder,** manifested especially by emptiness, low self-esteem and shame, fear, anger, confusion and numbness.
7. It produces **relationship difficulties** with self and with others.
8. It is **primary.**
9. It is **chronic.**
10. It is **progressive.**
11. It is **malignant.**
12. It is **treatable.**

I will describe the first three cardinal characteristics of co-dependence in this chapter and continue discussing the remaining nine in Chapter 4.

Learned And Acquired

We develop co-dependence unconsciously and involuntarily. In its primary form, it begins with mistreatment or abuse to a vulnerable and innocent child by its environment, especially its family of origin, and later by its culture or society. In contrast to addictions, co-dependence does not appear to have a genetic transmission. Rather, it appears to come about by the following process, which I call *wounding*. In this description of the wounding process, I use terms from self psychology, object relations theory and from the recovery literature[105,266,363,672,645,652].

The Process Of Wounding

Like most psychological wounding, this process is largely unconscious.

1. Wounded themselves, the child's parents feel inadequate, bad and unfulfilled.
2. They project those charged feelings onto others, especially onto their spouse and their vulnerable children. They may also project grandiosity. They look outside themselves to feel whole.
3. In a need to stabilize the parent and to survive, the child denies that the parents are inadequate and bad, and internalizes (takes in, introjects, accepts) the parents' projected inadequacy and badness, plus a common fantasy: "If I'm really good and perfect, they will love me, and they won't reject or abandon me." *The child idealizes the parents.*
4. Because of the above, the child's vulnerable True Self (lost heart of the self, libidinal ego) is wounded so often that to protect its True Self it defensively submerges ("splits off") itself deep within the unconscious part of its psyche. *The child goes into hiding* (see Figure 3.1).
5. The child takes in whatever else it is told — both verbally and nonverbally — about others, and stores it in its unconscious (mostly) and its conscious mind (sometimes and to some degree).
6. What it takes in are messages from major relationships. The mental representations of these relationships are called "objects" by the object relations theorists. These representations are laden with feelings and tend to occur in "part-objects" (such as good parent, bad parent, aggressive child, shy child, and so on).
7. The more self-destructive messages are deposited more often in the false self (which has also been called the

internal saboteur, anti-libidinal ego, negative ego, or the internalized or introjected, rejecting or otherwise mistreating parent).

8. *A tension builds:* The True Self strives to come alive and to evolve. At the same time, the negative ego (the most destructive aspects of the false self) attacks the True Self, thus forcing it to stay submerged, keeping self-esteem low. The child's grieving of its losses and traumas is not supported. This resulting "psychopathology" or "lesion" has been called a schizoid compromise[266], multiplicity of repressed egos, and a splitting off of the true self[672]. The outcome can be a developmental delay, arrest or failure.

Suzette Billedeaux

Figure 3.1. The Child Goes into Hiding

9. Some results include chronic emptiness, sadness and confusion, and often periodic explosions of self-destructive and other-destructive behavior — both impulsive and compulsive — that allows some release of the tension and a glimpse of the True Self.
10. The consequences of the continued emptiness or repeated destructive behavior keep the True Self stifled or submerged. The person maintains a low self-esteem and remains unhappy, yet wishes and seeks fulfillment. Compulsions and addictions ("repetition compulsions") can provide only temporary release, can lead to more suffering and ultimately block fulfillment and serenity.

The result of the above described wounding process is co-dependence in its primary form. It can also be called the adult child syndrome or condition. Co-dependence is a practical and expansive concept that describes some of the most important manifestations of being an adult child of a troubled, unhealthy, or dysfunctional family. I find it most useful to view co-dependence as being a major manifestation of the adult child syndrome.

11. Recovery and growth involves discovering and gently unearthing the True Self (Child Within) so that it can exist and express itself in a healthy way, day to day. It also means restructuring the ego to become a more flexible assistant (positive ego) to the True Self. Some other results are aliveness, creativity and growth.
12. Such self-discovery and recovery is most effectively accomplished gradually and in the presence of safe, compassionate, skilled and supportive people. With commitment to and active participation in recovery, this healing process generally takes from three to five years and often longer[645,652].

Developmental

While many of the definitions of co-dependence in Table 1 suggest or imply an involved developmental factor, several address it directly. In their definition Freil and Freil include "arrested identity development," (Weinhold and Weinhold) "failure to complete psychological autonomy" and Robert Subby elaborates on the developmental blocks in co-dependence in *Lost In The Shuffle* [225,605,634a].

If continued, the mistreatment or abuse that begins the *wounding* process *interrupts, damages* and *blocks healthy human development* and *growth.* These developmental stages involve learning to connect, love, feel, trust, explore, initiate, be autonomous, think, cooperate, master, create, develop morals, skills and values, evaluate, regenerate (heal), evolve and grow, recycle — all crucial for healthy human life (See Table 3.1). Blocking these developmental stages paralyzes healthy growth and threatens survival. During the wounding process, when we are in a survival mode, we focus outside ourselves and neglect our inner life. We gradually become more and more distant and eventually become alienated from our True Self in all its dimensions, including these developmental phases of growth. This leaves us unskilled and deficient in whichever crucial inner life ability has been blocked.

In spite of these developmental blocks, our society's emphasis on thinking and doing allows us to function intellectually and do various physical and mental tasks well. But in our relationship with self and others we often have difficulty — from the perspective of our inner life — achieving the other developmental tasks, including connecting, trusting, mastering and loving.

Thus, if a child's parent is dysfunctional in the role of healthy parent — that is, if the parent cannot assist the child in healthy psycho-spiritual growth and development — then that will *block* (to varying degrees) the *child's ability to work through* whichever *developmental task* may be appropriate, and thereby block the *ability to grow and evolve.* If this parental inadequacy continues, the child will likely remain blocked at that point until that particular developmental task can be worked through in a healthy way at any age.

Recovery may provide the person a *second chance to work through* these developmental stages in a healthy way. But in early recovery we can feel as though we are starting all over — even from a kind of infancy — as we risk authentic interaction with self, others and, if we choose, our Higher Power. And if we persist in our recovery work, we can complete these otherwise incomplete developmental tasks. While important and necessary, this particular work is but a part that fits and meshes into the total work of the recovery process (see also Figure 10.4 on page 119).

Table 3.1. Tasks in Human Development*
(reading from bottom to top)
(compiled in part from references[137,201,363,384,385,389,414,451,563,672])

Tasks	Approximate Age In First Cycle	Realm Of Being	Stage In Recovery
Be Co-creative Expand love Transcend ego Self-realize	Later in life, usually second half, when have a sense of self that can let go of its ego	Spiritual	3
Recycle	19		
Evolve & grow Regenerate (heal)	13	Emotional	
Evaluate Develop morals, skills & values Create (make)	6		
Master	4		2
Cooperate	3		
Think		Mental	
Separate	2		
Initiate			
Explore			
Trust	1		1
Feel		Physical	0
Love			
Connect			
Be			
	0		

*We recycle these tasks throughout our life[384]. Healthy adolescents repeat the first 14 to 16 tasks. Parents usually cycle in parallel with their children.

Outer Focused

This characteristic is addressed in the definitions and dynamics of co-dependence throughout this book. There is nothing harmful or wrong with looking outside of ourself. In fact, doing so is useful not only in everyday life, but in our survival at any time. However, co-dependents overdo it by focusing outward to such an extent they neglect their inner lives and suffer inordinately and unnecessarily. This suffering often leads to dysfunction in their relationship with themself, others and their Higher Power. Table 3.2 lists some characteristics of states, experiences or dynamics that may develop in a co-dependent relationship that has reached an advanced stage. I will continue exploring the cardinal characteristics of co-dependence in Chapter 4.

Table 3.2. Some Characteristics of Co-dependence

- My good feelings about who I am stem from being liked by you and receiving approval from you.
- Your struggles affect my serenity. I focus my mental attention on solving your problems or relieving your pain.
- I focus my mental attention on pleasing you, protecting you or manipulating you to "do it my way."
- I bolster my self-esteem by solving your problems and relieving your pain.
- I put aside my own hobbies and interests. I spend my time sharing your interests and hobbies.
- Because I feel you are a reflection of me, my desires dictate your clothing and personal appearance.
- My desires dictate your behavior.
- I am not aware of how I feel. I am aware of how you feel.
- I am not aware of what I want. I ask you what you want.
- If I am not aware of something, I assume. (I don't ask or verify it in some other way.)
- The dreams I have for my future are linked to you.
- My fear of your anger and rejection determines what I say or do.
- In our relationship I use giving as a way of feeling safe.
- As I involve myself with you, my social circle diminishes.
- To connect with you, I put my values aside.
- I value your opinion and way of doing things more than my own.
- The quality of my life depends on the quality of yours.

Source: Anonymous, modified from paper circulated by Co-Dependents Anonymous.

4

How To Identify Co-dependence, Part II

Disease Of Lost Selfhood

Whether we call it our True or Real Self, Child Within, consciousness, ego ideal, psyche, mind or identity, this being appears to be who we really are. And this, our true identity, is lost in co-dependence.

Our True Self does not yet know how to handle the pain of living in a mistreating, abusing or otherwise dysfunctional environment. Feeling overwhelmed, it goes into hiding. Then our false self, ego or co-dependent self comes in to help us survive and function.

This "absence" — which is actually only *hiding* — of the True Self usually brings about a feeling of *emptiness,* which we may then try to fill with things outside of ourself. But doing so doesn't fill us in a lasting or fulfilling way. Only after experiencing the repeated pain of the consequences of addictions, compulsions or other disorders — combined with the ongoing feeling of the emptiness — are we often forced to look within, into our True Self.

Only when we can realize our True Self and connect it to our Higher Power, can we begin to recover and to feel fulfilled.

Personal Boundary Distortions

A boundary is a personally initiated and maintained dynamic that protects the well-being and integrity of the True Self[649,652]. A boundary distortion can be simply stated as "not knowing where I end and you begin." The co-dependent person has numerous boundary distortions. While boundary distortions are implied throughout the definitions of co-dependence (See Table 1.1), two of these address boundary problems directly: "boundary distortions around intimacy and separation" (Cermak) and "difficulty with setting functional boundaries" (Mellody).

Co-dependence cannot develop without distortions in personal boundaries, and a person cannot recover from any disorder, including co-dependence, without forming healthy boundaries.

A Feeling Disorder

In co-dependence we lose touch with our crucial inner life, which includes especially our feelings. We become alienated from our feelings. Yet these feelings don't disappear. They continue to surface, most commonly as emptiness, low self-esteem and shame, fear, anger, confusion and numbness[645,652]. These feelings are usually masked in other disguises, since actively co-dependent people have difficulty recognizing and dealing directly with their feelings. In recovery the co-dependent learns experientially what these and other feelings are, how to recognize them and how to use them in everyday life.

Relationship Difficulties

Relationship difficulties are among the most basic of these cardinal characteristics, since co-dependence is about a distortion of healthy relationships. We have difficulty relating to ourself, to others and to our Higher Power. These relationship difficulties are reflected throughout our life, and in our core recovery issues (described in Chapters 15 and 16). Recognizing and working through these issues is an integral part of recovery from co-dependence[258,652].

Primary

Most co-dependence is primary in that it occurs from childhood, as described in the wounding process discussed in Chapter 3. Primary also means that no other disorder in the co-dependent person causes it, although one or more disorders — including addictions — may exist concomitantly (See Figure 4.1).

Figure 4.1 describes any of these disorders that may exist with co-dependence as "Stage Zero conditions." The Stage Zero condition or disorder represents the tip of the iceberg, with the bulk of the iceberg being co-dependence (the iceberg model is illustrated in Figure 6.2). Depending on genetic, familial and environmental factors, each person will likely manifest a different disorder (Stage Zero condition) or set of disorders.

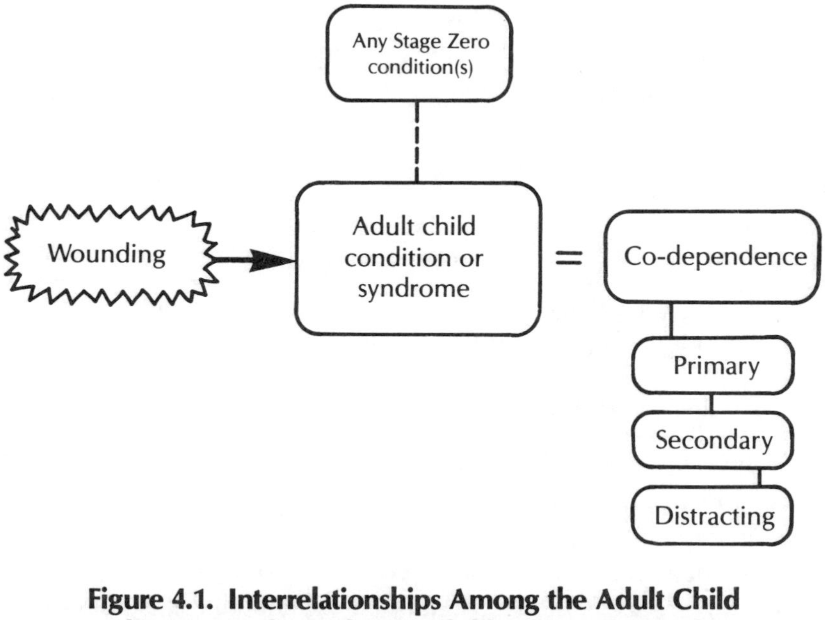

Figure 4.1. Interrelationships Among the Adult Child Syndrome, Co-dependence, Child Mistreatment/Abuse and Medical and Psychological Disorders

A person who obtains specific treatment for the Stage Zero disorder reaches Stage One recovery, which usually takes a few months to a few years to stabilize (See Table 4.1). In Stage One any addiction, compulsion or related disorder may be addressed. Once stabilized, the person may wish to address the underlying co-dependence (which in perhaps 95 percent of people with co-dependence is the same as the adult child syndrome or condition). This Stage Two recovery usually takes from three to five years or longer in the best full recovery program[652]. In Stage Three recovery the person is then more able to address and realize spirituality successfully[646] (See Table 4.2).

Table 4.1. Recovery and Duration According to Stages

Recovery Stage	Condition	Focus of Recovery	Approximate Duration
3	Human/Spiritual	Spirituality	Ongoing
2	Adult Child	A C Specific Full Recovery Program	3-5 years
1	Stage Zero Disorder	Basic-Illness Specific Full Recovery Program	½ to 3 years
0	Active Illness	Addiction, Compulsion, Disorder — — — — — — Woundedness	Indefinite

When to focus on Stages 2 and 3 recovery usually depends upon the person's prior healing and present condition.

Secondary Co-dependence

Even if we grew up in a healthy family, a less severe form of co-dependence may occur when we enter into a close or important relationship with an actively addicted, disordered or otherwise dysfunctional person. I call this secondary co-dependence.*

One difference is that secondary co-dependence is often milder and easier to treat and to recover from. With appropriate treatment (as described in Part II), the person may make a successful

*Frequently, associated Diagnostic and Statistical Manual Of Mental Disorders (DSM-IIIR) diagnoses for secondary co-dependence may include adjustment disorder (309.28), dysthymic disorder (300.40) or anxiety disorder (300.00). (Even so, overall, most people with any of these three diagnoses will have primary co-dependence.)

recovery in a matter of a few months and most can do so in a year or less. This is because they have as base a healthier self and therefore healthier use of ego defenses and coping mechanisms to assist in their recovery.

This view of secondary co-dependence differs somewhat from that of Cermak, who views it as occurring when someone who has co-dependent *traits* becomes enmeshed with someone with unhealthy narcissism[145]. While this concept has some theoretical interest, I find it more healing to identify such a person with these co-dependent traits as already having primary co-dependence, although not usually in as severe a form as a person with more advanced co-dependence (see also Figure 5.1).

Table 4.2. Summary of The Stages of Recovery

- **Stage Zero**

  Stage Zero is manifested by the presence of an active illness or disorder, such as an addiction, compulsion or another disorder. This active illness may be acute, recurring or chronic. Without recovery, it may continue indefinitely. At Stage Zero, recovery has not yet started.

- **Stage One**

  At Stage One, recovery begins. It involves participating in a full recovery program to assist in healing the Stage Zero condition or conditions. (A *partial* recovery program is less likely to be as successful as a full one.)

- **Stage Two**

  Stage Two involves healing adult child or co-dependence issues. Once a person has a stable and solid Stage One recovery — one that has lasted for at least a year or longer — it may be time to consider looking into these issues. An adult child is anyone who grew up in an unhealthy, troubled or dysfunctional family. Many adult children may *still* be in a similar unhealthy environment, whether at home, in one or more relationships, or at work.

- **Stage Three**

  Stage Three recovery is spirituality and its incorporation into daily life. This is an ongoing process.

Distracting Co-dependence

Distracting co-dependence can be recognized in a person who comes to a therapist requesting assistance in doing adult child recovery work, yet is too distracted to do the necessary and appropriate amount of introspection and family-of-origin work. The distraction is often due to being in a close relationship with an actively addicted or other dysfunctional person. The person's own active addiction or other disorder may also provide a distraction that prevents productive adult child recovery work.

Chronic

Co-dependence is chronic. A person who does not work appropriately and for a sufficient duration in a specific recovery program that addresses any Stage Zero disorder (in a Stage One recovery program), and then co-dependence (Stage Two recovery), is unlikely to make a successful recovery.

Progressive

Without specific and appropriate treatment and recovery, co-dependence usually gets worse over the course of time. While partial treatment interventions — such as psychoactive medication, psychotherapy that does not address the core of co-dependence and the adult child syndrome, and behavior therapy — may offer some brief periods of relief, successful ongoing recovery is unlikely without a specific program of sufficient duration.

Malignant

Sometimes co-dependence takes a malignant course. It may do so in the form of serious accidents, overt or covert suicide, homicide, relapses of addictions and possibly some medical illness such as cancer.

Treatable

Co-dependence is treatable. With sufficient motivation by the person and appropriate treatment interventions and assistance by the helping professional, with long-term treatment the co-dependent person is *likely* to make a *successful recovery.* This will usually also depend on the nature and response of any Stage Zero conditions to any specific Stage One treatment prior to the person's recovery work from co-dependence.

There is a potential trap in using the words "treatable" and "treatment" here. This is because they imply that treatment is something that is done *to* a person and comes from the *outside.* A preferable term here is *recovery,* for which the individual takes responsibility by changing from within — with appropriate, skilled and safe *assistance* from the outside. I discuss this concept further in Chapters 19 and 20 on the new paradigm.

5

Personality Components And Roles, Traits And Disorders

Co-dependence can disguise itself in people and present to helping professionals and others in a number of ways. At least 15 manifestations of co-dependence may appear as various traits, patterns or guises of behavior and personality. Any individual may experience and present with any one or a combination of the following.

1. **Rescuers** and **fixers** try to rescue, fix or help others while neglecting themselves. They lose their identity in others[138]. Helping professionals often manifest co-dependence in this way. As is true of most of these guises, they usually learned it as a survival technique growing up in their dysfunctional family of origin.
2. **People pleasers** have unhealthy personal boundaries and limits[649,652]. They would rather acquiesce and comply with others than express their own healthy wants and needs. They have a hard time saying no to others. Part of their recovery includes learning to say no. People pleasing is a subtle form of manipulation and control.

3. **Overachievers** feel empty from the loss of their True Self, and try to fill the emptiness with achievements. But because the emptiness was not due to lack of achievement, it tends not to be relieved for very long with each achievement. The child who takes the role of family hero is at especially high risk for this manifestation[631].
4. **Inadequate Ones** or **Failures** feel as empty as their seeming opposite, the overachievers. Failures have low self-esteem and a recurring feeling of shame. They feel imperfect, incomplete, inadequate, not good enough, bad, rotten and flawed at their core. A feeling of inadequacy actually underlies and runs the overachiever's drive to overachieve. It also underlies and is a major dynamic in nearly all the other manifestations and consequences of co-dependence.

   In recovery co-dependents discover that this sense of shame was only a protective covering like the outer layers of an onion, that covered and blocked their True Self from fully knowing and expressing itself. Nearly all of the shame they felt was projected onto them by others. It does not belong to them. Cognitively and experientially discovering this fact and integrating it into their life is a major part of the recovery process[645,649,654].
5. **Perfectionists** are driven by fear of failure and the need to avoid being wrong or making any mistakes. They can drive themselves and those around them nearly crazy in the attempt. There can be a fine line between the healthy wanting to do one's best and learning from mistakes, and the unhealthy preoccupation with perfection to one's own detriment[583].
6. **Victims** can present as the "sick one" with chronic illness, or as the "bad one," the delinquent or scapegoat who is always getting into trouble. The victim admits and expresses self-pity — "no one understands" them. They often whine while telling their story of woe. Although they may toy with getting help, they rarely commit or follow through. They admittedly run from taking responsibility for self-improvement. They often lure rescuers, fixers and helping professionals to try to help them, so they can shame or otherwise punish them for not really helping. Victims often eventually tell would-be helpers, "You've just made it worse."

Victims live mostly in the past, reciting an endless string of "If only's." Victims admit that they are losers, and ask others to feel sorry for them[377]. Until they begin to take responsibility for being victims, their prognosis with any therapeutic assistance is poor at worst and guarded at best. Even so, they tend to be one step ahead of the martyr.

7. **Martyrs** are more difficult to assist in recovery than victims because they deny most of what the victim admits, such as their self-pity and feeling misunderstood, unappreciated, burdened and hopeless. Nonetheless they may manifest these feelings by their actions and their treatment of others — their behavior speaks louder than their words. They often sigh, refusing all suggestions or help, and say they already know all of these, have tried them and they don't work.

   The martyr's victimhood is more difficult to recognize because they can look good on the surface. Yet they won't take responsibility for their lives. Martyrs often suggest that they have "too much" responsibility and may disguise themselves as rescuers or fixers. Both martyrs and victims want someone else to take responsibility for them and want to see the other struggle and suffer.

   Martyrs live mostly in the future, pretending to be done with the past. They may also be overly religious. While victims admit they are losers, martyrs won't — and don't even know it. Both martyrs and victims refuse to face and feel their pain[377]. Martyrs are among the most difficult to help of all the people that helping professionals see.

8. **Addicted ones** may seem to be in their own category. But in the 20 years I have worked clinically with alcoholics and other chemically dependent people, I have yet to see a person with these disorders who is not also co-dependent. In addition, each addict grew up in a dysfunctional family, and thus acquired primary co-dependence.

   People may be addicted to things other than alcohol or drugs, including other people, places, things, behaviors or experiences. Common addictions are eating disorders, sex addiction, workaholism or work addiction, money-related addictions such as compulsive spending or shopping, compulsive or pathologic gambling, and relationship addiction (which itself is another guise of co-dependence).

9. **Compulsive Ones** are similar to addicted ones. Compulsions are another manifestation of co-dependence and include the addictions listed in item 8, above. While it may be difficult to differentiate some compulsions from addictions, one important difference is that compulsions tend to have less severe consequences. Because of this, people with mild or socially acceptable compulsions, such as a person who is compulsively neat, may not be identified as easily by their family and friends or by helping professionals.
10. **Grandiose Ones** may present as over confident and even grandiose. Men may be "macho"; women may have overexaggerated femininity or be fragile or frail — and either may also be grandiose and overconfident. This guise is related to ego inflation[191], and is the opposite of the healthy characteristic in recovery described as humility. Being humble here does not mean groveling or being like a doormat, but rather being open to learning about self, others and one's Higher Power.
11. **Selfish** or **Narcissistic Ones** — Having underlying low self-esteem, they may try to fill themselves with an over-attention on *self* to the detriment of *others.* This is the opposite of what most co-dependents do, who focus on others to the detriment of self. Yet underneath they are still co-dependent because they have a lost self due to focusing on others to fill their need for perfect mirroring. But with narcissists, who may at times be grandiose, compulsive or addicted, abusive and so on, others can never mirror them perfectly enough[414]. Narcissists usually abuse or mistreat others, often subtly, and display unhealthy narcissism (described later in this chapter).
12. **Bullies** are so insecure about and alienated from their True Self that they may lash out at others in order to feel stronger and more in control.
13. **Abusers,** like bullies, are insecure and alienated from their True Self. They try to control others physically or emotionally in order to feel in control themselves.
14. **Lost Children** are often the third-born or later child in a dysfunctional family. They feel so overwhelmed by trying to get appropriate attention and to get their needs met in

competition with the older sibling (often the hero or over-achiever) and the second born (often the delinquent, bully, or bad one), that they give up and withdraw[631]. In an attempt to help handle their frequent psychosomatic illness, they may become victims, martyrs or stoic.

15. **Comedians** or **"Little Princesses"** also called "mascots" or "family pets," learned to get attention and survive in their family by being funny or cute. This behavior can be carried on into adult life to defend against intimacy and pain or to manipulate, control or hurt others. Like nearly everything in life, humor is a double-edged sword. It can be used in healthy or unhealthy ways.

In recovery, co-dependents may draw on any of these less desirable traits as they transform them into healthier ones. For example, bullies can learn to be assertive in a healthy way; and martyrs or victims can learn to be more sensitive to their inner life and take responsibility for making their life a success. The person thus transforms the curse into a gift.

Historical Evolution Of These Roles And Personality Components

In the 1950s and before, a few of these roles and personality components or traits were described by several clinicians and authors, including Virginia Satir. Based in part on these descriptions and on her own observations, Sharon Wegscheider began to clarify various roles manifested by members of alcoholic families: the dependent (alcoholic or dysfunctional one), the chief enabler (the spouse), and their children: the hero, scapegoat, the lost child and the mascot[631]. Black, Ackerman and others also described these roles, sometimes by different names, and added new and important dimensions to their dynamics. I summarize these roles and some of the key characteristics from their work in Table 5.1.

An *enabler* is a person who usually unconsciously (or sometimes consciously) facilitates the destructive behavior of a dysfunctional person or persons. This facilitating may include repeated attempts to rescue or fix the dysfunctional person[138,630]. Another guise of looking outside oneself for fulfillment, enabling is a common behavior among actively co-dependent people, and it usually contributes to their detriment and that of the dysfunctional person.

While some co-dependents and adult children may fit these roles neatly, others do not. In 1984 I, and independently Ackerman[9], described how these roles may vary, not only from person to person, but also by birth order and other life experience. Thus the variations from the *classical*, as shown in Table 5.1, include: *sequential* (person moves from one role to another over time); *mixed* (person experiences and manifests more than one role at a given time); and *non-classical* (many of those in my list of 15 behaviors, roles and personality components or traits above, that were not originally described by Wegscheider, Black, Ackerman and others).

To Table 5.1 I also add the untrained and unrecovered helping professional. There have been several books and articles written about the wounded healer[185a,398,478]. Since most helping professionals, like most people, grew up in unhealthy troubled, or dysfunctional families, not all of them will be recovered from their resulting woundedness. They may also not be trained appropriately to deal with many of these problems and issues, due in part to the non-recovery and old paradigm-oriented training from their teachers in their professional schools.

Yet today a remarkable thing is happening. Progressively more of these helping professionals are not only awakening to their own woundedness, but are entering into a recovery program for their co-dependence and adult child syndrome. By so doing they are contributing to and are an example of the effectiveness and success of this movement.

Degree Of Wounding

There is variation — not only in roles and personality components among co-dependents and adult children — but also in the *degree of wounding* that the individual may experience. I describe some of the factors that may contribute to such wounding in Tables 5.2 and 5.3. These factors include: the degree of *parental dysfunction*, the degree of *physical* and/or *sexual abuse;* the *duration* of the *parental dysfunction;* the *gender* of the dysfunctional parent; the *severity* of the *parental co-dependence;* the *personality* of the *child* and also the *child's perception;* the *presence* and *severity* of chemical

Table 5.1. Originally Described Roles among Members of Dysfunctional Families
(Modified from Wegscheider, Black, and my own work)

Role	Primary Feelings	Identifying Symptoms	Payoff For Person	Payoff For Family	Possible Price
Dependent, most dysfunctional and/or intimidating	Shame Anger Fear	Addiction or other disorder or dysfunction	Relief of Pain	Attempt at Stability or Flexibility	Addiction or other disorder and its consequences
Chief Enabler (often spouse)	Shame Fear Anger	Helplessness (despite controlling behavior)	Importance; self-righteousness	Responsibility	Illness; martyrdom and depression
Hero Responsible child usually first born	Shame Guilt	Overachievement; Caretaker Perfectionist	Attention (positive)	Self-worth; pride	Compulsive drive; often marry CD or other dysfunctional
Scapegoat, "Acting-Out," Troubled child usually second born	Shame Hurt Anger	Delinquency; (Least in denial)	Attention (negative)	Focus away from dependent	Self-destruction addiction
Lost Child Adjuster often third born	Loneliness Shame Confusion	Isolation; shyness	Escape	Relief from tension and responsibility	Social isolation; Often ill
Mascot, with features of Placating child, often last born	Fear Shame	Clowning; hyperactivity "cute"	Attention (amused)	Distraction Fun	Immaturity; emotional illness
Unrecovered/ Untrained Helping Professional	Desire to help; Shame	Overwork; partial or unsuccessful treatment results	Temporary symptom relief	Temporary relief	Treatment failure in patients/clients; frustration & burn-out

Patterns may include: **Classifical** (i.e., person remains in one role), **sequential** (goes from role to role), **mixed** (more than one role at once), **non-classical** (some other pattern).

Table 5.2. Clinical Impressions of Some Factors Associated with Varying Degrees of *Severity of Woundedness* among Children of Alcoholics and Other Dysfunctional Families

Characteristic	**Less**		**Woundedness**				**More**
Degree Parental Alcoholism/Dysfunction	Mild		Moderate				Severe
Degree Physical/ Sexual Abuse	None	Mental-Emotional	Physical		Sexual		Extreme cruelty
Duration Parental Alcoholism/Dysfunction	Onset Elderly (parent)	Before Age 45 of CoA/DF	Before Age 17	Before Age 12	Before Age 5	Since Birth	Multiple & Severe Family Dysfunction for Past-Generations
Gender of Alcoholic Dysfunctional Parent	Father		Mother				Both
Severity of Parental Co-dependence	None	Mild	Moderate				Severe
Personality of CoA/DF (or perception)	Healthier	Average "Neurotic"	Advanced "Neurotic"				Major Psychiatric Illness — Mild-Moderate-Severe
Chemical Dependence, other Addictions in CoA/DF	None	Harmfully Involved	Early		Middle Stage		Severe or Advanced
Other Stress Factors & Cultural Factors	Few		Moderate				Many

Table 5.3. Clinical Impressions of Some Factors Associated with Varying Degrees of *Severity of Woundedness* among Children of Alcoholics and Other Dysfunctional Families, as Related to the *Recovery* of the Person and the Family.

Characteristics	**Less**	**Woundedness**			**More**
Age of person & CD **Duration when entered** adequate recovery	Young	Teen	Adult	Elderly	No Recovery
Strength of **Program**	Strong	Moderate			None
Type Program	Spiritual plus . . .	Adult Child Group Therapy	Twelve Step Alone Conventional Psychotherapy or Medicine Alone		None
Recovery of **Parents**	Strong & When CoA/DF Younger				Weak & When CoA/DF Older
Recovery of **Siblings** and **close others**	Strong & When CoA/DF Younger				Weak & When CoA/DF Older
CoA/DF Skills of **Therapist**	High				Low

dependence or other addictions or *dysfunctions* in the child or adult child; and *other stress* and *cultural* factors (see Table 5.2).

Table 5.3 shows six additional such factors that are related to recovery in the person and in the family members. These include: the *age* of the person upon *entering* an adequate recovery program; the *strength* and the *type* of that program; the *recovery* of the *parents;* the recovery of the person's *siblings* and *close others;* and the *skills* of the *therapist* in assisting people in recovery from co-dependence and the adult child syndrome.

Personality Traits And Disorders

The DSM-III-R differentiates personality *traits* from personality *disorders*[24,449]. Personality traits, such as generosity, selfishness, passivity and aggressiveness, are according to DSM-III-R, "enduring patterns of perceiving, relating to and thinking about the environment and oneself . . . exhibited in a wide range of important social and personal contexts." These traits may become a disorder when a personality is narrowed down to only a few traits which have become "inflexible and maladaptive and cause either significant impairment in social or occupational functioning or significant subjective distress."

Cermak says that while co-dependent traits may be widespread, the diagnosis of co-dependence, which he prefers to call Co-dependent Personality Disorder, can be made only when there is identifiable dysfunction resulting from excessive rigidity or intensity associated with these traits[145]. As such he has suggested five diagnostic criteria for co-dependence, shown in Table 5.4.

Currently, there is no such disorder listed in the DSM as co-dependent personality disorder. Cermak suggests that co-dependent personality traits may create such dysfunction that co-dependence may then fit most easily under the DSM-III-R diagnosis of "Personality Disorder Not Otherwise Specified (NOS)." He says that researchers may need to use criteria such as his for validity and reliability studies, which through revising and retesting should eventually achieve a level of diagnostic sophistication at least comparable to that which exists for currently accepted personality disorders[145].

Table 5.4. Suggested Diagnostic Criteria For Co-dependence
Adapted From Cermak 1986; 1990.

1. Continued investment of self-esteem in the ability to control both oneself and others in the face of serious adverse consequences.
2. Assumption of responsibility for meeting others' needs, to the exclusion of acknowledging one's own needs.
3. Anxiety and boundary distortions around intimacy and separation.
4. Enmeshment in relationships with personality disordered, chemically dependent and impulse disordered individuals.
5. Exhibits at least three of the following:

   - Excessive reliance on denial
   - Constriction of emotions (with or without dramatic outbursts)
   - Depression
   - Hypervigilance
   - Compulsions
   - Anxiety
   - Alcohol or other drug abuse
   - Recurrent victim of physical or sexual abuse
   - Stress-related medical illnesses
   - Has remained in a primary relationship with an *actively mistreating or abusing person* (my substitute for his "alcoholic or other drug addict") for at least two years without seeking outside support.

Cermak's suggested diagnostic criteria are useful in the evolution of our understanding of co-dependence. Unfortunately, by its limitations it may end up excluding nearly 70 percent of people with co-dependence, as shown in Figure 5.1. If the estimate by Virginia Satir and others that 95 percent of people in the United States grew up in dysfunctional families is true, then nearly all of these people will be wounded to some degree from that painful experience. And if co-dependence is a major manifestation of the adult child syndrome, then most adult children will have some degree of wounding manifested by co-dependence. Yet Cermak's criteria would cover only people with the most extreme degree of co-dependence — about 25 percent of the population by his estimate[145]. However, I and others believe that those people who identify as being co-dependent by any one or more of the *definitions* in Table 1.1 or by its many other *characteristics* are equally entitled to any use that they can make of the concept and experience of being co-dependent, including working through their own healing in a full recovery program.

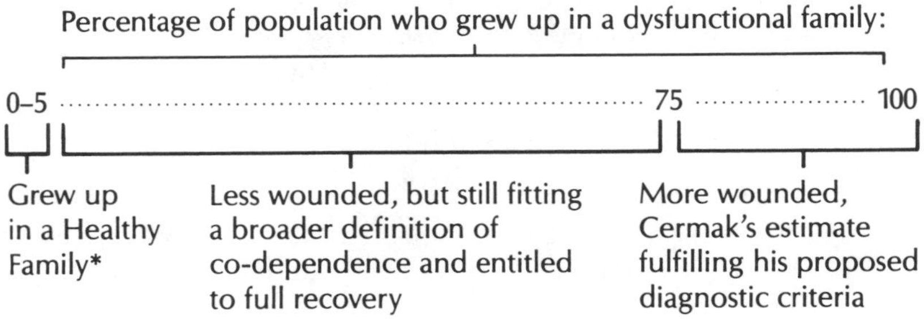

*While not usually co-dependent, these people are susceptible to secondary co-dependence.

Figure 5.1. Spectrum of Co-dependence in Progressively Increasing Degrees of Severity
(reading from left to right)

Narcissus And Echo: Interaction With An Unhealthy Narcissist

Cermak's suggested diagnostic criteria include several of the core recovery issues later described in Chapter 15 (fear of abandonment, low self-esteem and shame, control, over-responsibility for others and difficulty with feelings); several basic dynamics (boundary distortions, enmeshment, addictions and compulsions[649,652]) and other manifestations of co-dependence and of post-traumatic stress disorder (PTSD) (fears and hypervigilance) described throughout this book. Two of these criteria are *giving to a dysfunctional person* to such an extent that doing so becomes *to one's own detriment,* and constitute Cermak's suggestion that the co-dependent is like Echo in the Greek myth of Narcissus and Echo, while the dysfunctional other is like Narcissus.

Interaction With An Unhealthy Narcissist

The myth of Narcissus and Echo, here paraphrased from Cermak[145], can help expand our understanding of several important aspects of co-dependence.

> Echo was fairest of the wood nymphs and one of the most talkative. But her talkativeness got her into trouble with Hera, the wife of Zeus. Known for her jealous outbursts, Hera thought that Echo was purposely distracting her with talk while Zeus was cavorting with her friends. So Hera condemned Echo to remain speechless, except for repeating what others said. This was hardest to bear when Echo, like many before her, fell in love with the handsome Narcissus. She had no way to tell Narcissus how she felt. All Echo could do was follow him about, hoping for a crumb of attention.
>
> Her big chance came one day when Narcissus called out to his companions, "Is anyone here?" Thrilled, but too shy to meet him face-to-face, Echo instead remained hidden behind a tree and called back, "Here . . . here!" Narcissus looked but saw no one. "Come!" he shouted. That was what Echo had been waiting for, and stepping forward, she beckoned to Narcissus and said sweetly, "Come." But Narcissus turned away in disgust from her outstretched arms, and said, "I will die before I give you power over me," to which Echo responded forlornly, "I give you power over me." His rejection left her feeling ashamed. She could not be comforted, yet she continued to love Narcissus.
>
> Because Narcissus scorned those who adored him and was oblivious to their affection, Nemesis, the goddess of righteous anger, punished him. Furious over his treatment of Echo, she made Narcissus lean over a clear pool for a drink and fall hopelessly in love with his reflected image. Consumed by the futile desire to have his affection returned, Narcissus slowly wasted away. When death eventually overtook him, Echo was helpless to reach out to him until his last breath. As he said his final "Farewell, farewell," to his own image, she repeated the same words to him. Then Echo's flesh also wasted away, and her bones turned to stone. Today, all that remains of Echo is her voice, in canyons and caves, still repeating only what others have said.

Narcissus is an archetype for the dysfunction of unhealthy or pathological self-adoration, or unhealthy narcissism, and Echo is an archetype for the unhealthy dependence of co-dependence. The myth shows us how people with many of these same characteristics are often drawn to one another. They may be attracted simply because they are used to the other's behavior, since they grew up in a family and a society that taught them to behave and to respond in that way. But, on a deeper level, they may also be drawn to one another in a search to heal their unfinished business[288] and, perhaps more important, their lost self.

The myth of Narcissus and Echo is a caricature of only two aspects of co-dependence, and other mythological figures and stories illustrate other components of co-dependence[85,86]. Perhaps because co-dependence is "the human condition," there are numerous examples of co-dependent behavior and dynamics in classical myths and legends. For example, the myth of Amor and Psyche[471] (co-dependence as love addiction), of Icarus and Daedalus[191] (inflation of the co-dependent self or ego), of Chiron (the wounded healer)[185a] and numerous stories of child abuse[86].

An important part of the recovery process is to learn to get our healthy needs met, to be self-caring — also called healthy narcissism — and to learn about some characteristics of unsafe people, which includes unhealthy narcissists. Let's review some of the characteristics of each.

Healthy Versus Unhealthy Narcissism

Narcissism — focusing on my self and getting my wants and needs met — can be healthy or unhealthy. Healthy narcissism is also called self-caring. We care for our healthy wants and needs in our own way and in our own time, without hurting anyone. Having healthy boundaries helps us to accomplish this. That is, we get what we want and need without invading another's boundaries and by setting our own healthy boundaries.

Unhealthy narcissism is focusing on my self to the detriment of others — the opposite of the usual view of co-dependence, which is focusing on others to the detriment of self. That detriment may be manifested and characterized by a number of behaviors and dynamics, as shown in Table 5.5. While some of these unhealthy traits may be present at times in people with ordinary active co-dependence, and while several may be present in those with other personality disorders, such as borderline personality disorder, and in active addictions, most of them tend to be present in the psychodynamics and behavior of people with an uncommon condition called *narcissistic personality disorder.* In part because of this association, the terms "narcissism" and "narcissistic" have taken on a negative connotation, even though narcissism, that is, self-focusing, can be and often is *healthy,* as shown in Table 5.5.

The person with unhealthy narcissism is acting the way our parents probably meant when they told us not to be "selfish." Yet what many of our parents *didn't* teach us was a healthy self-caring. Before we can be in a healthy relationship, we have to know how to be self-caring in a healthy way. Part of the way we can do this is by having healthy boundaries[649,652].

People with unhealthy narcissism frequently invade others' boundaries. Unless they work long and hard through a full recovery program, it is highly unlikely that they will change and become narcissistic in a self-caring, healthy way. And so it is difficult, if not impossible, to have a healthy and fulfilling relationship with them. Recovery from co-dependence allows us to come to that realization when we are in such relationships.

Co-dependent Relating To An Unhealthy Narcissist

With this understanding of healthy and unhealthy narcissism, we can return to some of the differentiating features in the relationship between the co-dependent and the unhealthy narcissist, as summarized in Table 5.6. First, they are each attracted to one another: The narcissist demands perfect mirroring and the co-dependent, in the most extreme form, is preoccupied with mirroring the other. Even so, each gives the other unhealthy mirroring. The narcissist has an overpowering need to feel important and special, and the co-dependent has a strong need to help others feel that way. Thus the focus of the narcissist is both on the false self and somewhat on the (still unconscious) True Self, while the focus of the co-dependent is on the narcissist. The narcissist *cannot see* the *other as separate* from self; while the co-dependent has the opposite view, that is, *not seeing self as separate* from the other. Finally, the narcissist *overdoes* all self-caring and demands it from others, while the co-dependent *underdoes* or may even do almost no self-caring.

Table 5.5. Some Characteristics of Healthy and Unhealthy Narcissism.

Characteristic	Healthy	Unhealthy
Orientation	True Self	Negative ego
Humility	Present	Absent; ego inflated
Assertion	Self-assertive	Aggressive
Boundaries	Healthy	Unhealthy; often invades others boundaries
Indulgence	Self-indulgent (as appropriate)	Selfish
Sees others	As separate individuals with own needs and feelings	Primarily as how others can be useful to them
Responsibility	Assumes appropriate personal responsibility	Blames others; avoids personal responsibility
Character defects	Owns character defects	Tends to project own character defects onto others
Needs to control	Values balance rather than control. Uses dominion rather than domination	Seeks to control or dominate people, places and things
Self-awareness	Self-aware (of needs and feelings)	Tends to be unaware (numb) or hypersensitive
Sensitivity	Sensitive to perceived criticism or rejection	Hypersensitive to criticism or rejection
Anger	Expresses appropriately	Inappropriate outbursts of anger or rage/or internalized rage and anger
Honesty	Tends to be honest	Often dishonest
Empathy	Feels and expresses	Lack of empathy
Flexibility	Realistic and flexible	Perfectionistic
Values	Values intimacy, love, productivity and creativity	Values "power," money, beauty and attention
Being around them is	Enlivening	Toxic and draining

Table 5.6. Some Reciprocal Characteristics of the Unhealthy Narcissist (dysfunctional other) and the Co-dependent.

	Unhealthy Narcissist	**Co-Dependent**
Attraction	For the co-dependent	For the narcissist
Mirroring	Demands perfect mirroring by the co-dependent; gives unhealthy mirroring in return	Gets and gives unhealthy mirroring by primary involvement with narcissist
Focus	False self (narcissistic self or negative ego)	The narcissist
Need	To feel important and special	To help others feel important and special
View of self and **other**	Cannot see other as separate from self	Cannot see self as separate from other
Self-caring	Overdone	Underdone or absent

Source: Compiled in part from Masterson 1988 and Cermak 1991.

Even with all of these differences, they tend to have at least four things in common: They each (1) grew up in a dysfunctional family and (2) have thereby lost their True Self; and each is (3) seeking acceptance, intimacy and love; while each also (4) fears that intimacy. They also often participate together in a form of an ego-defense system called projective identification that is common to such relationships (see discussion at end of Chapter 8).

Beyond Narcissus And Echo: The Hero/Heroine's Journey

While the myth of Narcissus and Echo is helpful in increasing our understanding of some of the dynamics of the interaction of unhealthy narcissism and co-dependence in their extremes, there are other myths, legends, and stories, as mentioned above, that are more expansive in our understanding of co-dependence and especially of the recovery process. Perhaps the most useful is from the work of Joseph Campbell and others, wherein they describe the hero or heroine's journey[121,645,646]. Whether the hero is Ulysses, Parsifal, Helen Keller, or the Little Prince, their journey is *our* journey. Whether we are wandering aimlessly in the fog of any Stage Zero disorder or are recovering in a more focused way through the several stages of our healing process, *we* are the hero. We go through trial after trial, adventure after adventure, as we heal our human condition and discover our true identity in our own way and in our own time.

In ancient times, creating, focusing upon and blaming mythical gods and our interactions with them was a way to begin to make some sense of our human condition. Perhaps co-dependently, rather than own it, we projected our shadow stuff onto these gods. In trying to heal this unfinished business, we can project aspects of our positive and negative, light and dark, conscious and unconscious material outside of ourself and onto these made up characters and their families. It is only when we bring them *inside* of ourself — and take responsibility for working through their dualities and conflicts — that we can begin to get free of their painful hold on us. In doing so, we *own* our shadow, all of our unfinished business that until now has remained painfully unconscious inside of us.

In recovery we can thus make some use of these myths and their dynamics. In them are all of the material that we talk about today — only expressed in different language. While these gods and their families were quite dysfunctional — repeatedly mistreating and wounding their children and each other — they also showed many strengths, some of which were transformed from their weaknesses. In their dysfunction, they illustrated composite and often outrageous "case histories" of what today we might call adult child and co-dependent issues. These characters experienced and acted out a number of core recovery issues, including abandonment, all-or-none thinking and behaving, control, high tolerance for inappropriate behavior and difficulty being real. As we heal, we can study them when and where appropriate, and use them in our recovery.

6

The Natural History Of Co-dependence

Now that we have seen some of the ways that the co-dependence/adult child syndrome may present, let's look at how such a life might unfold. I call this "the natural history of co-dependence."

We may become co-dependent at any time in our life, but most of us learn it from birth. As children, when we get into conflict or experience a loss, we hurt. The important people around us — our parents, teachers and so on — often do not support us or allow us to express or heal our hurt, and so we stuff it. The genesis of co-dependence begins with the repression of our observations, feelings and reactions. Eventually we begin to invalidate our own crucial internal cues (see Figure 1.1).

This lack of attention to ourself makes others assume greater importance, and we begin to pay more attention to them. Because we focus so much on the needs of others, we begin to neglect our own needs. By so doing we stifle our True Self. Usually early in this process we begin to deny a family secret, such as a parent's alcoholism or some other dysfunction. Such secrets are often so charged with painful feelings — also part of our True Self — that we have to push them away and out of our experiential view, into our subconscious mind[652].

But we still have feelings, often of hurt. As we continue to stuff our feelings, we become increasingly tolerant of emotional pain in an unhealthy way. We may become so tolerant that we become numb. And because we stuff our feelings, we are unable to grieve our everyday losses to completion[654].

So our True Self, the part of us that acknowledges our real feelings, is in hiding. But we still need some part of us to run our lives. To survive, we begin to construct a false or co-dependent self. Making and identifying with this false self further blocks our mental, emotional and spiritual growth and development.

Yet we have a desire to contact and know our True Self. We learn that "quick fixes," such as addictive and compulsive behaviors, will allow us to glimpse our True Self and, by letting some feelings emerge, will let off some of the tension. However, if the compulsive behavior is destructive to us or to others, we may feel shame and a resulting lower self-esteem. At this point, unable to contact our True Self, we may begin to feel more and more out of control, and we try to compensate by the need to control even more. We may end up deluded and hurt, and often project our pain onto others.

We continue to be alienated from our True Self. Our tension has now built to such an extent that we may develop stress-related illness manifested by aches and pains, and often by dysfunction of one or more body organs. We are now in an advanced state of co-dependence and may progressively deteriorate so that we experience one or more of the following: extreme mood swings, difficulty with intimate relationships and chronic unhappiness. This advanced state of co-dependence may seriously interfere with the recovery process of those who are attempting to recover from alcoholism, another chemical dependence or another condition or illness.

I summarize the development or genesis of co-dependence in Table 6.1.

Early in this development two core issues emerge: fear of abandonment and shame. We are afraid that if we are real, that our parent or other will leave us. And why else would they leave us?

Because we are inadequate, bad, not enough. And so we feel ashamed. These core issues, and several others, will surface regularly — whether conscious or unconscious — in the daily life of the person with active co-dependence[645,654].

Table 6.1. Genesis Of Co-dependence

1. Wounded and inadequate parents; and unsupportive other environment.
2. Invalidation and repression of inner life and its internal cues, such as our observations, feelings and reactions.
3. Neglecting our needs.
4. Beginning to stifle our True Self (Child Within).
5. Beginning to construct our co-dependent (false) self.
6. Denying a family secret or other toxic secret.
7. Increasing tolerance of and numbness to emotional pain.
8. Distortions in personal boundaries.
9. Development of high tolerance for inappropriate behavior.
10. Inability to grieve a loss to completion.
11. Blocking of growth (mental, emotional, spiritual).
12. Compulsive behaviors in order to lessen pain and to glimpse our True Self.
13. Progressive shame and loss of self-esteem.
14. Feeling out of control. Need to control more.
15. Delusion and projection of pain.
16. Stress-related illness develops.
17. Compulsions worsen.
18. Progressive deterioration:

   - extreme mood swings
   - difficulty with intimate relationships
   - chronic unhappiness
   - interference with recovery from alcoholism/chemical dependence, compulsions and other conditions

Whether we are an infant or a child growing up with such alienated and dysfunctional people, or whether we are an adult living with or close to them, it is highly likely that — with our present awareness and coping skills — we will be negatively affected. By the process described in this book and elsewhere, our True Self will be stifled[266,263,645]. We learn to focus outside of ourself and on others as a survival tool, to stop the hurting and to help our lives work better. However, it doesn't work well, and persistently doing so develops into co-dependence.

We Had To Give Away Our Personal Power

To survive, we have unconsciously been forced to give away our personal power. To understand some of the dynamics of reclaiming our personal power, we can use a simple formula: **P = A + R.** That is, Personal Power equals Awareness plus Responsibility.

Awareness

Awareness means cognizance of our inner life. In recovery we become progressively more aware of each and every component of our inner life. This includes our beliefs, thoughts, feelings, decisions, choices, needs, body sensations, intuitions, daydreams and night dreams, other experiences and more. Before recovery it might have felt frightening and confusing to enter too far into our inner life. As we reclaim our personal power and begin to experience our inner life, it may still feel that way sometimes; but it also begins to feel exciting and enlivening. It begins to feel *real.*

Responsibility

To claim our personal power we take responsibility for doing several things with our inner life. We can experience it by letting go into being in and with whatever comes up for us from our inner life. An important part of recovery is to learn to tolerate emotional pain in a healthy way. As we experience our inner life, we can also begin to observe it.

We take responsibility to treat everything that comes into our awareness from our inner life as being valid, real and owning it. Just this act of owning can empower and enliven us. We can then consider it, begin to process it, and then if doing so is appropriate, begin to express some of it with one or more safe people.

We become empowered by being aware and by taking responsibility for doing all of the above. Finally, we consider how it may be useful for us now or in the future, in living, growing and co-creating our life. We also take responsibility by setting healthy boundaries and limits around our True Self and its inner life.

Where We Give It Away

Most of us never learned much about our personal power. We simply were not shown, taught or allowed to claim and use it. To survive, we gave our power away. And we may still be giving it away, even though we no longer need to do so to survive.

To whom might we give away our personal power? As children we gave it to our parents and other family members. We gave it away to our educational system, including our professional schools, by allowing it to teach us mostly useless and irrelevant information. We gave it away to organized religion, which in part made up its own rules about us and our Higher Power and shamed and guilted us for not following them[86a,88,219,298a,577].

We gave away our personal power to relationships with people who did not accept us as our own unique True Self in all of its love and its glory. And we gave away our personal power to our colleagues and peers — from "peer pressure" to all kinds of toxic conformity[299]. We gave it away to "experts." We gave it away to politicians, most of whom are unrecovered co-dependents and adult children, who work in a dysfunctional bureaucracy that we call our local, state and federal government.

We gave it away to chemicals and food, to addictions and compulsions. And we gave it away to our law enforcement system. Just look at how this system works: Crime continues to besiege us and is worsening, and we are "losing" the "battle" in the "war" on drugs — a war that nearly totally ignores the legal drugs of alcohol, tobacco and prescription drugs. Both government and these legal systems try to fight drugs in a typically co-dependent way — by trying to "control" them[84].

We gave and still give away our personal power to the media, which has an emphasis on politics, selling and sensationalizing, in a practice of non-stop unhealthy competition[405]. And we gave it away to "authority figures," while mostly ignoring our own inner authority (our True Self connected to its Higher Power). We give it away to the written word, with the illusion that if it is in print or published, it is somehow more true than if it is not. This literature includes not only popular literature, but also so-called "scientific" and academically oriented books and articles.

We gave it away to helping professionals who patched us up without assisting us in deeper healing. And we gave it away to celebrities and to gurus who may have misled us away from our True Self. Finally, we gave it away to perhaps the most incompetent one of all: our ego, our false self — our co-dependent self.

Reviewing these and other possibilities can be useful in considering the genesis of our wounding and our co-dependence. But in recovery we discover that we now have a choice: to be authentic and real or to continue to be false and co-dependent.

Two Roads

Robert Frost's poem "The Road Not Taken" ends: "Two roads diverged in a wood, and I took the one less traveled by, and that has made all the difference." These are the roads of being real or false (see Figure 6.1), and certainly being real is the less-traveled road. If we choose to be real, and live from and as our True Self through our awareness and responsibility, we can then have authentic experiences in relationships with our self, others and with the God of our understanding. In the process of our recovery, we can then realize self-knowledge, growth and serenity. This appears to occur in a never-ending cycle of wounding and recovery, regression and progression, involution and evolution, as we live the unfolding Divine Mystery of being our True Self in experiential connection with our Higher Power.

But we often make the other choice. We choose, often involuntarily, our false self with its existence of active co-dependence, addiction and attachment to people, places, things, behaviors and experiences. While we may gain some life experience here, it will be by definition incomplete and not authentic. And from our continuing unresolved conflicts, which the ego in large part participates in making, we experience no resolution and no self-knowledge. We feel like martyrs or victims: stagnated or regressed, chronically unhappy.

The choice between those two paths is ours. We usually make it when we are well into our recovery.

The "Iceberg" Model Of Co-dependence

Another way to describe important parts of the natural history of co-dependence is by the "iceberg" model. Figure 6.2 shows the

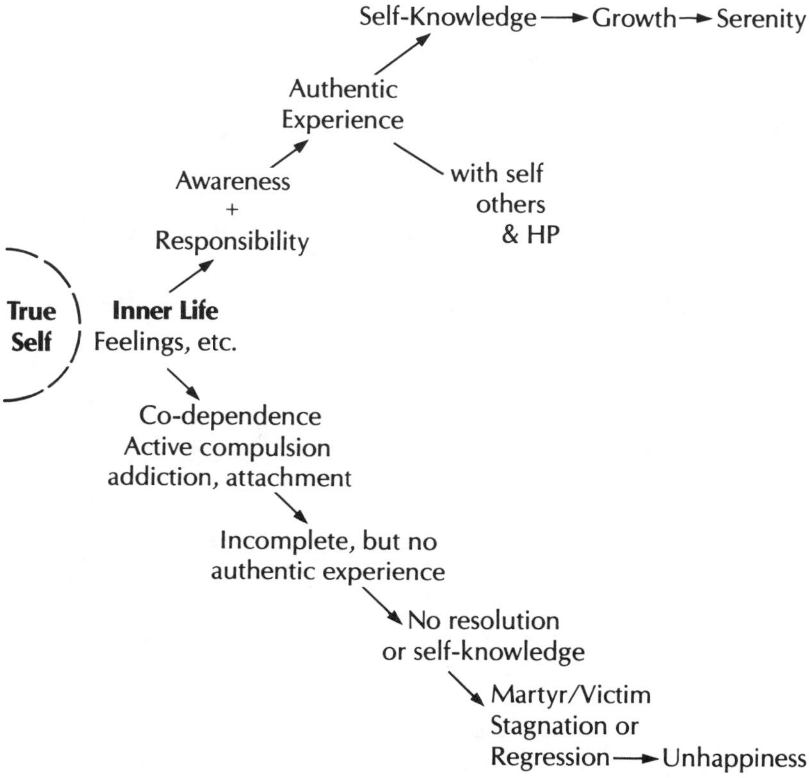

Figure 6.1. Two Choices In Recovery

relationship of co-dependence to some of its origins and consequences. Let's take a closer look at the sequence of events.

An Unhealthy Family And Society

We grow up in an unhealthy family of origin and in an unhealthy society. In that setting we do not get our healthy human needs met, including the ability to be real. In the unfolding of this process, at least two major incidents later become core recovery issues: fear of abandonment and toxic shame. What is being abandoned is our True Self.

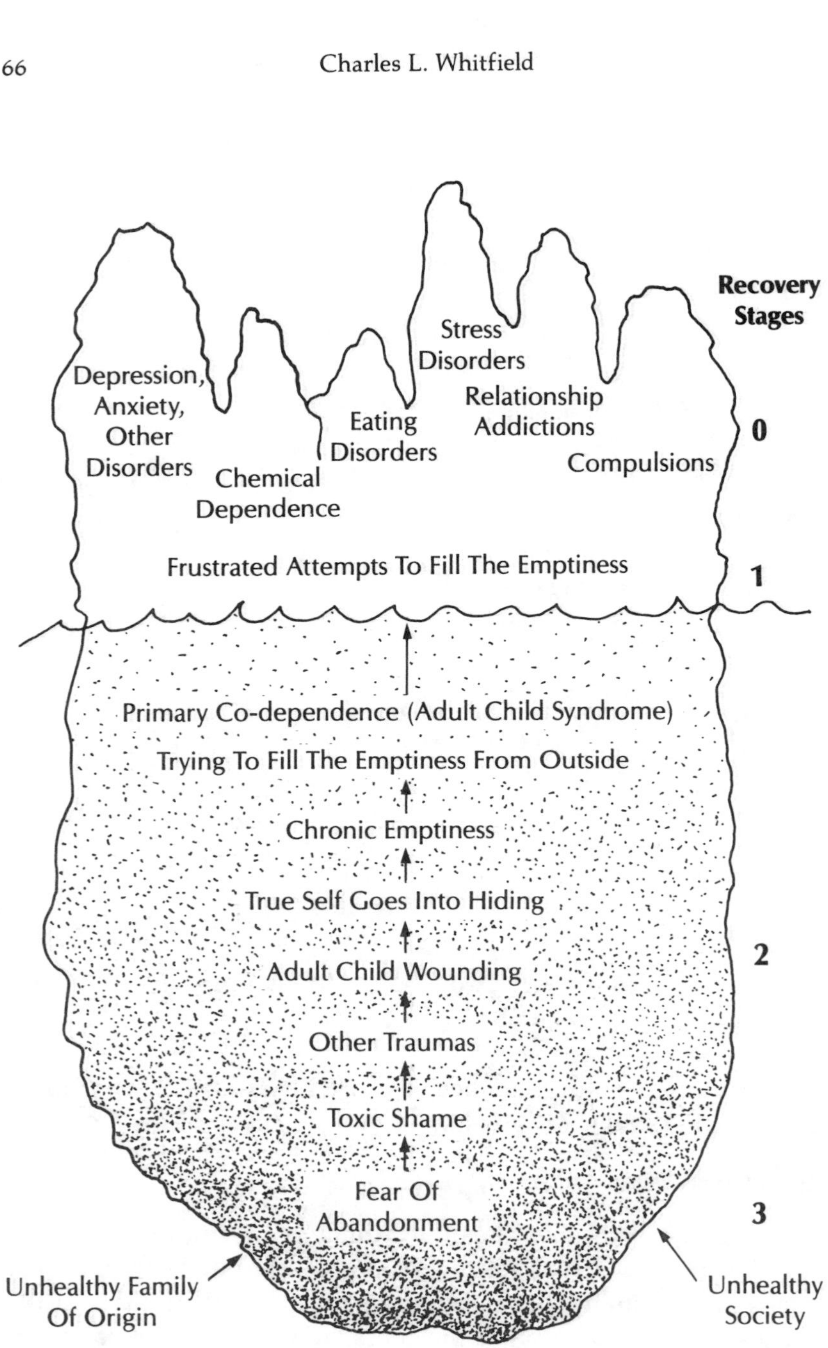

Figure 6.2. The Iceberg Model: Relationship of Adult Child Wounding, Co-dependence and Various Disorders

Modeled after Travis and Ryan 1988, Friel and Friel 1987 and Whitfield 1987.

Fear Of Abandonment And Toxic Shame

And why would anyone abandon me? Because I must not be good enough. This constant abandonment of our True Self, combined with the projected inadequacies and other "poisonous pedagogy" of our parents, peers and others in society, generates toxic shame.

Because of the continued and overwhelming pain from the abandonment, toxic shame and other traumatic events, our True Self goes into hiding — deep within the unconscious part of its psyche. This is the wounding that becomes what we call the adult child syndrome.

While as children we experience many feeling states, a predominant one is *emptiness.* It seems that no matter what we may experience, gnawing away in the background is always a feeling of emptiness, which aches and cries to be filled.

Trying To Fill The Emptiness From The Outside

And so we set out on a long journey of trying to fill the emptiness. At the same time, the false or co-dependent self has come forward to try to run our life. This combination of the child in hiding and the false self's trying to run our life and fill our emptiness from the outside is the crux of co-dependence.

And all the while our True Self is trying, often desperately, to come out of hiding to connect, experience, express, create, celebrate and be. This tension between the True Self and the false self is the basic conflict in co-dependence — the human condition.

We may attempt to fill our emptiness from the outside in numerous ways, with all sorts of people, places, things, behaviors and experiences. These may result in experiencing any of several possible painful consequences, including:

- Depression, anxiety and related disorders
- Chemical dependence
- Eating disorders
- Relationship addiction
- Stress-related disorders
- Compulsions

Just which one or more of these we get depends in large part on our hereditary makeup, our environment and other factors. While co-dependence is not the single cause of any of these disorders or conditions, it is usually a major causal and aggravating factor in the genesis and the relapse process of the specific disorder or condition. And thus it is important to eventually heal the co-dependence as a beginning part of the total treatment of whatever disorder may have been present on the surface.

Repeated and frustrated attempts to fill our emptiness from the outside may eventually teach us that the cause of our emptiness is due to only two closely related factors: our True Self is in hiding and is not experientially connected to God.*

The Wounding And Recovery Curve

Still another way to describe key events and concepts in the development or genesis of co-dependence and its recovery is the *Wounding and Recovery Curve* (see Figure 6.3). It is modeled after the curve for the pathogenesis and recovery from alcoholism designed by Glatt[249] and Jellinek[316] and can similarly describe some of the sequences for co-dependence. This chart summarizes, integrates and expands most of the concepts described above in this and previous chapters.

The Process Of Wounding

The process of wounding begins with the spiritual and proceeds through the mental, emotional and then the physical aspects of our life (see Figure 6.2). The recovery process goes in reverse, from the physical (Stage One recovery), to the mental and emotional (Stage Two) and finally to the spiritual (Stage Three). Wounding and recovery. Involution and evolution.

We start out as a spark of Consciousness, of Love — an innocent Child of God. We separate from that Source and forget our Identity as being part of the Divine. We are born into a family and a society of wounded and unrecovered adult children, where our

*I develop these concepts further in parts of *Healing The Child Within, A Gift To Myself* and *Spirituality In Recovery*.

healthy needs are not met. Fearing abandonment by our parents or other important relationships, we internalized their projected pain and inadequacies. We continually experience their invalidation of our uniqueness and our inner life and incorporate it as toxic (unnecessary and traumatic) shame. Because of this overwhelming pain, our True Self goes into hiding. As a result, we feel empty.

While at some level we may sense that something is wrong and that we are in an unhealthy family, we know that there is little we can do about it. If we faced up to that fact, the pain and confusion might be too overwhelming. To survive we internalize the projected painful messages that we are inadequate and bad and that our parents and others are adequate and good. We thus idealize our parents and other authority figures.

We neglect our healthy needs and deny our internal and external reality in order to survive. Even with continued trauma, however, our True Self never dies. It struggles to come alive in all kinds of ways. *But its being real* is still stifled, so we try to fill our emptiness with the only way that others model and accept — from the outside. When this doesn't work, we experience an increasing unhealthy tolerance of and numbness to emotional pain. This inability to feel and to grieve, coupled with distortions in our personal boundaries, may cause us to become "people pleasers."

The Wounding Deepens

Operating out of fear and shame means that if we are afraid important people will leave us, we learn to tolerate their inappropriate behavior to such an extent that we develop the condition associated with the core issue of high tolerance for inappropriate behavior. Arrested or stunted in our development, and outer-focused to the detriment of our True Self, we now have the condition of primary co-dependence, a major manifestation of the adult child syndrome.

During this time we have likely experienced multiple and repeated episodes of age regression — suddenly feeling small and helpless when experiencing any kind and degree of trauma. These repeated age regressions tend to reinforce our fear, shame and confusion (see also page 147).

Figure 6.3. Curve of Adult Child /

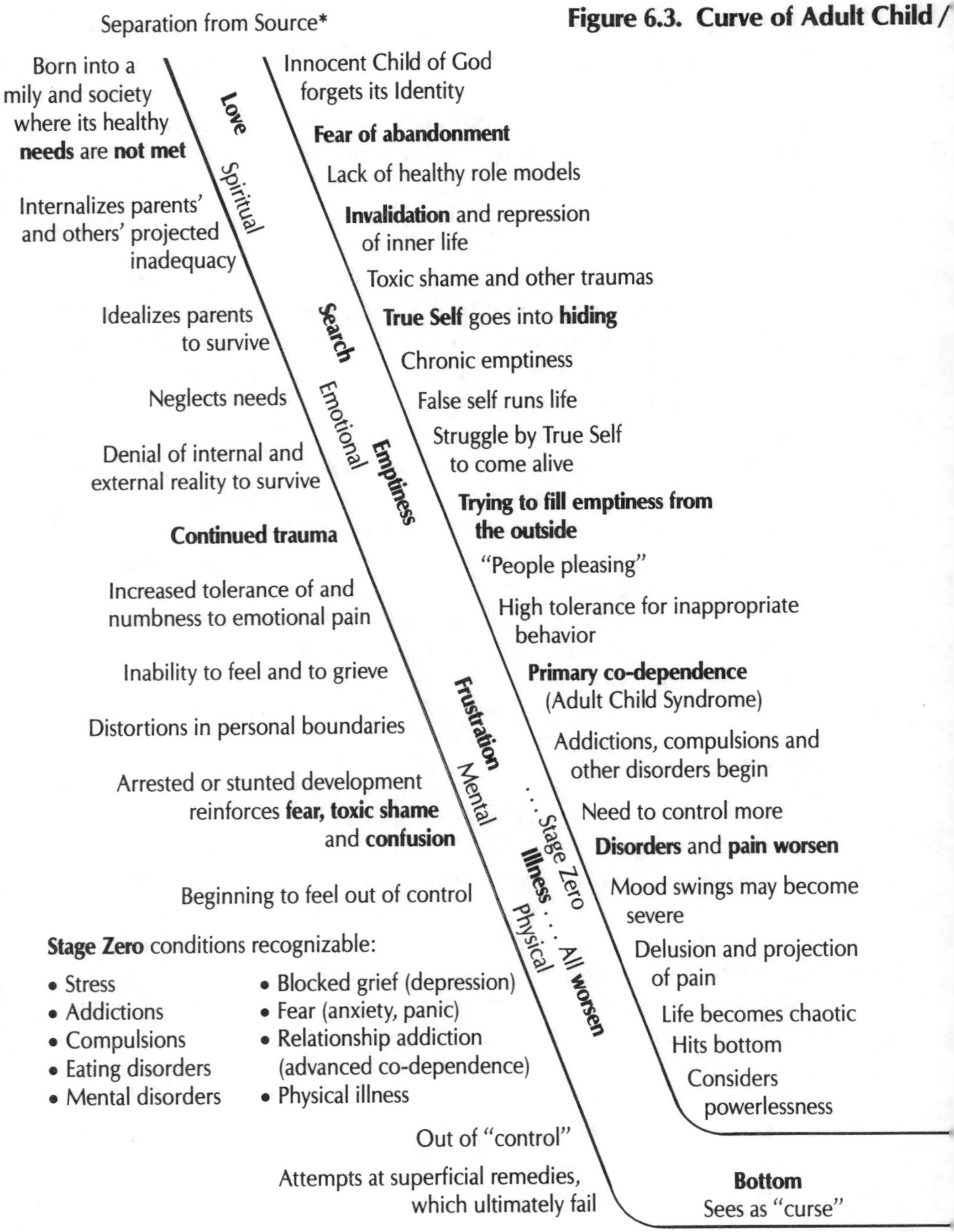
Separation from Source*
Born into a
mily and society
where its healthy
needs are **not met**
Internalizes parents'
and others' projected
inadequacy
Idealizes parents
to survive
Neglects needs
Denial of internal and
external reality to survive
Continued trauma
Increased tolerance of and
numbness to emotional pain
Inability to feel and to grieve
Distortions in personal boundaries
Arrested or stunted development
reinforces **fear, toxic shame**
and **confusion**
Beginning to feel out of control
Stage Zero conditions recognizable:
• Stress
• Addictions
• Compulsions
• Eating disorders
• Mental disorders
• Blocked grief (depression)
• Fear (anxiety, panic)
• Relationship addiction
(advanced co-dependence)
• Physical illness
Out of "control"
Attempts at superficial remedies,
which ultimately fail
Love
Spiritual
Search
Emotional
Emptiness
Frustration
Mental
Illness
Physical
. . . Stage Zero
. . . **All worsen**
Innocent Child of God
forgets its Identity
Fear of abandonment
Lack of healthy role models
Invalidation and repression
of inner life
Toxic shame and other traumas
True Self goes into **hiding**
Chronic emptiness
False self runs life
Struggle by True Self
to come alive
Trying to fill emptiness from
the outside
"People pleasing"
High tolerance for inappropriate
behavior
Primary co-dependence
(Adult Child Syndrome)
Addictions, compulsions and
other disorders begin
Need to control more
Disorders and **pain worsen**
Mood swings may become
severe
Delusion and projection
of pain
Life becomes chaotic
Hits bottom
Considers
powerlessness
Bottom
Sees as "curse"

*Higher Power, God/Goddess/All-That-Is

Co-dependence Wounding and Recovery

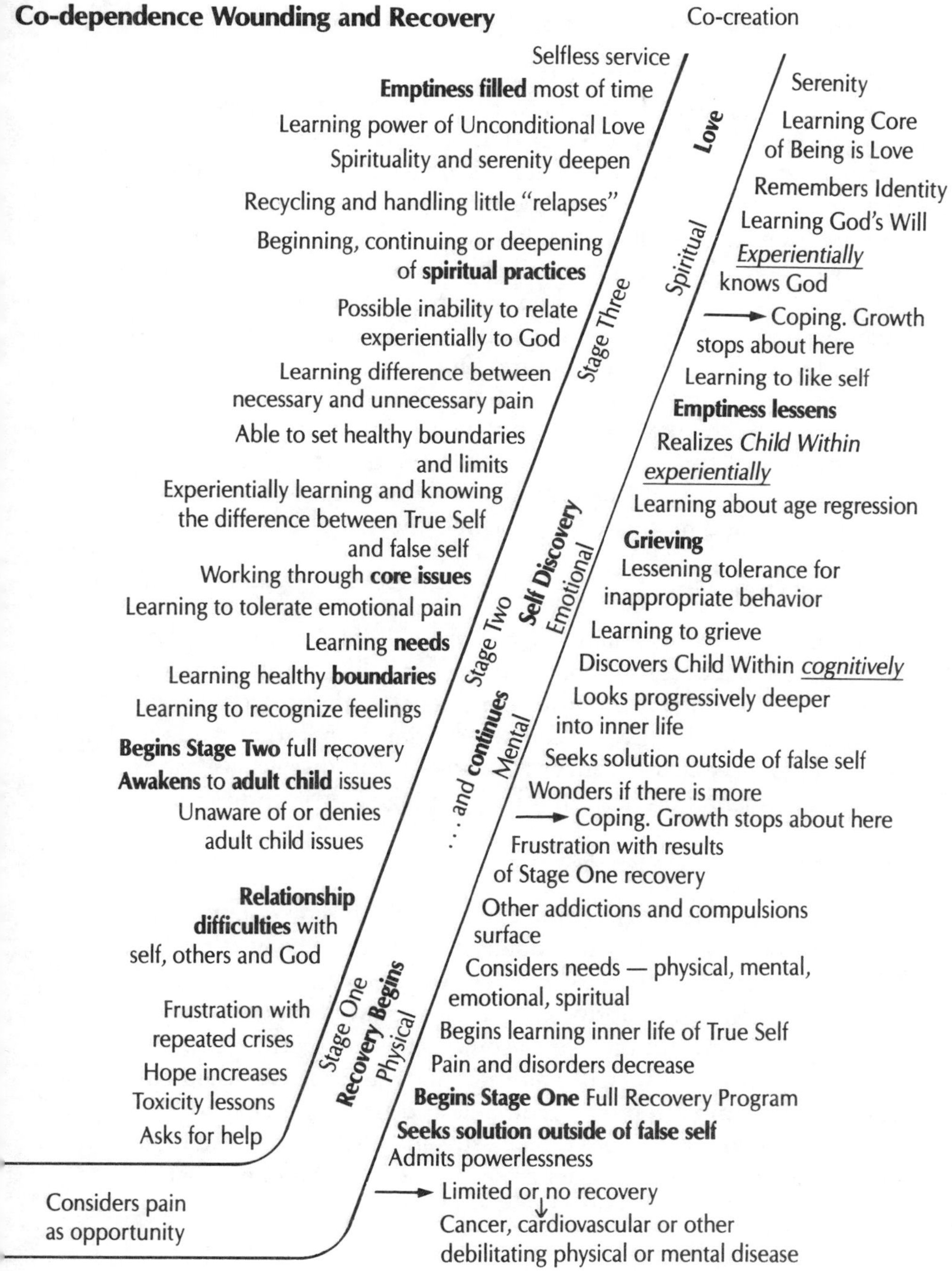
Co-creation
Selfless service
Emptiness filled most of time
Learning power of Unconditional Love
Spirituality and serenity deepen
Recycling and handling little "relapses"
Beginning, continuing or deepening of **spiritual practices**
Possible inability to relate experientially to God
Learning difference between necessary and unnecessary pain
Able to set healthy boundaries and limits
Experientially learning and knowing the difference between True Self and false self
Working through **core issues**
Learning to tolerate emotional pain
Learning **needs**
Learning healthy **boundaries**
Learning to recognize feelings
Begins Stage Two full recovery
Awakens to **adult child** issues
Unaware of or denies adult child issues
Relationship difficulties with self, others and God
Frustration with repeated crises
Hope increases
Toxicity lessons
Asks for help
Considers pain as opportunity
Stage Three
Stage Two
Stage One
Love
Spiritual
Self Discovery
Emotional
. . . and **continues**
Mental
Recovery Begins
Physical
Serenity
Learning Core of Being is Love
Remembers Identity
Learning God's Will
Experientially knows God
Coping. Growth stops about here
Learning to like self
Emptiness lessens
Realizes *Child Within* *experientially*
Learning about age regression
Grieving
Lessening tolerance for inappropriate behavior
Learning to grieve
Discovers Child Within *cognitively*
Looks progressively deeper into inner life
Seeks solution outside of false self
Wonders if there is more
Coping. Growth stops about here
Frustration with results of Stage One recovery
Other addictions and compulsions surface
Considers needs — physical, mental, emotional, spiritual
Begins learning inner life of True Self
Pain and disorders decrease
Begins Stage One Full Recovery Program
Seeks solution outside of false self
Admits powerlessness
Limited or no recovery
Cancer, cardiovascular or other debilitating physical or mental disease

Addictions, Compulsions And Disorders Appear

Eventually, one or more addictions, compulsions or other disorders may appear. These may also include: stress-related or psychosomatic illness; blocked grief, often called depression; unhandled fears, often called anxiety or panic disorder; relationship addiction, which happens commonly in advanced co-dependence; and any of a variety of mental or physical disorders or illnesses.

During any of these we may begin to feel out of control. Because of this, we experience the need to control more, accompanied by mood swings that may become severe, and delusion and projection of our pain onto others. Our life may become chaotic. We may make various attempts at superficial remedies for all of this pain, which may or may not help. But ultimately, we hit bottom. It is at this point that we have the opportunity to begin to recognize and heal this entire wounding process through the self-initiated and motivated experience known as *recovery*.

The Process Of Recovery

No one knows how many people are able to use "hitting bottom" as an opportunity for recovery and life transformation. Many who hit bottom seem to experience little or no recovery. They continue living lives of noisy or quiet desperation, and end with often premature cancer, cardiovascular disease, or other physical or mental disease, that is, any Stage Zero conditions.

Searching Outside Of The False Self

But some people do awaken. Perhaps the common denominator in this awakening is admitting powerlessness in some way, enough so that we are able to seek answers outside of our false or co-dependent self, ego, adaptive or grandiose self. During our period of descent or involution, we become attached to the false self, which convinced us that it was the only way that we could survive. Having forgotten our True Self and its connection to God, we did not know that we were already and always safe and on an eternal journey and experience, a part of the Divine Mystery, and that this adventure was but a part of it.

Some Triggers To Recovery

Recovery begins at the moment we admit powerlessness and reach for help outside of our false self. At that time several different possibilities may occur to help trigger an awakening to our actual, current condition. These triggers can occur to initiate any of the three stages of recovery. They may include experiencing any one or more of those awakening experiences listed on page 100.

Stage One Recovery

At this point we may reach out and ask for help. If we find competent help and begin to take responsibility for our recovery, we may then begin a Stage One partial or full recovery program. Our Stage Zero disorder and its pain and toxicity may begin to lessen.

Soon we become more hopeful and start the earliest beginnings of learning about our inner life. We also begin to consider our physical, mental, emotional and spiritual needs and start getting them met. During this time one or more crises may occur, but we can now begin to learn to use each of these as a growth experience. Repeated crises, however, may frustrate us. Because we have not yet realized our True Self and connected experientially to God, we may still feel empty. As we continue to search for fulfillment outside of these, other addictions and compulsions may surface. We may need to address *these* now with another, somewhat different Stage One full recovery program.

Even though we are doing better, we may become frustrated with parts of our recovery in Stage One. This frustration may be aggravated by continuing difficulties in our relationships with ourself, others and God. And while our Stage One recovery may eventually be mostly stable, we may be unaware of — or even deny — our co-dependence or adult child issues. At this point in our recovery we may continue just coping, and our growth may stop about here. And with no further growth, we may remain actively co-dependent and slowly spiral back down toward chronic unhappiness and a premature death.

Stage Two Recovery

We may hit bottom more than once. At this point something may trigger our awakening into the possibility of Stage Two: adult child or co-dependence recovery. As we thus awaken to our adult child condition and wonder if there is more to our life, we may again seek help outside of our false self. As before, if we find competent help and then take responsibility for our recovery and our life, we can begin a Stage Two partial or full recovery program (see Part II of this book and *A Gift To Myself* for details of the recovery process).

As we enter Stage Two recovery, we begin to look deeper into our inner life. In this process of recovery we will be learning:

- To recognize our *feelings* and use them constructively
- What our *needs* are and how to get them met
- To *grieve* our ungrieved losses, hurts and traumas
- To *tolerate* emotional *pain*
- To set healthy *boundaries* and limits
- To work through our *core* recovery *issues.*

We will also be learning about the important phenomenon of age regression and how it can help us in our recovery. And we will be learning cognitively about our Child Within.

This is usually a time of great confusion and emotional pain. But it is also a time of gradually increasing clarity, excitement and eventually peace. Soon we will begin to lose our high tolerance for inappropriate behavior. As conflicts come up in our daily life, we will *experientially connect* them to our *past,* and thereby work through our ungrieved hurts and losses. Throughout this experience we will be learning the difference between our True Self and our false self.

Over a period of from three to five years — or longer — we will experientially realize our Child Within, and our feeling of emptiness will begin to lessen. As we work through much or most of our toxic shame, we will be learning to like ourself. We will also be learning the difference between necessary and unnecessary pain.

During all this time we may or may not have been developing a growing relationship with our Higher Power. If we continue and deepen this relationship experientially — if we feel it in our hearts — then we can move into Stage Three recovery. If we do not, we may continue just coping. Even though we are much more aware of our True Self, our growth may stop here. If that happens, we may not discover and know God's Will and Love for us and may not learn to be a co-creator with that One.

Stage Three Recovery

While some people may experience yet another bottom to enter Stage Three recovery, many will not. This is because they will be beginning, continuing or deepening their spiritual practices, such as meditation, prayer, reading spiritual literature, working the Twelve Steps and the like. In this stage we can thus learn that *we can grow without suffering* — through these spiritual practices and by practicing and extending Unconditional Love[279].

Here we will continue to get our healthy needs met. When "little relapses" or "recycles" come up, we will handle them, with the assistance of our Higher Power. We will experientially know God, and our spirituality and serenity will deepen.

We will also be learning what God's Will is for us (see Chapter 23 and such books as *A Course In Miracles).* As we progressively get to know our True Self and its connection to God, our emptiness will be filled most of the time. We will learn more and more how to let go of our false self. As if it were some long-forgotten melody, we will begin to remember our true Identity: as a Child of God.

From here on, a large part of our life may be about progressively knowing the power of Unconditional Love. We can do this through experiencing Unity Consciousness; learning that the Core of our Being is Love; and by practicing selfless service, which is distinctly different from being actively co-dependent. Having realized the strength of our humility and innocence, we may now begin to co-create our life: We do all that we can do, and then surrender to God to do the rest.

7

How Co-dependence Becomes Physical Illness

During the middle or advanced stage of co-dependence, physical illness may develop. It may be due to stress that is mishandled to such a degree that it becomes distress, which then develops into stress-related illness. Physicians spend most of their time treating stress-related illnesses of all sorts[185,572,646]. In an attempt to avoid the pain of short-term stress, co-dependents stuff their feelings and attempt to please others. Such avoidance usually ends up producing long-term stress called *distress.*

Toxic Rules That Block Grieving

Physical illness may also develop through disallowed or repressed grieving. From birth we are taught dysfunctional family rules, the incorporation of which is part of the genesis of co-dependence. For example:

1. It's not OK to talk about problems or to talk about or express our feelings openly.
2. It's not OK to communicate indirectly through another person than the one you need to talk to.

3. Don't be "selfish."
4. Always be strong, good, perfect and happy.
5. It's not OK to be playful and have fun.
6. Don't rock the boat (adapted from Subby 1987).

These kinds of rules may serve to protect us from short-term conflict and pain, but they set the stage for hiding our True Self, including its needs, wants and feelings.

Unexpressed Feelings

Inevitably, we will have losses. These rules tend to prevent us from grieving our losses in a healthy way. And what we do not grieve healthily, we tend to act out in physical, mental, emotional or behavioral ways that are often problematic. For example, *anger* unexpressed and unprocessed may manifest as depression, compulsion and addiction; family and child abuse; and probably a lowering of our body's immune response — which is a major factor in our ability to fight off infection and cancer.

Unexpressed *fear* can result in anxiety disorders, insomnia, heart arrhythmias, sexual dysfunction and other stress-related illnesses. Unexpressed *guilt* may lead to self-neglect, compulsion and addiction, other self-destructive behavior and other chronic conditions. And unexpressed *shame* can result in self-neglect, compulsion and addiction, other self-destructive behavior, sexual dysfunction and other chronic conditions. Our feelings do not just happen in our minds: they are complex physiological interactions within our True Self's sophisticated system of internal cues.

Research suggests that writing and sharing our feelings strengthens our body's immune response. In one study 25 adults kept a diary of disturbing life events for five days and wrote how they felt about each of them. Another 25 adults kept a diary about superficial life events only. Their immune response was measured at six weeks, and then six months later and compared with their baseline. The former group had an improved immune response, whereas the latter group had no change[490,491]. Studies like these, coupled with clinical observations[576], indicate that when we do not grieve in a healthy way — when we do not let our True Self experience and express itself — we often get sick.

For the first ten years my medical practice involved mostly conventional, somatically oriented medicine. The last sixteen years has been progressively devoted to an eclectically oriented psychotherapy. In all this time I have observed more than a thousand co-dependent patients. I noticed a pattern of chronic functional, psychosomatic or physical illness in these people, covering a spectrum from asthma, to migraine headaches, to arthritis, to hearing loss, all of which tended to improve or clear with treatment that was specific for their Stage Zero disorder *and* for their co-dependence.

The Relationship Between Co-dependence And Chronic Fatigue Syndrome

Nearly any physical illness may be aggravated by co-dependence. One that particularly appears to be related to overwork and neglecting one's needs in co-dependence is chronic fatigue syndrome (CFS), which is caused by an inability of the body to contain a virus, possibly the Epstein-Barr virus[327]. This virus is present in about 90 percent of the population, but does little or no damage unless the immune system is overstressed or weakened.

The fatigue of CFS is often so debilitating that it requires long periods of total bed rest. Other symptoms may vary from headache, sore throat, muscle and joint pain to gastrointestinal disturbances, inability to concentrate and remember, blurred vision, night sweats, depression and the inability to sleep soundly despite chronic fatigue[110,303,603].

Many who are afflicted with CFS push themselves beyond their limits. These people tend to be caretakers or high energy expenders, who ignore the signs that their bodies are giving them. Some co-dependents tend to use a chronic busy-ness, including helping others to the detriment of self, as a way of self-medicating their chronic emotional pain. As they recover from both the CFS and their co-dependence, they learn to work more moderately, acknowledge and meet their physical needs for rest and recreation, and say no whenever they feel any warning signs, no matter what they may have committed to. CFS is but one example of *many illnesses* that may be *aggravated* or even partially caused *by co-dependence.*

Future Directions

I believe that the concept of co-dependence will eventually affect the practice of medicine, including psychiatry.

Is it possible that co-dependence is a co-factor in the pathogenesis of cancer? How might co-dependence affect the development of cardiovascular disease and many other medical and surgical conditions, including AIDS?

Many people are writing on the important and often crucial effect of the mind and spirit on the body[185,415,572,720,723,727], but none has related it clearly to co-dependence. We may be on the brink of breakthroughs in this puzzling area of medicine. The field is wide open for the exploration and sharing of observations and research.

8

Co-dependence And Psychological Illness

Since its inception the mental health field has been helping people with co-dependence. What is now changing are the ways we describe these people's conditions and help them recover. For a while we used fancier descriptive terms such as "neurosis" and other disorders, "undifferentiation," "passive aggressive," "locus of control," "other directed" and "outer focused." And we also used simpler terms such as "victim," "martyr" and "stress." We helped these people get to know themselves better and take more responsibility for their lives. Now, however, we are reframing and broadening the dynamics of the conditions that we have for so long observed. As a result we have a more precise and sophisticated way of helping people.

Relationship To Other Disorders

How does co-dependence impinge upon or fit in with the various psychological disorders? And how useful will it be to describe co-dependence as an independent disorder or disease entity?

For those helping professionals who are aware of and treat people with co-dependence, it is useful to describe it as a discrete disorder. Whatever guise it may first present as, co-dependence is involved as a primary or secondary factor in the person's difficulties or suffering. This is practical because co-dependence is such an imminently understandable and treatable condition. It is understandable for both the recovering person and the helping professional, and this fact enhances the movement of the recovery process for both. As described throughout this and other writings, there are effective treatment approaches and techniques available for co-dependence as a specific disorder. It is likely that these will be progressively refined with time and experience, and that we will create additional helpful treatment approaches and techniques.

When we describe co-dependence as a specific disorder, how broad should our description be? And will it be most useful to fit it into a category of disorders? Cermak[142,145] describes it under the category of personality disorders, specifically most like mixed personality disorder. But describing it as a personality disorder alone is limiting for clinicians and others. This approach has advantages and disadvantages. For example, it makes available discrete diagnostic criteria for those who may be less familiar with co-dependence to help them identify advanced co-dependence. The diagnosis then has potential to be more available to the general mental health professional, as well as the public. However, as of this writing co-dependence is still neither understood nor accepted by the mainstream of mental health. In fact, while a beginning recognition is growing slowly, many are not even aware of the importance of its existence. Yet co-dependence is so basic and so pervasive that it likely affects not just most people who come for some sort of psychotherapy or counseling, it affects most *people.*

Stage One Psychological Disorders

Since co-dependence is not currently accepted as a diagnosis in our diagnostic code books, insurance companies are not aware of its existence and therefore will not pay for its treatment[24]. So we have to find, from the patient or client's history, an acceptable additional (Stage One) diagnosis if they are to be considered for reimbursement for treatment, as they are entitled when they are covered by health insurance. The following are the most frequently associated with co-dependence:

- Avoidant personality disorder (DSM code 301.82)
- Dependent personality disorder (301.60)
- Obsessive-compulsive personality disorder (301.40)
- Mixed personality disorder (now called personality disorder not otherwise specified (301.90)
- Dysthymic disorder (300.40)
- Anxiety disorder (300.00)
- Post-traumatic stress disorder (309.89)
- Various addictive disorders

Less frequently, other DSM diagnoses may be appropriate:

- Obsessive-compulsive neurosis (301.40)
- Histrionic personality disorder (301.50)
- Passive-aggressive personality disorder (301.84)
- Borderline personality disorder (301.83)
- Paranoid personality disorder (301.00)
- Bipolar disorder (296.6)
- Major depression (296.2)

While co-dependence may play a part in the genesis of and in the relapse of the *psychotic* disorders, we are just beginning to explore whether and where co-dependence treatment may help in their total management. Early observations suggest that once stable, using an approach that addresses their underlying adult child syndrome is helpful in their overall recovery. Some disorders, such as advanced narcissistic personality disorder and antisocial personality disorder, would likely not be very responsive to treatment for co-dependence.

We can consider viewing co-dependence as lying within a diagnostic category (for example, of personality disorders). And we can also view it — and probably more accurately so — as a general and pervasive part of the painful side of the human condition such that it is *itself* a category under which many, if not most, conditions can be subsumed.

Personality disorders are said to be less treatable than other conditions. However, with a specific and full recovery program, co-dependence is usually more treatable. Recovery is generally slow, and varies from person to person. Yet when approached from the dynamic of co-dependence, the same person who otherwise might have been diagnosed as having a personality disorder and therefore "less treatable" would now have a greater chance for recovery. This would depend, of course, on the severity of wounding and on the person's persistence in being self-motivated for recovery. It would also depend on whether the therapist had specific training and skills in treating co-dependence and in recognizing and treating, or referring, other major and treatable psychological disorders.

Disadvantages

There are some disadvantages to having co-dependence as a distinct diagnostic entity. For example, Schaef suggested that it may lose its power as we recognize it as a general and pervasive part of the painful side of the human condition[553], and thus as a focal point from which we can begin to get free. I doubt that this is an issue any longer. Another disadvantage is that because it is as much a category as a distinct disorder, there is the potential that counselors and therapists may diagnose *it alone,* and neglect or miss other important or treatable Stage Zero conditions.

Yet another concern arises when the terms "co-dependence" or "co-dependent" are used to describe a certain symptom, sign, behavior or dynamic in place of a more precise description. Other words in the mental health field have been and are still being so misused, such as "schizophrenic," "depression," "borderline" and "stress."

Post-Traumatic Stress Disorder (PTSD)

People with PTSD are usually also co-dependent (even though not everyone with co-dependence can fit the diagnostic criteria for PTSD as presented in DSM-III-R). Many of us[247,260,652] believe that PTSD is one of the ways that co-dependence can manifest, although we do not know just how often that may occur. Part of the reason is that the DSM-III-R diagnostic criteria for PTSD are based heavily on post-military combat experiences. These criteria are described in DSM itself and in several other sources. They include having (1) a history of a recognizable stressor (although DSM continues not to include growing up in a dysfunctional family as one of its listed stressors); (2) symptoms or signs of re-experiencing the trauma, such as bad dreams or panic attacks; (3)

psychic numbing or inability to fully feel our feelings and express them; (4) hyperalertness or hypervigilance; (5) survivor guilt and (6) avoiding activities associated with the trauma.

Based on his clinical experiences working with people with severe PTSD and multiple personality disorder, Giles[247] adds the following symptoms or signs: (7) fear of (a) repetition of the trauma or (b) loss of control over aggressive impulses; (8) anger or rage at (a) the source of the trauma or any figure who might be blamed or died or was associated with the trauma and (b) at those exempt from the trauma; (9) sadness and grief over loss of aspects of the True Self; and (10) isolation, alienation, paranoia, addictive disorders, somatic complaints and search for a geographic cure.

PTSD is one of several related manifestations of growing up in a dysfunctional family and of the resulting co-dependence that can be included in the spectrum of conditions called dissociative disorders. I find it useful to view PTSD as a dissociative disorder, since it tends to merge so often with dissociative disorders and because people who have it tend to dissociate fairly frequently.

Dissociative Disorders

Growing up in an unhealthy or dysfunctional family — or even now being in any similar environment — is painful. The pain can often feel overwhelming. One of the ways we handle such pain is by our psychological pain-dampening mechanisms, commonly called "ego defenses." Here the ego or false self is defending the True Self against overwhelming pain[363], and there have been many descriptions of these defenses. Co-dependents may use any and all of these defenses, including repressing and minimizing. Two of these, however are important examples: the defenses of dissociation and projective identification.

Dissociation

Dissociation is a multi-faceted way of distancing from the memory and the feelings of one or more painful experiences. Some of its characteristics include a state of confusion and using any combination of several other emotional defenses against pain, including repression, projection, rationalization and reaction formation.

There is also often the addictive use of people, places, things (including caffeine, nicotine and sugar), behaviors and experiences to further distance from the pain[584].

It may be manifested in many ways among adult children and co-dependents, including periodic or frequent "numbing out." This includes the "psychic numbing" of PTSD and, for example, smiling while describing a painful experience. People who have experienced abuse or trauma frequently report, "I went numb," "I just wasn't there" or "I left my body." Diagnostic surveys such as the Dissociative Experiences Scale (DES) can be helpful in assessing the type and degree of dissociative experiences that a person may have[504]. However, the recommended cutoff score of 30 points on the DES appears to be too high, in that it may miss many co-dependents who dissociate frequently.

Dissociation is an important dynamic and experience in age regression, panic attacks, PTSD and other similar phenomena. Dissociation is one of the many manifestations of the Child Within's going into hiding. The True Self goes into hiding to protect itself from the overwhelming pain of mistreatment, abuse, lack of being affirmed and mirrored in a healthy way, and the double and other negative messages from toxic others around it.

A growing number of mental health professionals has developed a special interest in disorders of dissociation, which may cover a spectrum from mild to severe[504]. As with all ego defenses, dissociation has positive and negative aspects. It is healthy and useful in normal daydreaming — an important part of the creative process — and in breaking away from parents during normal adolescence. It is also a protective and useful survival defense for growing up in an unhealthy family. But after we grow up and leave that family, to dissociate frequently in such an unhealthy way may no longer be necessary, especially if we are now around safe people.

Healing Disabling Dissociation

In recovery, as we heal in the company of those safe people, we can begin to *recognize* when we are dissociating. If we are in group or individual therapy, the others can mirror what they see and hear. Our group can mirror what is coming up for them from their inner lives as we tell our story and describe how we are feeling.

Whether alone or with a safe person, we can experiment with *deliberately* trying to *dissociate.* Bringing what was formerly unconscious into our conscious awareness can be empowering[243]. As we dissociate — that is, alter our state of consciousness in this way — we can practice increasing or decreasing the intensity of our experience. In this way we can gain more awareness and control over what once may have felt out of control for us.

Identifying what people or situations may *trigger* the experiences of dissociation is also useful. Then we can begin to set healthy boundaries and limits around them so that they will not continue to hurt us.

Age regression is a dissociative state, and many of the principles for its healing apply for many of the other varieties of dissociation[652].

In all my years of practice I have never seen a person with a dissociative disorder who grew up in a healthy family. These dissociative disorders are mostly disorders of fear, and they also have in common co-dependence. Each of these people grew up in a dysfunctional family and is thus an adult child. It is exciting and encouraging that mental health professionals with a special interest in dissociative disorders are beginning to recognize the effectiveness of using an adult child and co-dependence approach in their work.

Advantages To Dissociation

When we dissociate we alter our state of consciousness. The person who can move spontaneously from one state of consciousness to another can have several advantages. One is that in recovery they may eventually be able to access their unconscious feelings and other inner life material more easily. And they can go in and out of therapeutic trance more easily. While fear is often still a block for some, they may be able to make more constructive use of experiential techniques in their recovery.

People who can dissociate consciously may eventually be able to experience more easily a loving relationship with their Higher Power. For example, many people have had near-death experiences

(NDEs) in which they seemed to leave their body and enter a realm of light and peace where they met beings who told them it was not yet time to die. People who are aware of having come from dysfunctional families may report a more loving NDE than do people who are not aware that their family is dysfunctional. In their study of 128 people, 74 of whom had NDEs, Ring and Rosing discovered some of these connections[521]. Their story is striking:

> We begin by postulating that a history of child abuse and trauma plays a central etiological role in promoting sensitivity to NDEs. Our assumption, which reflects a now increasingly widespread understanding of some of the consequences of childhood abuse and trauma, is that growing up under such conditions would tend to stimulate the development of a dissociative response style as a means of psychological defense. Children who are exposed either to the threat or the actuality of physical violence, sexual abuse or other severe traumata, will be strongly motivated selectively to "tune out" those aspects of their physical and social world that are likely to harm them by splitting themselves off from the sources of these threats, that is, by dissociating. By doing so, they are more likely thereby to "tune into" other, nonsensory realities where, by virtue of their dissociated state, they can feel safe regardless of what is happening to the body. In this way . . . dissociation would be predicted to allow, in turn, relatively easy access to alternate, nonordinary realities.
>
> When, in later life, such persons undergo the trauma of a near-death incident, they are thus more likely than others, because of their prior familiarity with nonordinary realities, to be able to "flip" into that state of consciousness, which, like a special lens, affords a direct glimpse of the NDE.
>
> What we are suggesting, then, is that such persons are what we might call psychological sensitives with low stress thresholds, and that it is their traumatic childhoods that have helped to make them so. From our point of view, however, these individuals — our NDErs — are the unwitting beneficiaries of a kind of compensatory gift in return for the wounds they have incurred in growing up: that through the exigencies of their difficult childhoods they also come to develop an extended range of human perception beyond normally recognized limits. Thus, they may experience directly what the rest of us with unexceptional childhoods may only wonder at[521].

A Course in Miracles defines dissociation as being caught up in or stuck between two worlds: God's and the ego's. It says, "Dissociation is a distorted process of thinking whereby two systems of belief which cannot coexist cannot be maintained." This observation emphasizes the usefulness of spirituality in recovery. Since the dissociator in recovery can perhaps know God more easily, we are here transforming the curse of being wounded in this way into a gift.

As we advance in recovery we can make many important observations and have many empowering experiences. One of these is the discovery that, once we know in our hearts just what our destructive defenses and pains are, we can ask our Higher Power to transform or to remove them. The *Course* says, for example, "Defenses, like everything you made, must be gently turned to your own good, translated by the Holy Spirit from means of self-destruction to means of preservation and release." (I recommend the *Course* only toward the end of or after completing a full recovery program in adult child and co-dependence healing.)

Giving And Receiving: Projective Identification

Giving and receiving are core dynamics in relationships, whether they are healthy or unhealthy. Learning about projective identification as the unhealthy dynamic can open us to understanding and using the healthy dynamic.

Dissociation is a somewhat complex defense against emotional pain, and projective identification is even more complex. Both are commonly used to our detriment in active co-dependence. Yet recognizing and understanding these defenses can be empowering in recovery.

Projective identification has been given many names, including trading of dissociations, irrational role assignment, scapegoating, identifying with the aggressor, evocation of a proxy, split-off part objects, joint personality, family projection process, fusion, enmeshment, and family ego mass[685a]. But these are all the same process, and it occurs frequently in co-dependence.

Expanding on Klein's descriptions in the 1930s, Segal[563] defines projective identification as "the result of the projection of parts of the self into an object. It may result in the object's being perceived as having acquired the characteristics of the projected parts of the self, but it can also result in the self becoming identified with

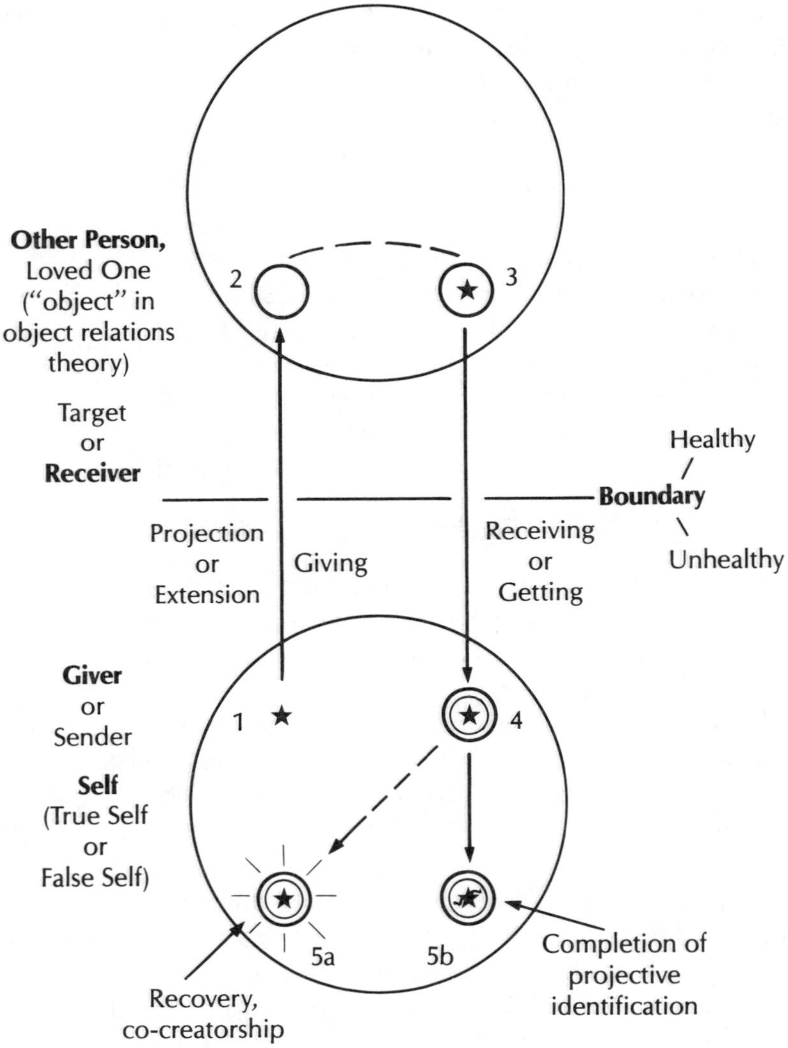

Figure 8.1. Cycle of Giving and Receiving in Human Interaction

the object of its projection." Although this observation was somewhat helpful in its time, this kind of jargon can confuse and distance us from the reality of our actual inner life experience. Cashdan is clearer, defining projective identifications as "patterns of interpersonal behavior in which a person induces others to behave or respond in a circumscribed fashion. This differs from ordinary projection, which is essentially a mental act and need not involve overt responses of any sort."[137]

Five Part Sequence Of Giving And Receiving

I clarify projective identification by the following expanded translation, arranged in a sequence of five events (see Figure 8.1). Projective identification begins when (1) I unconsciously relate to another (the "object") by sharing a part of my inner life ("parts of the self") with them. This sharing may include any feeling, need, wish, expectation, or idea that I may want to extend, give, connect or heal (project) to or with you, or about which I may want to be affirmed. Finally, like this step and all of the following ones, this inner life material may be either *received* from another or *made* by me, or *both.*

Whatever message I send to you may be mostly about me. But (2) what you do with that will be related to your inner life and your ability to respond. And so, based on those factors, (3) you may respond by sending me a message in return. This return communication may be your extension or projection of whatever you think, perceive and experience that I originally sent to you. Next in the sequence is (4) my perception of what you sent to me, which is what I take in or experience from you in return.

Each of these steps generates thoughts, feelings and other bits of inner life experience in each of us. What we do with all of this depends on the perspective from which we are experiencing our life in the moment. If I am living as my True Self (column 5a in Table 8.1), for example, then I use my experience to grow as a co-creator of my life. If all of the above is healthy, I may feel affirmed and have a more accurate and expanded sense of myself. And when there is conflict and pain, I may grow from the experience. But all of the above is still not yet projective identification, because I have remained with full awareness as my True Self and with healthy boundaries — and have not taken on anything that is not actually mine *or* tried to give you anything that is not yours. Rather than being projective identification, it is instead a healthy interaction.

Examples Of Projective Identification

However, if I ignore my True Self (5b) and identify with and exist from my false or co-dependent self, then I may stagnate or regress and remain feeling like a martyr/victim, with a contracted sense of myself. This projective identification may also allow me to continue to deny or disown a part of my inner life that I may have tried to project onto you. For example, if I am angry or resentful about something and I don't want to feel and handle that feeling, then I can unconsciously dump (project) it onto you. If you buy it, also unconsciously, and act it out by expressing it for me to others and also back to me, then I won't have to own and deal with my own feelings of anger and resentment. And what is more, if you express your now taken-on anger "too much" to others and to me, I will criticize and berate you — or hold it against you in some other way — for being so angry so often (Table 8.1, column B).

Or if I feel ashamed and inadequate, and I don't want to feel and handle that feeling, then I can likewise unconsciously attempt to transfer those feelings to you. And if you unconsciously buy it, then you can act it out and perhaps express it for me. Then I can shame you even more for being so inadequate (Table 8.1, column C).

Notice that in these examples (Table 8.1, columns B and C) nearly every message and movement is delivered and proceeds *unconsciously,* just as do nearly all of the same dynamics in unrecovered co-dependence. In fact, this dynamic is an example of co-dependence in action. This is in contrast to healthy interaction, where the giving and receiving tend to occur on a more conscious level of awareness on the part of both people. Also observe that to use projective identification requires the unhealthy co-operation, also unconscious, of two or more people or "Co-'s". Both partners are here each actively co-dependent because each has a lost self and is focusing (that is, projecting, using and blaming) on the other, their partner, to their own detriment.

We learned this detrimental defense the same place that we learned most of our other defenses against emotional pain: from our dysfunctional relationships. We watched others model it and we found that it may have helped us to survive the overwhelming pain of all of these unhealthy relationships. Fortunately, what is learned can also be unlearned.

Healing Projective Identifications

To heal our attachment to this damaging and eventually imprisoning defense is to heal our True Self. Three basic and interrelated actions and processes that are especially important here include: (1) realizing our True Self; (2) bringing the unconscious material of our inner life into our conscious awareness and owning it; and (3) setting healthy boundaries and limits. Boundaries are key here, as shown in Figure 8.1. If we have unhealthy boundaries, we are like sponges that absorb the painful conflicted material others send from their inner life. It is clearly *not ours,* yet we soak it up. And unless we have healthy boundaries, others may absorb whatever of ours that we send back to them. To have a healthy relationship, we each need healthy boundaries.

We can begin to bring our unconscious material up into our conscious awareness in countless ways that we can learn during the long course of the recovery process. Once we do, it will become progressively easier not only to recognize and heal our unconscious hurts, traumas and repetition compulsions, but to prevent stuffing (repressing and suppressing) present ones. In fact, rather than stuff them, we will experience them and use them for our growth and well being.

Being aware of and expressing parts of our inner life without dumping them onto others is a delicate balance[551]. Hearing the shared inner life of others without taking on what is not ours is also empowering. Healthy boundaries help us in this balance. Compassion (page 131) and what psychologists call "empathy" are also a healthy form of receiving. Table 8.1 shows examples of these dynamics in *healthy interactions* in columns D and E.

We get what we give. If we give out pain (projection) we get more pain in return. If we give (extend) love, we get more love in return. Understanding these principles and dynamics can help us heal our co-dependence[165].

Table 8.1. Giving and Receiving: Projective Identification in Co-dependence, with Some Dynamics and Examples

	Description of Dynamics	Individual Dynamics Examples
	A. Healthy Interaction	**B. Co-dependent Cycle with Anger**
1.	Aspect of my inner life needing connection, sharing, affirmation, extension or healing (projection). For example: a feeling, need, wish, expectation or idea. This material is received from another or made by me.	Unconsciously angry and resentful of parental abuse as a child, Dick projects his anger onto Jane. He does not fully experience or own his anger, but unconsciously entices her to feel and express his anger for him.
2.	Other's material and ability to respond. Received or made.	Jane has some unhealed anger of her own, and unconsciously takes on Dick's projected anger.
3.	Other's response, extension or projection. Received or made.	Jane openly expresses this anger at Dick's parents, at others and back to Dick.
4.	My perception. What I take in or experience. Received *and* made.	Relieved of the responsibility of handling his own anger, Dick perceives Jane as being too angry and resentful, and criticizes her for it. He remains calm and in control.
5a.	Staying fully aware in my True Self, I use my experience to grow as a co-creator. Affirmation. Expanded sense of self. Co-created. Healthy interaction.	Potential space for transformation and healing.
5b.	Ignoring my True Self, coming mostly from my false self, I stagnate or regress and remain as a martyr/victim. Contracted sense of self. Continue to disown part of me. Made. *Projective identification.*	Unaware of his True Self, Dick lives from his false self, remaining Jane's martyr/victim (as she is his). This allows him to continue to disown his still unexpressed anger, which continues to build and make him ill. They both avoid intimacy and blame the other for their unfulfillment.

C. Co-dependent Cycle with Shame

★ 1. Roy is unconsciously ashamed and feeling inadequate from being abused as a child. He projects his shame and inadequacy onto his employee, Jim. Instead of helping or supporting him, Roy shames and berates Jim for any slight mistakes.

2. Jim has unhealed shame from his own family of origin, and unconsciously takes on Roy's projected shame.

3. Hoping for Roy's and other's support, Jim openly talks of his mistakes when they occur, while protecting Roy from taking responsibility for Roy's own mistakes.

4. Roy continues to shame and berate Jim, including what he terms Jim's "lack of enthusiasm and involvement" in assisting Roy with their business.

5a. Potential space for transformation and healing.

5b. Unaware of his True Self, Roy lives from his false self, and criticizes Jim even more for being a "wimp" and a victim. This allows Roy to continue to disown his own shame, which continues to make him ill. They both avoid working together constructively, and blame the other for their pain.

D. Co-dependence Transformed to Healthy Boundaries

Peg, an elderly parent, projects to her adult child Kim the responsibility for helping Peg with her conflicts and pain.

Hero and caretaker, Kim wants to help and perhaps even fix her mother, and begins listening. Staying awake to her inner life, she soon becomes uncomfortable and realizes that this exchange is inappropriate.

Kim tells her mother politely that she is uncomfortable in this role, thus visualizing and strengthening her boundaries. Kim suggests that Peg needs her own therapist.

At first Peg responds by being confused and hurt. A few days later, however, Peg finds peers and a therapist with whom to talk.

Peg uses these new supports to begin to realize her True Self and to begin to learn her own healthy boundaries. Kim and Peg each begin to learn to extend unconditional love to the other. At times Peg reverts back to asking her daughter for help with her conflicts and pain. When this happens both recognize it and reestablish healthy boundaries.

E. Cycles of Extending Unconditional Love

1. Even though they have conflicts which they continue to work through, Marshall extends love to Barbara.
2. Previously uncertain of Marshall's love, Barbara now recognizes that love. She affirms and receives it.
3. Barbara then returns her love to Marshall.
4. Marshall openly receives Barbara's love and feels expanded by it.

5a. Marshall extends more love back to Barbara progressively and unconditionally. Both begin to experience their relationship as safe and trusting.

5b. At times Marshall reverts back to withholding love from her, and he begins to feel progressively increasing pain. Eventually, he remembers the love, often asking his Higher Power for assistance, and reextends his unconditional love to Barbara. Their relationship continues to grow.

9

Spiritual Illness

Spirituality has to do with relationships: our relationship with-our self, with others, and with the Universe (that is, our Higher Power). Similarly, we learn to heal the woundedness of our True Self in three states of being: (1) when we are alone — that is with our True Self; (2) when we are with others, especially close others; and (3) when we are with our Higher Power. These three states eventually merge as we heal, and all are imbued with a sense of the spiritual.

Spirituality is subtle yet powerful, and thus paradoxical. It is personal, practical and experiential. It is inclusive, supportive and nurturing. Yet it also transcends the physical and psychological realms of our existence. Spirituality is an aspect of understanding co-dependence that can assist us in expanding and eventually transcending more conventional psychology[579a,646].

Frustrated Mystics

Psychologist and philosopher William James once described alcoholics as being "frustrated mystics." Mystics are people who want to and often do experience everything fully, including non-ordinary realms of awareness or consciousness, and especially their relationship to God/Goddess/All-That-Is[376]. I believe that co-dependent people are also frustrated mystics. Thus, rather than being simply an escape from reality, co-dependence is also a search. It starts out as a search for happiness and fulfillment outside ourself. After repeated frustration it ultimately becomes a search for inner wholeness and completion.

In my workshops on spirituality in recovery I have listened to the detailed stories of 30 men and women from various backgrounds. When I asked them to "Tell us about the evolution of your spirituality and your relationship with God," all but two of them showed the following pattern: They first became a "religious co-dependent" by taking on a set of religious or spiritual beliefs and expectations that others told them they should incorporate. And they tried to do that — looking for the answer outside of them — repeatedly, until they became so frustrated that they gave up.

Some of these people become atheists and others agnostics. But the essential feature was that they gave up any serious consideration of whatever religion they may have been associated with up to that point. Then, consciously or unconsciously, they began a search on their own. This search included any one or more of several possible paths, such as meditation, working the Twelve Steps, reading spiritual literature and the like. In the end they each found a relationship, in various degrees of fulfillment, with the God of their understanding. They found and experienced that relationship in *their own way* and in their *own time.*

Special Versus Holy Relationships

One way to describe this spiritual journey, this search through both outer and inner world in relationships, is to use a model from *A Course in Miracles.* This is a modern book of spiritual or transpersonal psychology that increasing numbers of recovering people are examining. The *Course* describes two kinds of relationships: special and holy[165,627].

Special (Co-dependent) Relationship

The *Course* describes the co-dependent or addicted relationship (which it calls a "Special Relationship") by at least ten characteristics:

1. It denies the need for relationship with or assistance from Higher Power.
2. It is based on self-hate from shame and guilt.
3. It hides this shame and guilt under the guise of love of another.
4. It thus places the answer to our shame/guilt outside of us.
5. It assumes that something is lacking in us that we need to be happy.
6. It fixes expectations on the other, that is, the special relationship. By so doing, it denies the other's true Identity in Higher Power, that this person is part of God.
7. It is based on the scarcity principle, that there is only a limited amount of love to go around.
8. It becomes the focus of our anger and resentments.
9. It shifts responsibility for our happiness to the other, that is, the special relationship. For example, "If only you were or would be such and such, then I would be happy."
10. The ego (false or co-dependent self) uses the special relationship to attack the other by projecting shame and guilt and thus promising salvation, that is, happiness and fulfillment.

I see this description and concept as an expansion of co-dependence. These characteristics are related to some of the core issues of co-dependence, such as denial, control, difficulty trusting, low self-esteem, difficulty handling conflict, and difficulty giving and receiving love.

Holy (Healthy) Relationship

When I first read these characteristics in the *Course*, and in the writings of Ken Wapnick and others on the *Course*[627], I felt discouraged and even hopeless. If most relationships are this way, how can relationships ever work? The *Course's* answer to the special relationship is that we do not have to control more by being something we are not, that is, by doing more, better or different, which the ego would egg us on to do. Rather, all we need is a "little willingness" to open to our awareness of the healing power of God, which it refers to as "Love's presence," among other terms. When we do so, a miracle happens. We shift our perception, and we heal.

We simply shift our way of thinking. We change our mind about our mind. What results is a process that continues as the *Course's* answer to the special relationship, which it calls the *Holy Relationship*. Its characteristics are as follows:

1. It is based on my love of Higher Power, and True Self/Higher Self.
2. I see this love in everyone.
3. I take responsibility for my suffering by looking within myself.
4. I address and release my shame, guilt, hurt, anger and resentment through the forgiveness process.
5. I realize that there is only abundance of Love, and that the scarcity principle is only an illusion.
6. I know that there is nothing lacking in me, that I am a perfect child of God, and that my natural state is Serenity.
7. I respect my positive ego and use it as an assistant in my growth[376].
8. I use daily spiritual practices.
9. I live and relate in the present moment or Holy Instant, the Now.
10. In relationships, I am open and communicating, trusting, gentle, peaceful, joyful and celebrating.

These characteristics are of a healthy relationship, which includes a balance of healthy dependence and healthy independence. And they are compatible with Twelve-Step programs and with the core teachings of the world's great religious systems, both Eastern and Western, including Christianity and Judaism.

Ancient and modern spiritual teachers and literature say that to realize Serenity, we first have to discover who we are. The second of the Twelve Steps says, "Came to believe that a Power greater than ourselves could restore us to sanity," wherein sanity means wholeness or completeness. By so doing we become progressively more aware of all parts of our Self (who we are), including our lower self (physical, mental, and emotional) and our Heart — which is our True Self, and is the bridge to our Higher Self (intuition, creativity, compassion and God consciousness).

We thus have within us a Divine part. This means that Higher Power is in us, and that we are in Higher Power. Jesus said, "The

Kingdom of Heaven is within." When we so discover our Whole Self, we then begin to forgive it and love it. And when we have done so, we are free. We realize Serenity[528,646].

Our True Self is the only part of us that can connect experientially to God. I will address spirituality further in Chapters 22 and 23.

Part II

Co-dependence Treatment And Recovery

10

Treatment And Recovery Of Co-dependence: An Overview

The First Step of the fellowship of Co-Dependents Anonymous (CoDA) reads, "We admitted we were powerless over others — that our lives had become unmanageable." To treat and heal the suffering and dysfunction of co-dependence, we first realize that we are powerless over others. We are powerless over their beliefs, thoughts, feelings, decisions and choices, and their behavior. But we discover that we *are* powerful over ourselves, our *own* beliefs, thoughts, feelings, decisions, choices and behaviors. We begin to reclaim our personal power through a process of increasing awareness and by taking responsibility for our well-being and functioning: Power = Awareness + Responsibility.

Co-dependence is a disease of lost selfhood. So we can increase our awareness and responsibility by beginning to heal that lost self. To rediscover our True Self and heal our Child Within, we can begin a process that involves the following four actions:

1. Discover and practice being our True Self or Child Within.
2. Identify our ongoing physical, mental, emotional and spiritual needs. Practice getting these needs met with safe and supportive people.

3. Identify, re-experience and grieve the pain of our un-grieved losses or traumas in the presence of safe and supportive people.
4. Identify and work through our core issues.

These actions are closely related, and need not be accomplished in any particular order. Working on them, and thereby healing our True Self, generally occurs in a circular fashion, with work and discovery in one area a link to another area[645,652].

This approach addresses the traditional domains of the *cognitive* (the "head"), the *emotional* and *experiential* (the "heart") and the *personality* (which has both constitutional and learned factors). These are each important aspects of the True Self. It also expands the potential for healing, since it includes not only the physical, mental and emotional, but also the spiritual realms of our existence. Vehicles, techniques or methods to help us in this healing and recovery include:

Regular and **long attendance** at:

1. *Group therapy* that is specific for either co-dependence or adult children of dysfunctional families, depending on the person's recovery needs (this may take from three to five years of recovery work).
2. *Self-help groups* such as CoDA, Al-Anon, Adult Children of Alcoholics/Dysfunctional Families/Anonymous. Here we can hear others' stories, increase our awareness about what happened and begin working a Twelve-Step program.

As needed:

3. "Detoxification" or *detachment* from whatever person, place, thing, behavior or experience that may distract or block our work of recovery from co-dependence.
4. *Individual counseling* or psychotherapy, which may include extended family work.
5. Inpatient or other *intensive* recovery *experiences.*
6. *Education* experiences about co-dependence[349,350].
7. Conjoint family therapy. (*Caution:* use only if in advanced recovery or for crisis and do not expect to fix any family member. Discuss with your therapy group or individual therapist first.)

An **ongoing support system,** which may include:

8. Any of 1, 2 or 4 above.
9. *Journaling* or keeping a personal diary.
10. *Regular* contact and *sharing* with one or more trusted and safe friends.
11. Continuing, *conscious contact* in a relationship with a Higher Power.

All of these methods work better if we have first handled through detoxification or detachment, any active primary addictions or compulsions that may block ongoing recovery from co-dependence. Sedative-hypnotic drugs, anti-anxiety agents, and tranquilizers usually worsen co-dependence and are generally contraindicated.

The following chapters explore these components of recovery and treatment in more detail. First, however, let's look at the substages of adult child recovery[258].

The Stages Of Recovery

Awakening

Recovery begins with awakening, as shown in Figure 10.1. This awakening may be sudden and dramatic (less common) or slow and less dramatic (most common). It usually happens in a series of several separate but related awakenings stretched over a prolonged period of time — from many months to several years.

These awakenings are usually triggered by the experience of one or more events:

- Hearing someone's story of identification and/or recovery
- Reading literature and identifying as being co-dependent or an adult child
- Discovering and identifying in the process of psychotherapy
- A helping professional suggests or raises the possibility
- Attending a talk, workshop or conference and identifying
- Seeing a media presentation and identifying
- Praying to one's Higher Power or meditating and then opening to any of the above.

One of the most healing events and experiences in this awakening process is the act of giving an accurate *name* to what happened. Here we can begin to name any one or more of several parts of our identity, experience and inner life, as shown in Table 10.1.

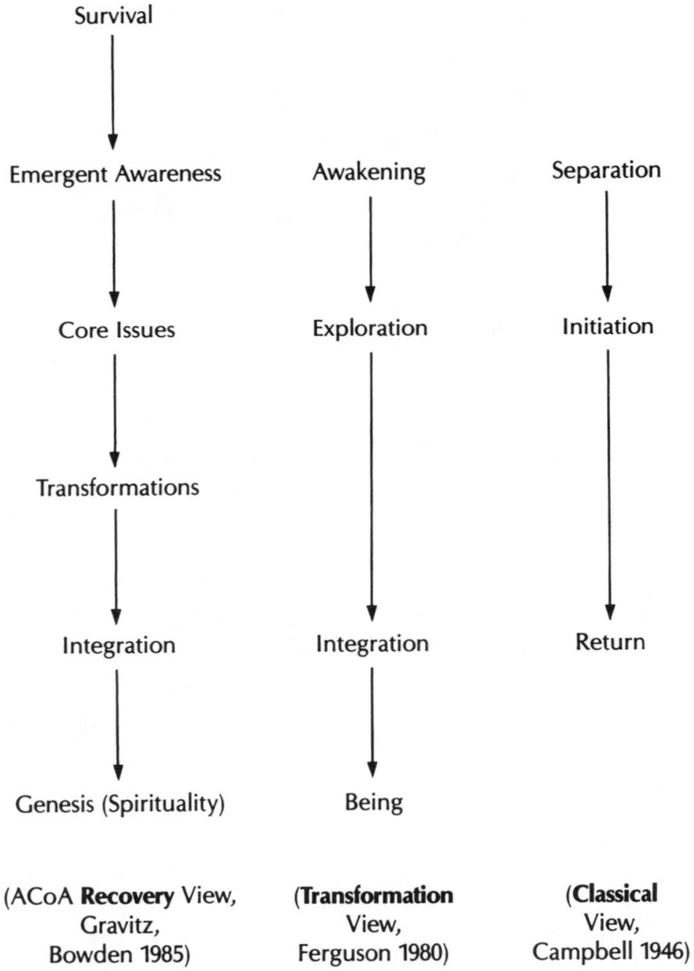

Figure 10.1. Stages of Adult Child Recovery as Shown by Three Views
(from *Healing the Child Within*)

Table 10.1. The Power of Naming Things in Adult Child Recovery, Wherein I Name . . .

Who I am	My Wants needs similarities or sameness differentness or uniqueness relationships addictions, attachments or compulsions
What happened	
How I was mistreated	
My ungrieved hurts, losses and traumas	
Any toxic secrets	My Core issues Basic dynamics (including boundaries & limits) Dreams Goals
Any chronic distress	
My Beliefs Thoughts Feelings Decisions Possibilities Choices Experiences	What is wrong What I want to happen How I can make that happen

To name things is personal Power.

For example, I may identify myself as an adult child of a dysfunctional family, and that I am co-dependent. This act of self-identifying is often a profound part of the awakening process. It is neither self-deprecatory nor is it about blaming others. Rather, it is about *naming* the truth of what happened. This naming is freeing. In doing so we discover that we are neither "bad," "sick," "crazy," or "stupid;" the truth is that we are just wounded. It is out of experientially realizing this woundedness and using it to grow in our recovery that we get free of its chains of unnecessary pain, confusion and suffering.

Core Issues

The core issues stage begins when we seriously begin an active recovery program such that we become aware of and name some of our specific core recovery issues. This stage is probably the second longest in duration and generally lasts for five years or longer. (See Chapter 15.)

Transformations

The transformations stage begins when we make our first major change in how we work through our conflicts. Through this work we learn to make lemons into lemonade. We eventually transform most of our co-dependence and adult child issues and weaknesses into opportunities and strengths.

What do we transform? We transform many of the symptoms and signs of our co-dependence, of our woundedness. We transform our lost selfhood into self-realization and aliveness, and our imprisoning roles into spontaneity. We transform being fused or enmeshed into healthy independence and healthy dependence, and being caught up into triangles into setting healthy boundaries and into intimacy. And we transform addictions and compulsions into making healthy choices and creativity[350].

Integration

We integrate when we work through a conflict or upset much more efficiently than before. For example, an upset, conflict or issue that used to take months to work through can now be worked through in a few hours, days or weeks. And we also do that work more completely. Doing so allows us more freedom to live and enjoy our life.

Spirituality

The spirituality stage, also called Stage Three recovery, illustrates several principles of the interrelationships among these stages. First, before we can move forward into any next stage, we need to have mostly completed the present one. For example, it is difficult to work very productively on core issues if we have not yet awakened sufficiently. From this principle we can realize that in each progressive recovery stage we then validate, support and nurture all of the prior stages, while at the same time we transcend them into that next stage. Thus, as we become more and more aware of our spirituality, we are at the same time able to attend to our needs in any one or more prior stages as they may come up.

Spirituality is the longest of the stages since it includes all of the prior stages. There is nothing that we do that is not spiritual. Spirituality is not about religion. While it includes and supports religion where appropriate, it also transcends it. Spirituality is crucial to identifying and healing co-dependence because it is about our relationships with self, others and God.

Peeling Away The Layers Of Co-dependence

One way to view the process of recovery is that it is like peeling away the layers of an onion. Each layer is a manifestation and consequence of the false self and our attachment to it. And each layer surrounds, constricts and imprisons our True Self, the core of our being.

There are three layers. The first consists of the numbness, pain and confusion that are but a part of the many foggy manifestations of the second layer. Until we cut through this often nebulous first layer, we are still in Stage Zero recovery — which is no recovery at all.

The second layer that binds our True Self consists of addictions, compulsions and various other disorders. To penetrate any of these usually takes from many months to several years of working in a Stage One full recovery program.

Underneath this layer is the third and final layer: adult child wounding and perhaps its major manifestation, co-dependence. This layer contains a lot of fear, shame and anger, three painful feelings that we have to deal with in the long and exciting process of Stage Two recovery.

We can also call these three constricting layers manifestations and consequences of our attachment to our false self (Figure 10.2). Underneath all of these layers, at the core of our being, lies the goal of recovery and our true identity: our True Self.

We peel away these layers throughout the entire process of recovery. The work of peeling away each layer involves recognizing, addressing, experiencing and healing multiple problems and concerns, called "unfinished business." While I described some of the influences of and approaches to handling Stages Zero, One

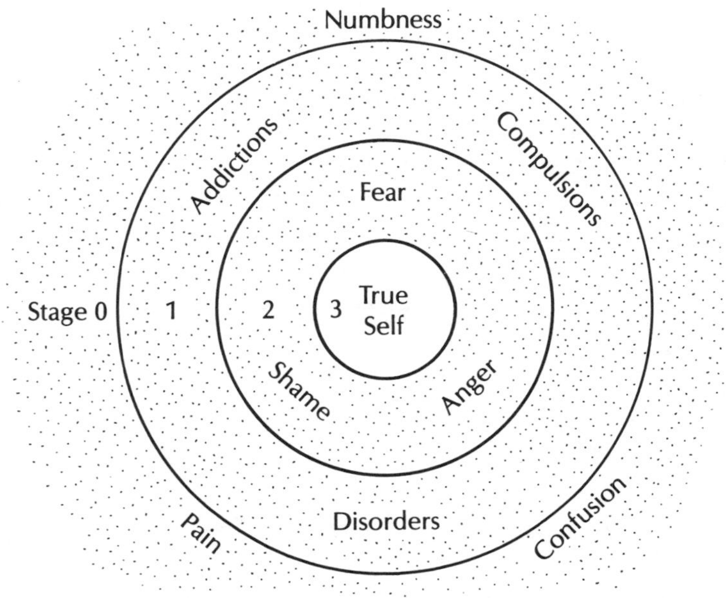

Figure 10.2. The Constricting Layers of Co-dependence

and Three here and elsewhere, my focus in this book is on the unfinished business of Stage Two recovery. Finishing this business includes the following areas of recovery work:

- Grieving
- Original pain work
- Working through core issues
- Doing "personality" work
- Completing developmental tasks
- Setting healthy boundaries

These kinds of recovery work interact and merge with one another. They are not necessarily distinct or separate areas of the healing process. Figure 10.3 shows a Venn diagram of their relationships.

Grieving

Unresolved grief festers like a deep wound that is surrounded by scar tissue, a pocket of vulnerability ever ready to break out anew[576]. It stifles our aliveness, creativity, and serenity. We need three elements in order to grieve our ungrieved hurts, losses and traumas: (1) skills about how to do the grief work; (2) safe and supportive others; and (3) enough time to complete the process. An important part of grief work includes what can be called "original pain work."

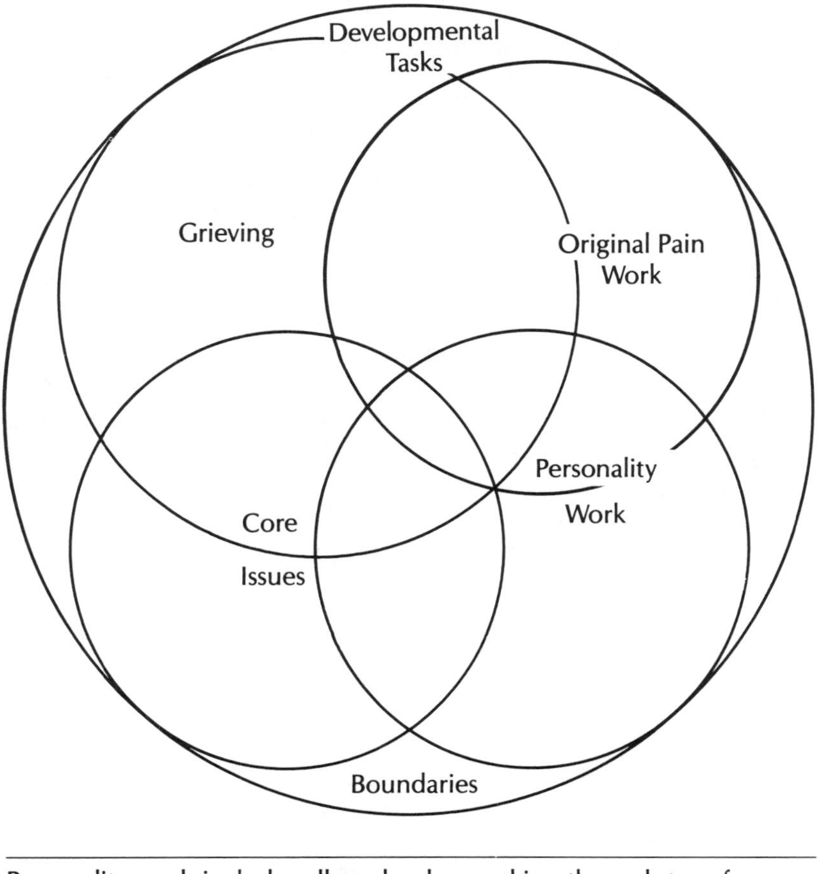

Personality work includes all work, plus working through transferences as they come up.

Figure 10.3. Key Areas of Recovery Work: Venn Diagram of Their Interrelationship

Original Pain Work

"Original pain work" is a term that helps us describe and heal a particular acute and deep part of our ungrieved hurts. It greases the wheel of the grieving process. Like grieving and recovery in general, this process cannot be forced or rushed, or our Child Within will likely go deeper into hiding. While there are many approaches to facilitating original pain work, the following eight actions can help in this process and are examples of some of its components in an effective healing sequence.

1. I tell my story of any current upset, as it may occur, to safe and supportive people, for example, in my therapy group or in individual therapy.
2. I cognitively and experientially connect my current upset, conflict and feelings around them to my past. To help with this process I can ask myself, "What does any of this current experience remind me of?" and then begin to answer.
3. I may write about it in my journal or in an unmailed letter. Or I may work through this conflict and its emotional pain by any of several other possible experiential techniques[652].
4. I bring in and read my unmailed letter (or describe whatever else I've done experientially) to my therapy group or therapist. I may also enact parts of the resolution of my original pain with these safe people, such as by using further experiential techniques (for example, gestalt or psychodrama techniques facilitated by my therapist).
5. In the company of these safe people, I then discharge the stored toxic energy until I feel as complete with it as I can for now.
6. Then I listen to feedback from the therapy group or therapist.
7. After listening to each person's feedback, I describe how my doing all of the above feels now.
8. I connect any future upsets and conflicts with what I have learned above.

Doing this original pain work can be an important stimulus to grieving our ungrieved hurts, losses and traumas. However, by itself this original pain work is not sufficient to complete our grief work, which usually requires several years to complete.

Working Through Core Recovery Issues

I describe some basic principles of working through core recovery issues in *A Gift To Myself.* These include the following.

Working Through A Problem, Conflict Or Issue

1. Identify and name my specific upset, problem or conflict.
2. Reflect upon it from my powerful inner life.
3. Talk about it with safe people (i.e., tell that specific part of my story).
4. Ask for feedback from them.
5. Name the core issue.
6. Talk about it some more.
7. Ask for some more feedback.
8. Select an appropriate experiential technique.
9. Use that to work on my specific conflict and feelings at a deeper level.
10. Talk and/or write some more about it.
11. Meditate upon it or pray about it.
12. Consider how I might learn from it.
13. If I still feel incomplete, repeat any of the above.
14. Whenever I am ready, let it go.

Doing "Personality" Work

The terms "personality" and "character" should not be equated with an individual's identity. While we are each unique and individual beings, as represented by the many aspects of our True Self, I believe that nearly all of the unhealthy and destructive aspects of our personality are due to a combination of our being wounded and to our attachment to our false self. Because these are so deep and unconscious, it takes some special work with a specially trained and experienced therapist to help heal them. Doing "personality" work means healing the results of our prior wounding. Even when these are influenced or caused by constitutional or "genetic" factors, I have observed that it is most conducive to the healing process to approach them as nearly all being due to wounding.

Some Therapist And Group Tasks In "Personality" Work

Personality work is complex. It requires trust and surrender on the part of the recovering person and experience and skills on the part of the therapist. This work is described in part in several books[137,145]. A helping professional who wishes to learn it will require clinical supervision by an experienced therapist. While using this work is not to be taken lightly, the following brief description may be helpful in providing an overview and outline of part of this process.

1. The therapist — and in the case of group therapy, the group — empathically connects with the person. This connection is important throughout their ongoing relationship.
2. The therapist (and group — with the facilitation of the group therapists when needed) accompanies and guides the person while working through their unfinished business.
3. The therapist recognizes the presence of: *transference* (projecting emotionally charged material that was acquired in the past onto others in the present); related *core issues;* and any "stuckness" in *developmental* tasks, and assists the person in working them through. When we over-react — that is, react beyond what is appropriate for the situation or circumstances — this is a sign of transference. While tranference can be dramatic in presentation, it is more often subtle. For example, transference occurs when we see and expect or experience the therapist or other as being an ideal parent while forgetting their human inadequacies; or when we attend to the therapist or other to please them, while neglecting our own healthy needs[137,145].
4. In such situations the therapist's constructive responses may include one or more of the following actions:
   - Listening to and tolerating any projected material, while empathically connecting.
   - Questioning with such questions as (infrequently and only when appropriate): "Does this remind you of anything from your past?"
   - Facilitating movement in any constructive way.
   - Supporting the person's needs as appropriate.

- And (rarely or seldom) interpreting a particular and appropriate dynamic or connection.

  In group therapy, if the group member appears to be transferring onto one group therapist, the co-group therapist steps in and works with and facilitates the group member's work through the conflicts and the transference.

5. By using constructive feedback the therapist (and other group members) validates, mirrors and supports the person during the work[652].
6. The therapist and other group members, as appropriate, sets healthy boundaries. These boundaries and limits, coupled with a therapist who does not talk too often or too much, help provide the person with a healthy amount of frustration that helps to fuel working through the unfinished business[145].
7. The group and the therapist(s) provide the recovering person with new, safe and healthy interpersonal experiences that are part of the "grist for the mill" of recovery work.

Healing the personality's woundedness includes all of the work of recovery plus the specific work around working through transferences as they occur. For a therapist to be able to provide healthy and skilled work requires a training experience of appropriately supervised work assisting many people over a duration of several years, as well as having completed a substantial portion of their own recovery as an adult child.

Completing Developmental Tasks

The work of completing developmental tasks is exacting and requires a working knowledge of the stages, issues and tasks of healthy and unhealthy human development. When appropriate, the therapist gently guides the person through these developmental stuck points[105,137,145,384].

Setting Healthy Boundaries

Learning to set healthy boundaries and limits is a crucial part of recovery. I will explore these further in Chapter 13.

Summary

Figure 10.4 graphically summarizes some of the components of the process of peeling away the layers of co-dependence that surround and constrict our True Self. This illustration also shows how most of recovery is experiential, while some important parts of it are cognitive and behavioral.

Using Experiential Recovery And Treatment Aids

My best guess is that about 90 percent of adult child recovery is experiential — in the realm of personal experience that occurs in and from our inner life. About 10 percent of healing and recovery is cognitive — in the realms of our intellect and mental understanding. Of course, much of the experiential can have cognitive dimensions, and vice versa. Nonetheless, recovery cannot proceed successfully only in our head. It must also be experienced in our heart, guts and bones — in the deepest fiber of our being. The behavioral part of recovery adds to and uses the experiential and the cognitive.

While healing is most effective when we initiate, work through and thus create our own healing and recovery, we now have available a variety of experiential recovery and treatment aids to assist us in that creative process. When we experience, we are aware of and are in our powerful inner life. A goal in healing is to continue experiencing that inner life, which is a major part of our True Self. Eventually, we learn that when our false self comes in and takes over, we just notice that, and then decide whether we need it right now. Chapter 22 describes letting go of our attachment to our false self.

We can begin to experience our inner life by choosing one or more experiential techniques that may help facilitate our experiencing. These techniques tend to have some of the following characteristics in common.

- **Being real** — we tend to be our True Self when we are using an experiential technique, although at the beginning we may feel uncomfortable when doing so.
- **Being focused** — we are focused on one or more aspects of our inner life.

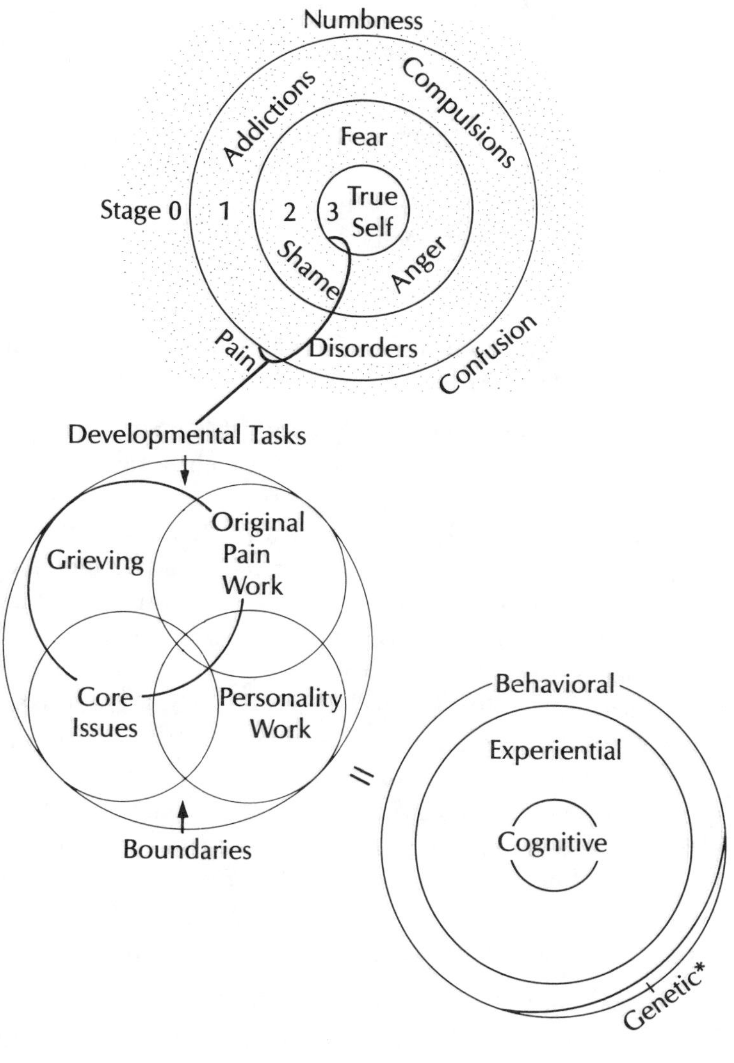

*Genetic Factors are more important in Stages Zero and One and less important in Stage Two recovery.

Figure 10.4. The Interaction of Key Areas of Recovery Work with their Cognitive, Experiential and Behavioral Components

- **Structure** — there is a structure or form to the technique itself.
- **Safe** — to be most effective and healing, it is generally done in a safe and supportive environment.

As our feelings or anything else from our inner life come up at any time, we can share them with one or more appropriate and safe people and then work through them toward a healthy resolution. Ask your therapist any questions that you might have about any aspect of experiencing[652].

Some Cautions

While experiential techniques usually help us in our healing, at times they can *block* our healing. Here are three potential blocks:

1. *Addiction* to their *"quick hit," "fix"* or *"rush."* Some of the more dramatic or fast-acting experiential techniques can open us to our deep feelings and other parts of our inner life so quickly or effectively that we believe that they are the only way that we can open up. As with any addiction, we may think there is no other way. This can limit our ability to open up to ourself and our feelings spontaneously and in a number of other healthy ways.
2. *Diversion from living life authentically.* If we focus too much on the technique, we can become diverted from living our life naturally — from, through and as our True Self.
3. *Excluding less dramatic techniques* that are equally or even more healing. Some experiential techniques are more subtle, and their healing works more slowly. For example, just being real and speaking from our heart can be as healing as the most dramatic, action-oriented family sculpture.

As we heal we can use experiential techniques constructively, while being aware if we become overly attached to their trappings and drama.

Prognosis

Two of the definitions of co-dependence (see Table 1.1) say that "recovery is possible." Indeed, one of the characteristics of co-dependence and the adult child syndrome is that by working through a full recovery program, recovery is not only possible, but is likely. Yet not everyone who begins this work will make a successful recovery. While this area requires more research, at our present state of knowledge we can consider at least seven variables that will likely influence the prognosis for a successful recovery (see Table 10.2).

Wounding Factors

Table 10.2 outlines a spectrum of wounding as it may affect adult child and co-dependence recovery. Perhaps the two most important factors in the wounding process are the *severity of the wounding* and the *age* at which it *took place.* The severity of wounding is related to the type and amount of mistreatment and abuse that the child and adult experienced. This severity is also inversely related to the child's age when the wounding took place, so that the younger the age when the mistreatment occurred, the more severe the manifestation of the wounding usually is.

Recovery Factors And Response

At least three factors are crucial to the completion of a successful recovery: (1) surrender to and working through the healing process; (2) awareness of our inner life; and (3) learning to tolerate emotional pain without any form of self-medication, so that it can be worked through. It is also helpful to have or develop patience for the entire healing process to proceed.

If these factors are full or maximal, then the person will have a much better chance for a good response to participating in a full recovery program for an appropriate duration of time. By contrast, if they are little to none, then the prognosis is uncertain, and the chance for a successful recovery may range from none to fair. However, even the most severely wounded people can recover successfully if they incorporate the above factors while they work a full recovery program for a sufficient duration of time.

Distracting Stage Zero Disorders

The person may have now or have had in the past one or more Stage Zero conditions. It is important that the person be free enough of these and other distractions to focus on adult child recovery. These distractions may include any Stage Zero condition, including any addiction or compulsion, and for recovery to go smoothly, it is important that they be addressed and stablized for a sufficient length of time before adult child work is begun.

Table 10.2. Spectrum of Wounding as It May Affect Adult Child and Co-dependence Recovery

Recovery Response			
likelihood to full recovery program for sufficient duration	Good to excellent	Fair to good	Little or none to fair
Wounding Factors			
Severity of wounding	Mild/moderate	Moderate/ severe	Severe*
Age at time of wounding	Any age	Before age 3	First 18 months*
Example DSM disorders (Stage Zero)	• Dysthymic disorder • Anxiety disorder	• Obsessive-compulsive disorder • PTSD	• Severe borderline personality disorder**
Recovery Factors			
Surrender to working through the healing process	Full or maximal	Moderate	Little or none
Awareness of inner life and ability to **tolerate** emotional pain	Full or maximal	Moderate	Little or none
Patience	Much	Some	Little or none
Blocks to recovery (See Chapter 17)	None	One or more	One or more, but not worked through

*This alone does not mean that the prognosis is poor. The prognosis may be good with these if other poor prognosis factors are absent.

**Narcissistic and antisocial personality disorder usually indicate a poor prognosis; exceptions are rare to uncommon, and even then the diagnosis may be in question.

These distracting Stage Zero conditions are screened for in the initial evaluation before the person starts group, individual or residential therapy. At times, however, they may be missed and recognized only later in the course of treatment. For recovery to proceed efficiently, it is important to address the condition or conditions seriously with a full recovery program of its own.

11

Self-Help Groups

A variety of self-help groups is oriented to assisting co-dependents and adult children in their recovery. These include the fellowships of Al-Anon or Nar-Anon, Adult Children Anonymous (or Adult Children of Alcoholics, or Adult Children of Dysfunctional Families) and Co-Dependents Anonymous (CoDA). Each of these self-help groups uses some form of the Twelve Steps and Twelve Traditions originated by Alcoholics Anonymous as the basis for their recovery program.

Meetings are free of charge and last about one hour. The size varies from as little as two people (rarely) to 50 or more. A secretary usually reads a preamble and introduction, then there is sharing of personal stories, experience, strength and hope. People usually do not use their last names and in this way the meetings are anonymous.

"Cross talk" or direct feedback during the meeting is generally and wisely discouraged; this differs from group therapy, where the therapeutic aid of feedback is facilitated by group leaders and by observations and the recovery experience of the other group members. While members do not give direct feedback in these meetings, they do give nonverbal support in the form of

Table 11.1. Characteristics of Recovery Methods for Adult Children of Dysfunctional Families and for Co-dependents

	Methods							
	Al-Anon	ACA Self-help	Co-De-pendents Anonymous	Group Therapy (Inter-actional)	Individual Psycho-therapy	Short-Term Intensive Treatment	Workshops, Conferences and Educa-tional Groups	No Recovery Program
Potential for personal growth	1–2	2	2–3	1–4	1–3	2–3	1	0–1
Meeting size	2–100+	2–100+	2–100+	7–10	2	10–30	Small to large	0
Length of meeting	1 hour	1 hour	1 hour	1¼–2 hours	30–50 minutes	Multiple and vary	Varies	0
Consistency of attendance by others	1–3	1–2	1–3	3–4	4	4 (short term only)	Varies	0
Frequency of meeting	Daily possible	Weekly to daily possible	Weekly or more	Weekly	As scheduled	Daily short term	Short term	0
Professional therapists	0	0	0	Yes	Yes	Yes	Varies	0
Supervision in overall recovery	1–2	1–2	1–2	3–4	1–3	2–3	0–1	0
Fee	0	0	0	Yes	Yes	Yes	Yes	0
Depth of shared feelings	1–2	2–3	2–3	2–4	1–4	2–4	0–2	0–1

Level of intimacy	1–2	1–3	1–3	2–4	1–3	2–4	1–2	0–1
Confidentiality	1–3	1–3	1–3	3–4	4	3–4	0–1	0–4
Healthy family modeled	1–2	1–3	1–3	3–4	1–2	3	1–2	0+
Feedback	0–1	0–1	0–1	2–4	1–4	2–4	1–2	0
Suggested duration of attendance	Long term	Long term	Long term	3-5 years	As needed	Short-/long-term program needed	Short term	0
Commitment to attend	0	0	0	Long term	Varies	Yes	Varies	0
Availability of long-term support	As available	As available	As available	Yes	As scheduled	0	0	0
Comments: For guidelines on recovery, see Gravitz and Bowden 1985; Whitfield 1987, 1988, 1990; Subby 1987. Most experts agree that **group therapy** is the treatment of choice for adult children and for co-dependent people, supplemented by other methods shown here.	Focus: Relationships with alcoholics. Teaches detachment and self-awareness Useful for sharing, identifying, program structure and fellowship. Advice from others varies from excellent to poor. Get a sponsor. Work the program. Integrate these self-help group experiences with other methods as described here and elsewhere (see panel to left), especially group therapy.	Focus: Family-of-origin work. Awareness and expression of feelings.	Focus: Relationships past and current and awareness of self.	Co-leaders' specific experience and personal recovery is important.	Specific experience and personal recovery of the therapist is crucial. Ask around and test your intuition and personal growth in the therapy.	Varies from residential 5-30 days to weekends to "reconstruction." Long-term recovery program is up to the individual and may be weak. Can be dangerous if used alone.	Useful for awakening and general information. Supplements other recovery methods. Frustrating if used alone long term.	Depends on individual. Full recovery rare, if ever. Can enter any recovery method at any time.

Key: 0 = none 1 = minimal or some 4 = maximal or most

Source: Whitfield 1990.

identification, validation and affirmation, and often some informal feedback after the meeting. These Twelve Step programs have many uses, including sharing, identifying, fellowship, program structure, guidance and work.

Table 11.1 describes and compares some characteristics of all three self-help programs, as well as group therapy, individual therapy, short-term intensive therapeutic experiences and workshops, conferences and educational groups.

Co-dependent people, with or without the suggestion of their therapist, may make use of any or a combination of these three self-help groups. The general focus for Al-Anon (or Nar-Anon) is getting free of the unnecessary pain and suffering from living with or being in a close relationship with an alcoholic or other drug-dependent person. For Adult Children Anonymous or its equivalent, the general focus is on recognizing and sharing experiences around family-of-origin issues and getting free of unnecessary pain and suffering around these. And for Co-Dependents Anonymous the general focus is on getting free of unnecessary pain and suffering in any relationship, past or current.

It is useful to get a sponsor. This person should be the same gender as and have more recovery time than the newly recovering person, and be someone with whom the person feels comfortable. The sponsor acts as an assistant in working the Twelve Steps.

Relapse

AA's Big Book says, "Rarely have we seen a person fail who has thoroughly followed our path. Those who do not recover are people who cannot or will not completely give themselves to this simple program, usually men and women who are constitutionally incapable of being honest with themselves." Rather than being mostly "constitutional," as previously supposed, unhealed adult child and co-dependence issues appear to play a major role here and in those who repeatedly relapse from any addiction, compulsion and most other Stage Zero disorders[481]. Indeed, as opposed to many Stage Zero conditions, co-dependence appears to be acquired, not inherited or constitutional.

Working The Twelve Steps

When a person relapses from any disorder for the first time after starting an appropriate Stage One full recovery program, it is useful to sort out what might have happened to bring about the relapse and then to strengthen the program. Part of this strengthening may be to begin examining issues of co-dependence. At the second relapse it is definitely time to begin some specific measures to help the person deal with co-dependence. These measures are described throughout this book. But another measure that is useful is working the Twelve Steps.

The clinician who assists co-dependents and adult children should know the Steps and some principles of how they can help. And the person in recovery should also know them. Let's take a closer look at what the Twelve Steps say. I recommend using a workbook format for working each of the Steps, one at a time, taking as much time as you need for each, and also reviewing these, where appropriate, with your sponsor.

The Twelve Steps Of Co-Dependents Anonymous

The **First** Step says, "We admitted that we were powerless over others — that our lives had become unmanageable." Paradoxically, the act of realizing our powerlessness over others with whom we may be in conflict can be empowering.

The **Second** Step says, "Came to believe that a Power greater than ourselves could restore us to sanity." The self in "greater than ourselves" means our false self, our co-dependent self, which has for so long (and so unsuccessfully) been trying to run our life. And so we risk going outside of that false self for assistance. While the Power that we use may ultimately be the Higher Power of our understanding, early in recovery it can be whatever works for us in our healing process that is outside of our false self.

The **Third** Step says, "Made a decision to turn our will and our lives over to the care of God as we understood God." This one often scares and confuses people with active co-dependence because they may fear giving up control to a God that, in their experience, has often not been there for them. And control is a core recovery issue. But a key word that is often overlooked is "care." We do not turn our *entire* will and life over to God, which might even be a form of "spiritual co-dependence," but only to God's *care.* Thus we remain in charge of and responsible for our own life's success and joy, as a co-creator with our Higher Power. It can take some time to learn to be a co-creator. (See Chapter 23.)

The **Fourth** Step says, "Made a searching and fearless moral inventory of ourselves." This Step is best done in writing, and should include strengths as well as weaknesses. Weaknesses are the "character defects" as described in the Sixth Step, and these include many of what we now may call co-dependence issues. They may include the core recovery issues, basic dynamics in recovery and others[654].

The **Fifth** Step continues the Fourth. It says, "Admitted to God, to ourselves and to another human being the exact nature of our wrongs." Ideally, we should take this Step with our sponsor; but it may be done with any safe and trusted person who is also in recovery. Doing so helps us own and work through the pain of our weaknesses. Also, although it is not mentioned specifically in this Step, it helps us claim and affirm our strengths as well.

The **Sixth** and **Seventh** Steps enable further removal of our weaknesses: "Were entirely ready to have God remove all these defects of character," and "Humbly asked God to remove our shortcomings." Key words here are *entirely ready, remove* and *humbly.* Humility is the opposite of the toxic states of arrogance and grandiosity that frequently occur in active co-dependence. It means being open and willing to experience and learn from self, others and God.

Steps **Eight** and **Nine** address making amends: "Made a list of all people we had harmed, and became willing to make amends to them all," and "Made direct amends to such people wherever possible, except when to do so would injure them or others." Here we continue to heal our injured interpersonal bonds. We can consider and work through these two Steps carefully and without blame or anger to the "other" person. I recommend that people rehearse these amends with their sponsor or another safe person before talking with the actual people to whom they are making the amends.

Step **Ten** says, "Continued to take personal inventory and when we were wrong promptly admitted it." We work this Step daily. Healing our co-dependence allows us to focus on our inner life, which will help us with this personal inventory as well as owning our wrongs. Working this Step is an ongoing cleansing process. In working this Tenth Step it is important not to shame ourself by assuming that we are defective and thus wrong. Our character defects do *not* mean that we as True Self are defective. Rather, our "wrongs" include our distorted beliefs (also called "old tapes"), thoughts, feelings and choices that can result as the behavior of our repetition compulsions, all of which may have resulted in pain for us.

The **Eleventh** Step allows us to go even deeper into our spiritual experience: "Sought through prayer and meditation to improve our conscious contact with God as we understood God, praying only for knowledge of God's will for us and the power to carry that out." This helps us move from active co-dependence into co-creation, as we seek through the spiritual practices of prayer and meditation for an aware and experiential relationship with our Higher Power.

To me, this experience is ultimately about feeling in our heart God's Unconditional Love and knowing that with It we are perfectly safe. We make that contact and feel that Love only through our True Self, since our false self is incapable of knowing God. And when we have realized our True Self and known God's Love for us in this way, we are mostly filled, and do not have to search co-dependently to fill our emptiness with people, places, things and behaviors outside of us.

The **Twelfth** Step says, "Having had a spiritual awakening as the result of these Steps, we tried to carry this message to others, and to practice these principles in all our affairs." This Step is rich in food for thought, learning and growth, as we heal from co-dependence. The spiritual awakening can take many forms: from the slow and gentle to the dramatic, from the painful to the joyous. This Step also implies that we have used these Steps as a vehicle for our awakening, and thus that spiritual awakening is not likely to come at the beginning of our recovery. It takes time[278].

Co-dependence Versus Compassion

The Twelfth Step also says, "tried to carry this message to others," and here we can begin to explore both cognitively and experientially some of the differences between active co-dependence and compassion (see Table 11.2).

Have you ever been moved by someone's story? We feel a similar empathy and passion in both compassion and co-dependence. But in true compassion we will feel those feelings and yet not feel compelled to jump in and rescue, fix or try to heal them. We are still there for people if they reach out to us in any way; but we are secure enough in ourself not to try to use fixing them to try to fill our own emptiness.

Table 11.2. Co-dependence and Compassion: Some Differences

Characteristics	Co-dependence	Compassion
Trying to fix, rescue, change or control	Yes	No
Ego attachment	Yes	No
Attachment to the outcome of being with the other	Yes	No
Living as True Self connected to God	No	Yes
Feeling	Apprehension to misery	Bittersweet peace
Focus	Outside of self	True Self, connected to God, *with* the other person

Compassion is one of the most evolved states of consciousness that we can experience and be. In active co-dependence, focusing outside of ourself, we live in the range of discomforts from apprehension to misery. In compassion we may feel a bittersweet peace. Although this peace may have a painful edge, we can abide as we contemplate or sit with the other. It is almost as though we are sitting there in attendance with the other, while practicing the Serenity Prayer:

God grant me the Serenity
To accept the things I cannot change,
Courage to change the things I can,
And the Wisdom the know the difference.[650]

If we are attached to the outcome and try to fix or rescue the other person, we are not practicing compassion — we are in a state of consciousness we can call passion. A way to help avoid such a complication and its resulting pain is always to bring a recovering person with us in making any Twelfth Step call on another who might be in need.

Co-dependence And Altruism

The Twelfth Step also suggests altruism: to give in any way without any ulterior motive. This is an expression of a basic positive attitude toward self and others without having any other narcissistic needs[304]. Co-dependents give to get, or to control or to avoid being hurt. The person at the level of genuine altruism gives only out of the love and joy of giving.

Yet there is a paradox here, because altruistic people usually eventually receive benefits in addition to experiencing the love and joy. Eventually, they receive in proportion to what they give. Part of the paradox is that to let all of this happen we cannot be attached to the outcome of the act. Selfless service is a form of altruism, and can be characteristic of an advanced and spiritual state of recovery from co-dependence.

Co-dependence On A Sponsor/Sponsee

Having and using a sponsor, or sponsoring another person in any Twelve-Step fellowship, can be a delicate balance. We cannot become overly dependent on the sponsor or sponsee and must learn to be just independent enough in a healthy way to avoid all or most of the common complications of co-dependence. The sponsor must have enough compassion not to become attached to the outcome of any aspect of the sponsee's life, including trying to fix them or transferring any of their unfinished business onto them. To do this requires constant vigilance and is helped by the sponsor's own ongoing recovery program.

12

Group Therapy

Group therapy is the crucial hub around which we can heal our co-dependence. If a person could use only one recovery aid, this is the one that I and most of my colleagues across the country would recommend. Thus, group therapy is the treatment of choice. However, working through the core issue of all-or-none (see Chapter 15), there is no reason to limit ourself to only one recovery aid.

Ruling Out Or Addressing Distracting Co-dependence

For people who have "distracting co-dependence" (page 38), I recommend a combination of individual psychotherapy and, if available, weekly group therapy. The group therapy should be short term (six months to one year in duration) and focused on the distracting features of their co-dependence. The purpose of these two aids is to stabilize early recovery so that they can then eventually begin to work without being so distracted on the major causes of the co-dependence, which are usually adult child issues[105,645,652]. If this specific type of group therapy is not available, regular attendance at Al-Anon in combination with individual therapy may be helpful. I also recommend Al-Anon in addition to group therapy.

The therapist should also rule out any *other Stage Zero disorders* or conditions. If these are present, the person should begin a Stage One full recovery program for a sufficient duration before beginning Stage Two recovery and adult child-specific group therapy, as discussed below.

Not everyone with co-dependence needs this specific kind of stabilization. I estimate from my clinical experience that perhaps 20 percent or less will need it, leaving about 80 percent who can enter directly into a full recovery program for being an adult child of a dysfunctional family. Attending an appropriate Twelve-Step fellowship such as Al-Anon, ACoA, or CoDA will strengthen this early recovery process.

Principles Of Group Therapy

The hub of the recovery process for those 80 percent of co-dependents, and for the 20 percent with distracting co-dependence once stabilized, is adult child-specific group therapy. Many therapists who assist co-dependents and adult children in their recoveries have found that for a number of reasons group therapy is a helpful treatment aid and probably the treatment of choice for these conditions.

The adult child-specific therapy group is most helpful for many reasons, including the following.

1. It is **safe.** While at times people may get some uncomfortable feedback, it is highly unlikely that they will be mistreated. The group generally follows principles of being safe.
2. It is **confidential.** Names and any identifying details of members and what goes on in the group stays in the group.
3. It **re-creates** many **aspects** of each member's **family of origin** and thus provides a vehicle to work through much unfinished business, such as painful emotional ties, conflicts and struggles (that is, transference or projections) associated with their family of origin.
4. It provides each member with **several "therapists,"** that is, people to listen, support, give feedback, witness and affirm, instead of just one, as in individual therapy.

5. It **models recovery** in various stages. Especially motivating and healing is the ability to see other people in beginning, middle and sometimes advanced stages of recovery. Many make definitive and at times dramatic positive changes in their lives and in healing their True Self. Seeing these changes modeled by others inspires people in their own healing process.
6. With appropriately trained and skilled group leaders, the group is able to **work** on specific **life issues** that span the range of physical, mental, emotional and spiritual recovery. I recommend two co-leaders who are not only trained and skilled in group therapy, but who are well into healing their own True Self.
7. It provides **supervision** and **guidance** in overall adult child and co-dependence recovery and healing.
8. It provides a safe place to use many of the **experiential techniques** described in the literature[621,652].
9. It provides the well-known advantages of group therapy in general, such as the ability to obtain **identification, validation, feedback,** appropriate healing confrontation, **support** and the **many other** useful factors and dynamics in group therapy[652,681].

The ideal size for such a therapy group is about eight or nine. The weekly fees range across a spectrum of a sliding scale, based on the person's income or ability to pay (found usually only in a few funded agencies) to fees that are in keeping with community standards (most groups). Just like each individual group member, each group has its own personality.

Working In Group Therapy

Working in such a group takes courage, risking, persistence and patience. Some basic principles in doing such work in group therapy include the following:

1. Make a serious commitment to using group therapy as a major part of your full recovery program. Don't just "try it out." Experts across the country say that it is the most efficient recovery aid for co-dependence and the adult child syndrome.

2. Keep a balance in your pace when you join a group. Don't rush too fast or say too much too soon. Take at least two weeks and listen to the group as it works. See how you can identify and notice what comes up for you in your inner life.
3. Speak from your inner life, as described in Figure 1.1. Our inner life includes our beliefs, thoughts, feelings, decisions, choices, experiences, wants, needs, sensations, intuitions and unconscious experiences, such as dreams, fantasies and repetition compulsions (that is, making the same mistake over and over unconsciously).
4. Learn to speak from an "I" perspective and with "I messages." Doing so will be far more healing for you than speaking from a distancing, second-person "you" perspective. Example: use the effective, "I'm angry and hurt about how my parents mistreated me when I was a child" instead of the much less effective, "You can get upset if someone doesn't ever do what you want them to."
5. Notice that there are four general stages in the evolution of your work in group: learning to trust, beginning to risk talking from your True Self, working (which takes a period of several years) and terminating.
6. There are several dynamics going on in every group session. These include working, giving and receiving feedback, process and content.
   - **Working** means talking about your concerns, problems, difficulties, conflicts and anything else that you choose, including what has happened and what is happening right now in your inner life. As you work, it may be helpful to tell the group what you want from them, such as to listen to you, give you feedback, identification, validation, problem solving, advice or whatever else you want or need.
   - Giving **feedback** includes speaking from your True Self. The most helpful, constructive and healing feedback in group may include any of the following:
     — What I see
     — What I hear
     — How I can identify with you
     — What came up for me in my inner life when I heard your story.

Focus and be specific. Describe specific behaviors, including what impact they have on your feelings. Focus on whatever the receiver of the feedback can change.

Advice and suggestions are usually not as helpful, and defensiveness, judgment or attacks are often destructive. Be brief enough in your feedback so that you do not detract from the overall time of the person who is working right now.

When listening to or receiving feedback from others, it is usually most healing to listen with an open mind and heart until everyone has spoken, before you respond to their feedback. Try not to be defensive or to make immediate decisions. Just let it sink in.

It is also useful to know the difference between process and content.

- **Content** is whatever is said or done in the group session. It is what is most obvious. While content is important, process is of equal and sometimes more importance.
- **Process** is everything else in the group, including how the group is discussing the content, who talks and who does not, voice and speech quality, nonverbal behavior, and what is not said or done, and especially any unfinished conflicts. Often we focus on content and exclude the crucial and more subtle process that is affecting the content.

Growing up in our family of origin, we may have had lots of things coming up from our inner life, like beliefs, wants, needs, and feelings about that process, but we may have learned to hold them in. In group and with other recovery aids, we can learn to let them out safely, use them constructively and then let go of them.

Exploring and talking about the process as it occurs increases closeness, understanding and intimacy. It can thus be one of the most scary and useful events in group or in any relationship. In most dysfunctional families talking about process material was not allowed. Usually group members experience sessions that focus on process as being among the most helpful and healing.

So as part of your healing in group, whenever you are in doubt about something or feel you are resisting saying something, you can choose to bring it up and express it. This helps to learn how to express what is in your inner life.

7. After you have been in group therapy for a month or two, consider whether you might benefit from making a recovery plan (see Chapter 13). I describe this in more detail in *A Gift to Myself* and *My Recovery Plan.*

   Read your plan to the group and ask them for feedback and to support you in accomplishing what you want to happen, your recovery goals.

8. While you will be going through your recovery at your own pace and in your own way, pay attention to and follow the group guidelines that your group leaders will give you. These guidelines include things like "housekeeping" items (time, place, duration of the group session, fee, absence policy and the like) to more process-oriented ones (e.g., minimizing socializing with members outside group).
9. It is ideal for each member to work in group at least once every three or four weeks. If you actively work much more often you may be taking time from other members, and if you work much less often, you may be missing out on valuable time for your own healing. If you need more time than that, you can consider individual therapy or counseling to supplement but not take the place of group therapy.
10. Realize also, however, that there is another powerful form of working in group: active listening, going within to your inner life, identifying, sharing and working both in and outside of group with what comes up for you that listening to others' issues and work may have triggered for you.
11. When you work, try to stay on focus. Try not to ramble, talk a lot about others in your life and their behavior, how you want them to change, or give too many details. Do try to talk about your own inner life, including your feelings, conflicts, wants and needs. Use "I" statements.
12. When you feel fairly complete with your work for that session, whether it has taken just a few minutes or nearly the entire duration of that group, indicate that you now feel complete by telling the group something like, "OK, thanks. I'm done for now." It may also be helpful to give the group some feedback about what it was like for you to have

worked by telling them something like, "That was helpful" or "I'm really glad that I talked tonight" or "That was scary to talk about, but I'm glad I did it. I feel better now."

Terminating Group Therapy

Somewhere in the course of the three to five years or more in group therapy, people begin to wonder about or even sense that they may be ready to terminate group therapy. A constructive and healing way to proceed would include the following:

1. Reviewing the *generic,* long-term recovery goals, estimate about how far you have reached each goal on a scale from 0 to 10. (I discuss recovery goals in Chapter 13.)

   Make this estimation first from your memory of about where you were with each goal just before you started group therapy, and write that number in the space to the left of the goal.

   Then estimate about where you sense that you are right now in reaching that goal, and write it in the space just to the right of the goal. Show these estimates to your group members and leaders, and ask for feedback on where each of them senses that you are right now.
2. Do the same with your specific *personal* recovery plan and its goals.
3. Review the overall criteria for healing our True Self (Chapter 18) and do the same with these. These are a bit more stringent than the recovery goals and may be more than you can do right now.
4. Ask your group and leaders for feedback about your recovery in general and whether they sense that this is an appropriate time for you to leave group therapy.

Take at least four to six weeks to complete this process. There is no need to rush through any of this.

If you are about 90 percent of the way, or 9 on a scale of 10 in your goals in experiencing the healing you wanted, and if the group and leaders sense that termination is appropriate right now, then you may consider terminating from group. When you do so, it is useful to have at least *three strong support systems* that are ongoing in your life. Tell the group about these and how you plan to use them.

It is also entirely appropriate and healthy to return for brief individual counseling or therapy whenever you sense the need. You may also return to group therapy later if you feel the need for more healing work in a group.

13

Developing A Recovery Plan

Making and using specific goals and objectives is a useful tool in recovery. In the therapy groups that I facilitate, my co-leaders and I encourage (but do not force) group members to establish a recovery plan, updated every few months, that is specific for their own needs and recovery.

Long-Term Recovery Goals For Co-dependents And Adult Children

To make these specific goals part of the plan, I have developed a list of general, generic or overall goals and guidelines for adult children and co-dependent people. They are grouped under four general areas: self-awareness, self-acceptance, self-responsibility and self-reflection.

Self-Awareness

- Discover, develop and accept my individual identity as separate from spouse or partner, parental or other authority figure, children and institutions.

- Identify my ongoing needs (physical, mental, emotional and spiritual).

Self-Acceptance

- Practice getting these needs met on my own and with safe people in healthy relationships.
- Identify, trust and process my internal cues (feelings, sensations and experience from my inner life). If not comfortable, check my responses with someone I trust.
- Assess my feelings, upsets, conflicts and similar situations and handle them in a healthy way (alone, with safe others and, if I choose, with my Higher Power).
- Learn to accept myself as an individual and unique child of God, with strengths and weaknesses.
- Learn to like myself and eventually to love myself, as my Higher Power loves me.

Self-Responsibility

- Identify, reexperience and grieve the pain of my ungrieved losses, hurts or mistreatment alone and with safe others.
- Identify and work through my major core recovery issues.
- Grieve the loss of my childhood while in group (for Adult Children).
- Develop and use an ongoing support system (at least three supports).

Self-Reflection

- There is no hurry for me to accomplish these goals right away. I can take my time.
- I don't have to reach every goal perfectly.
- I do not have to work on these goals in exactly this order.
- From these above goals I will — in my own time — make more specific and more personal goals for myself during my recovery.
- I can accomplish these goals through techniques such as risking and telling my story to safe people, through prayer and meditation, keeping a journal and other experiential techniques[652].

- When I use the above, I am caring for and healing my True Self.

Using The Recovery Plan

I encourage people in recovery to begin thinking about specific problems or conditions in their life that they would like to improve or change. They then list these conditions and create specific personal goals, or what they want to happen in their life. From these specific goals, they create a specific plan or method, also called "objectives," of just how they will reach these goals. Table 13.1 lists some examples.

Table 13.1. Sample Treatment or Recovery Plan

<table>
<tr><th>My Problems</th><th>What I Want to Happen (Goals)</th><th>How I Plan to Reach these Goals</th></tr>
<tr><td>Chronic unhappiness</td><td>Experience some happiness and serenity</td><td rowspan="2">1. Begin to heal my Child Within
2. Make a commitment to an adult child specific therapy group long term
3. Attend that group weekly and work on a personal problem or issue at least monthly
4. Whenever it comes up, share about my low self-esteem and shame</td></tr>
<tr><td>Low self-esteem</td><td>Raise my self-esteem</td></tr>
<tr><td>Difficulty with intimate relationships</td><td>Improve my participation in my intimate relationships

Have one successful intimate relationship</td><td>1. Practice 1 to 4 above
2. Work on my relationship problems in group therapy
3. Keep a diary or journal about my experiences in relationships
4. Seek individual therapy with a therapist knowledgeable in adult child recovery.</td></tr>
</table>

The complete healing of the co-dependence/adult child syndrome in group therapy takes about three to five years. For some it may take longer. This is not a negative reflection on the person, the therapist or the group. The use of a recovery plan as described above helps speed the healing process and gives the person, the therapist and the group some useful markers as to when terminating group therapy may be appropriate.

When the person has completed writing the recovery plan, I say, "It will be helpful now for you to share this plan with your therapist or group and ask them to support you as you work through it. You can also ask for feedback and suggestions. Keep a copy of your recovery plan handy and read it carefully every week or two."

I also say, "Every three or four months it is useful to review your plan and add to, subtract from or change it in any way that you choose. Then review it with your group or therapist. It is especially healing to tell your group and/or your individual therapist, if you choose, about everything that comes up for you around all of this."

Essentials For Recovery

At least twelve essential actions will make recovery go more smoothly and successfully:

1. Handling any distractions to recovery.
2. Learning to live from our inner life.
3. Learning about our feelings.
4. Learning about age regression.
5. Learning to grieve, and grieving.
6. Learning to tolerate emotional pain.
7. Learning to set healthy boundaries and limits.
8. Getting our needs met.
9. Experientially learning and knowing the difference between our True Self and false self.
10. Working through our core issues.
11. Learning that the core of our being is Love.
12. Learning to be a co-creator.

Let's look at each of these.

Handling Distractions

Learning to handle distractions includes identifying and stabilizing any Stage Zero disorders or conditions through working a Stage One full recovery program, so that we will be free to begin to know and heal our True Self. If we do not handle these distractions, they may prevent our ability to focus on our adult child and co-dependence healing.

Learning To Live From Our Inner Life

In co-dependence we focus on our outer life to an unhealthy degree. In recovery we learn to focus on our inner life so that we can more successfully live and enjoy our life, including interacting wth others.

Learning About Our Feelings

Feelings are a major and crucial part of our inner life. To learn about them, we have to "get down on the floor and wrestle" with each feeling. When we do that we get to know them so well that eventually we will be able to do any of the following for each feeling:

- Recognize it
- Feel it
- Experience it
- Work it through
- Use it, and then . . .
- Let go of it.

A particular feeling at a particular time may be either useful or useless, and it may even end up hurting us. Until we can recognize, feel, experience and work through a feeling, no matter how painful, we cannot use it and then let it go[652,654].

Learning About Age Regression

Age regression is a crucial concept and event in recovery, and we can learn it both experientially and cognitively. Age regression happens when we suddenly feel upset, confused and scared, like a helpless little child. There may be no apparent cause for it, and it may last a few minutes or longer. As we heal it, we learn that there is generally a trigger — usually some form of mistreatment, abandonment, invalidation or negative message or a threat of these — that initiates a rapid sequence of painful feelings. These feelings usually include: fear, hurt, shame, guilt, anger, confusion and disorientation. And we can end up feeling dysfunctional and out of control, almost like we want to scream. But our Child Within, our True Self, may feel too weak even for that, and so it may just want to go into hiding.

When age regression continues to wound us repeatedly, with no healing around it, we may remain paralyzed, confused and dysfunctional. When we recognize and heal it, age regression can be a great factor in our healing and well-being. To heal it we recognize it, work through it and learn from it. To do all of this can take many months, and more often from one to several years[652].

In recovery we discover that there are three kinds of age regression. The first is as described above, ending up in a sort of paralyzed or passive state and feeling. The second may have the same triggers and feelings, but we become much more active. We may throw a temper tantrum, verbally attacking someone close to us. The third type is a therapeutic variety of age regression, because it often occurs during the normal and constructive course of group or individual therapy.

All three of these kinds of age regression generate *conflict*, and we can use the occurrence of both the age regression and the conflict to help us go deeper into our pain and to heal. This intense feeling of conflict is a part of the phenomenon and defense of transference or projection. It can be experienced on at least three levels: (1) with those people with whom I am in current conflict; (2) with what the current experience reminds me of (a deeper level that addresses past unfinished hurts); and (3) what old tapes or messages I may be playing about all of this (the deepest level, and the way that I may often beat myself up).

To heal age regression, we need to have safe, close people to assist us. Learning about age regression opens doors to the richness and opportunity that lie deep within our inner life and helps us begin to sort out each of our feelings.

Learning To Grieve

Learning to grieve is crucial. When we grieve our ungrieved hurts, losses or traumas to completion, we get free of their chronically painful hold on us. A major part of recovery is about grieving.

As we work through grief, we first learn specifically what hurts, losses or traumas we have experienced. Then we begin to grieve them. Then we grieve some more, all the while learning progressively more about each of our feelings as they come up for us. Once we have grieved these major losses to completion, which usually takes several years, we are free to be our True Self and to grieve any current hurts, losses or traumas as they may occur, so that we do not become stuck in them — as we may have been in our past.

Learning To Tolerate Emotional Pain

Learning to tolerate emotional pain helps us to stay in our present discomfort long enough so that we can work through it and learn and grow from it. Sometimes people become so frustrated that they flee their particular recovery aid. A more constructive choice is to stay in the pain and ask for assistance from safe others, such as their therapy group, therapist, sponsor or best friend. I'll discuss later more specific approaches and options to healing emotional pain in this chapter in "Frustration With The Process."

Learning To Set Healthy Boundaries

Distortions in personal boundaries are a major dynamic in co-dependence. A boundary or limit is how far we can comfortably go in a relationship and how far someone else can comfortably go with us. A boundary is not just a mental construct: Our boundaries are real. Other people's boundaries are real.

Boundaries and limits serve a real purpose: They protect the well-being and integrity of our True Self, our Child Within. Our awareness of boundaries and limits first helps us discover who we are. Until we know who we are, it will be difficult for us to have healthy relationships of any sort. Without an awareness of boundaries, it is difficult to sort out who is unsafe to be around, including people who are toxic for us and people who may mistreat or abuse us.

In co-dependence, boundaries are distorted and invaded by both members of the dyad in a co-dependent relationship. When we heal our woundedness, of which boundary distortions play a major part, we are able to set healthy boundaries and limits.

Getting Our Needs Met

Learning to meet our healthy human needs is also crucial in the process of healing co-dependence. These needs include the physical, mental, emotional and spiritual aspects of our being. We get our needs met as we grieve, experience and live our lives in three relationships: with our self alone, with safe others and, if we choose, with our Higher Power (see Figure 13.1).

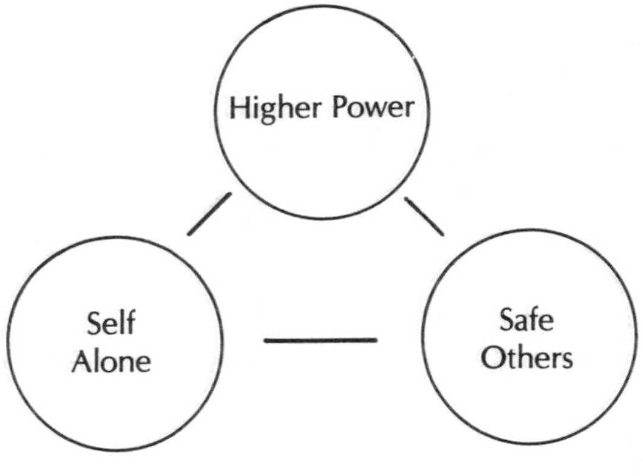

Figure 13.1. The Three Basic Relationships in the Healing Process

Learning The Difference Between True And False Self

In recovery it usually takes a long time to learn experientially the differences between our True Self and our false self. We can begin to explore this cognitively by looking at some of the differences, as shown in Table 13.2.

Table 13.2. Some Characteristics of the True Self and the False or Co-dependent Self

True Self	False or Co-dependent Self
• Authentic Self	• Unauthentic self, mask
• True Self	• False self, persona
• Genuine	• Ungenuine, "as-if" personality
• Spontaneous	• Plans and plods
• Expansive, loving	• Contracting, fearful
• Giving, communicating	• Withholding
• Accepting of self and others	• Envious, critical, idealized, perfectionistic
• Compassionate	• Other-oriented, overly conforming
• Loves unconditionally	• Loves conditionally
• Feels feelings, including appropriate, spontaneous, current anger	• Denies or hides feelings, including long-held anger (resentment)
• Assertive	• Aggressive and/or passive
• Intuitive	• Rational, logical
• Child Within, Inner Child; ability to be childlike	• Overdeveloped parent/adult scripts; may be childish
• Needs to play and have fun	• Avoids play and fun
• Vulnerable	• Pretends always to be strong
• Powerful in true sense	• Limited power
• Trusting	• Distrusting
• Enjoys being nurtured	• Avoids being nurtured
• Surrenders	• Controls, withdraws
• Self-indulgent	• Self-righteous
• Simplifies	• Complicates; is "rational"
• Wants to be real, connect, experience, create and love	• Wants to be right, control and win. Tells us the *opposite* of what we want and need.
• Non-defensive, though may at times use ego defenses	• Defensive
• Connected to its Higher Power	• Believes *it* is Higher Power
• Open to the unconscious	• Blocks unconscious material
• Remembers our Oneness	• Forgets our Oneness; feels separate
• Free to grow	• Tends to act out unconscious often painful patterns repeatedly
• Private self	• Public self

In 1985, when I began writing *Healing The Child Within,* I found it helpful to call the false self by another name: the co-dependent self, because the false self is the major "actor" and pretender in co-dependence.

The observer self is an important part of our True Self, the part of us that watches everything dispassionately and nonjudgmentally. When we step back into our observer self we begin to notice some more important differences between our True Self and our false self. In any conflict the false self wants to be separate, rational and logical, and it wants to avoid feeling any form of pain. It often sees things as being complicated, and will often complicate the conflict. It will persist even if doing so may be to our detriment.

By contrast our True Self wants to experience, connect, create and celebrate. It simplifies. It wants to heal and grow from any conflict and knows that it may have to go through its pain to do so. Finally, our True Self knows that it can co-create its life by connecting to its Higher Power — something impossible for the false self. Learning to differentiate these two is an ongoing process.

Working Through Our Core Issues

Our core issues may be about needing to be in control, all-or-none thinking and behaving, fear of abandonment or something else. Whatever it is, working through our core issues is intimately intertwined with nearly every aspect of recovery. Each of us has several or even all of these to work through as we get to know ourself, others and God better and better. I describe these core issues further in Chapter 15.

Learning That The Core Of Our Being Is Love

This task and the one that follows tend to come into our awareness in the most advanced stage of our recovery (Stage Three). While we can contemplate and even experience these to some degree at any time, they tend to come most easily after we have completed Stage Two recovery.

As we slowly peel away the constricting layers from around our true identity, we become progressively more free. These layers are a combination of the stuff of our false self and our collection of what others have dumped onto us over the years. As we slowly shed these painful layers, we begin to really experience the fact that at the core of our being we are a spark of creative, Unconditional Love. All we have ever wanted or needed is to be that Love and extend it to others. I explore this concept and experience in the last two chapters.

Becoming A Co-creator

To co-create is to join as our True Self in loving harmony with our Higher Power. By so doing we extend our Love and expand ourself so that, in concert with the God of our understanding, we can co-create success and joy in our life. This appears to be the most evolved experience that we can have as a human being. When we reach this final stage of our recovery, we have transformed our co-dependence into co-creation.

Frustration With The Process

But even if we cognitively know all of the above, we may become so frustrated in our recovery work that we want to stop all the associated pain. We need some approaches to handling this frustration.

When we are in group or individual therapy, we always have possibilities and choices related to our adult child recovery and to healing our Child Within.

There may come a time when we get so discouraged, frustrated or impatient that, in an all-or-none fashion, we leave the group or therapist without discussing how we are feeling and what our wants and needs are. This is not only disruptive to the group and to the healing process, but our True Self usually goes even deeper into hiding.

To help prevent this disruption to self and others, it is usually healing to discuss our urge to leave *in* group or individual therapy over a period of several weeks or longer. Some possible actions in such a situation might include: (1) terminating therapy; (2) staying and working through the pain and conflict; (3) working through it, then "taking a breather" by not actively working on any personal issues for a time, while still attending group regularly; or (4) some other possibility.

It is precisely at these times of frustration that we can heal our Child Within even more than had we left group or individual therapy without working through our pain and conflict. So, in a sense, these could be exciting times of opportunity, healing and growth.

Frustration is actually *part of* the process of *recovery.* When we feel frustrated with any aspect of our recovery, we can know that we are at a point where we can learn to work through a particular conflict. A key to getting free of the frustration is in tolerating its emotional pain long enough to explore and work through it.

In the past some of us may have run away from pain and conflict, or "beat ourself up" over it, stuffing our pain. It is in the safety and support of group or individual therapy that we can learn to tolerate emotional pain more clearly and successfully, work through conflict and grow from it.

Recovery is not just an intellectual or rational process. Nor is it easy. It is an experiential process, consisting of excitement, discouragement, confusion, pain and joy, with an overall pattern of personal growth. Recovery takes great courage.

14

Individual Psychotherapy, Intensive Experiences And Education Groups

Self-help and therapy groups are not the only options for healing co-dependence. Individual psychotherapy, intensive experiences and education groups also may be helpful in recovery.

Individual Psychotherapy

How can we tell if there is a need for individual psychotherapy or counseling? Here are some indicators.

- More time is needed for recovery work than the time available in group therapy or other treatment aids.
- The person does not yet feel comfortable talking about personal issues in group therapy. For example, sexual issues, incest, extremely embarrassing issues and the like.
- The person feels somehow blocked in group therapy or self-help fellowship program work, and wants to explore that block outside as well as inside group or self-help.
- The person simply wants to work on recovery in individual therapy.

The individual therapist should speak frequently, at least every three or four months, with the patient's therapy group leader to share such information as needs, goals and dynamics. It is helpful when these therapists mutually support one another in helping the person in the process of recovery. Of course, any such communication is done only with the full knowledge and written consent of the patient or client.

If you cannot afford a regular fee, you may want to see a therapist skilled in adult child recovery who works at a community mental health center in your area. Ask around or look in the telephone book to locate them. Principles of individual therapy are described in several sources, including Bruckner-Gordon's *Making Therapy Work,* and my own *Healing The Child Within, My Recovery Plan* and *A Gift To Myself.*

Intensive Residential Or Weekend Experiences

Another recovery tool is intensive weekend or longer residential experiences. These can be helpful in several circumstances:

- The person has difficulty working and growing in adult child-specific outpatient treatment, which ideally includes group therapy.
- The person has continued difficulty identifying and expressing feelings in an adult child-specific recovery program.
- The person worked well and grew initially and is now in a prolonged lull.
- The person persistently minimizes or denies family-of-origin issues.
- The person needs some more time to work than is available in group.
- The person is motivated and wants to have an intensive residential experience.
- The person has a marked dysfunction or crisis that cannot be managed by adult child-specific outpatient treatment. Some people who are especially dysfunctional may benefit from up to 30 days or longer in a hospital or residential facility that uses an adult child or co-dependence focus. Some health insurance plans may pay for part or most of this treatment.

Three Cautions

While these intensive residential or weekend experiences are generally useful and healing, they can be disruptive if you do not have the concomitant and ongoing support of a therapy group or individual therapy. I do not recommend that these experiences be used alone. Ongoing group or individual therapy for at least several months afterward is needed to help facilitate a healthy integration of these often powerful experiences into your healing and into your life.

If you attend such an experience, there is also a danger of "comparing out" a less intense and slower-paced outpatient recovery program. This is because in the intensive experience the "hit" of emotional experience and freedom can be so intense, almost like that of a drug. This can end up blocking your long-term healing and is an especially dangerous trap for people with a strong history of addiction. If any of this happens for you, discuss it with your therapy group or therapist.

Some outpatient therapy groups model themselves after these intensive programs. They encourage their members to work each week in these intensive and dramatic ways, using such action techniques as psychodrama, for six months to one year or more. While these techniques are certainly useful at appropriate times, and while my colleagues and I use them often in our outpatient therapy groups, it is questionable whether it will be in their best interest to expect a person in recovery and others in the group to do so at such an intensity.

There are two reasons for being cautious in this way. First, many people with co-dependence and the adult child syndrome have some degree of post-traumatic stress disorder (PTSD). An important therapeutic principle in assisting people with PTSD is that their therapy cannot be pushed, forced or rushed[145]. It must go gently, and at the person's own pace, or their True Self will retreat and go deeper into hiding. So in outpatient therapy the pace should be slow and the person given plenty of time to do their healing work in an unrushed fashion.

A second reason for going slowly has to do with another major dynamic of recovery: the grieving process. Simos, Bowlby and others have shown that the process of grieving a major loss takes at least two to four or more years[90,576]. Co-dependents and adult children usually have several major losses, hurts or traumas to grieve. Like recovering from PTSD, grieving cannot be rushed. For these reasons, short-term (one year or less) intensive (with several action oriented and dramatic experiences programmed into each session) therapy groups may not only be too short in duration but also may be detrimental to a successful recovery.

Watch out for all-or-none thinking here. Notice that I did not say that experiential and action techniques are not useful. They are . . . when used appropriately in the context of a slower-paced full recovery program as part of an interactional therapy group that is long-term, gentle, supportive, and does not push its members too deeply, too fast.

Inpatient Treatment

Since the late 1980s there has been a progressively increasing number of residential recovery or treatment units available across the United States that use many of the approaches described in this book. These are usually located in either addiction treatment facilities or in psychiatric hospitals. The duration of stay is usually from five days to 30 days or longer, dependent on the program offered and the individual's needs.

These residential experiences usually deliver care using the same principles and methods of identification and recovery as do outpatient programs. But since they are more concentrated over time, the experience feels more intense. The programs have a larger staff, often including a psychiatrist, who can help with the management of any major Stage Zero disorders, including the use of carefully selected medication if appropriate. This psychiatrist should be certified in the specialty of addiction medicine and trained in co-dependence and adult child issues. The staff should also be appropriately trained and skilled, and each should be well advanced in healing their own True Self.

Treatment planning and long-term follow-up are crucial in these residential programs. Even so, in my clinical experience I estimate that when they leave the facility from 20 to 40 percent of people do not continue in such adequate and long-term planned outpatient treatment. I have seen a small number of residential treatment staff who seem not to understand the importance of such long-term outpatient treatment, often suggesting that the person can complete recovery in a year or less. This suggestion is misleading and can be detrimental to full recovery.

A final concern is how institutional politics can affect the quality and delivery of care. For example, some psychiatric hospitals will convert a general psychiatric unit to one that offers or "specializes" in co-dependence or adult child issues. Sometimes the reasons for such a change of focus are based on institutional finances rather than recovery. Sometimes many of the staff are not appropriately trained and skilled in assisting people in this work, and some may be unrecovered adult children themselves. There will likely be more such political difficulties throughout the 1990s as mental health professionals trained in old paradigm (conventional) approaches discover the therapeutic advantages of expanding into those of the new paradigm, as described in Chapters 19 and 20. If the administration and staff remain mindful of these issues, the quality of care will likely be from good to excellent in most of these facilities, and inpatient psychiatric treatment may improve substantially.

Educational Group Experiences

Educational group experiences may consist of several sessions where didactic material on co-dependence or the adult child syndrome is presented by a therapist, counselor or teacher. They may also include some experiential exercises and some brief group interactions. While these are not meant to be formal group therapy, and while they alone are not sufficient to reach a complete recovery, they can be helpful in cognitive learning and in beginning to learn to heal with others, which can be of some assistance in recovery.

Another form of educational experience can be found in workshops, courses and conferences. Whether we attend any of these in person, view them on television or listen to them on tape, they may offer some cognitive assistance in recovery. As with the education groups above, these are of course also not sufficient for realizing a full recovery (see also Table 11.1).

Learning from these sources can be helpful. But there are some cautions of which to be aware. For example, it is easy to become attached to any speaker, teacher or guru, and their message, to the detriment of realizing True Self and its connection to its Higher Power and to close or intimate others. Indeed, the teacher or any other does not have the answer for us. If we look for answers in them or through them, we will likely end up suffering unnecessarily in co-dependence. While we can learn from their stories and suggestions, we still have to find our own truth in our own way and in our own time.

15

Core Issues

Core issues that are unhealed and unrecovered grease the wheel of active co-dependence and all its suffering and consequences. Recognizing and working through them is a major part of the healing process.

The Core Issues

An issue is any conflict, concern or potential problem, whether conscious or unconscious, that is incomplete or needs action or change. A *core* issue is one that comes up repeatedly. There are at least 15 core issues:

- Control
- Trust
- Being real
- Feelings
- Low self-esteem
- Dependence
- Grieving our ungrieved losses
- Fear of abandonment

- All-or-none thinking and behaving
- High tolerance for inappropriate behavior
- Over-responsibility for others
- Neglecting our own needs
- Difficulty resolving conflict, and difficulty giving and receiving love.

How They Help

Core issues reflect some of our areas of conflict as healthy human beings. They show up for us in our day-to-day lives in countless ways, especially in the following areas:

- Relationships — of any kind — with others, self and our Higher Power.
- Experiential recovery work — throughout our healing.
- Feedback given by therapy group members, therapists, sponsors, friends and others.
- Insight from reading, listening, reflecting upon or working through conflict.

Core issues can assist us in describing and framing — as well as working through — some of the origins and dynamics of problems in living, day-to-day conflicts, "character defects" and our struggle with our ego or false self.

Principles Of Core Issues In Recovery

Several principles of core issues are useful in the healing process. Reviewing them may begin to raise our awareness of how core issues affect us in our recovery.

1. Before we identify a core issue, most of its dynamics and effects are unconscious.
2. These dynamics and effects are often manifested by being a martyr or victim, and by enacting a repetition compulsion.
3. When working on material related to a core issue, it is useful eventually to name the specific core issue or issues.
4. It is useful to explore how the core issue came to be and how it manifested and still manifests in our life.
5. Bringing a core issue into our conscious awareness provides us the experience of the unfinished business, and improved

psychospiritual understanding and a movement to self-actualization, integration, wholeness and sanity.

6. In working through the core issues, we connect the pain (of experiencing the dynamics in action that the core issue exposes) to how we were mistreated and how our True Self went into hiding.
7. Core issues usually have opposites or all-or-none type components (for example, trust versus distrust).
8. Core issues can have at least four components: physical, mental, emotional and spiritual.
9. Focusing on a core issue sets in motion a flow to other issues, both core and non-core.
10. Core issues are also often interrelated with basic dynamics in relationships[649,650].
11. Most issues that we have with others, we also have with our self and with our Higher Power.
12. Our True Self uses recognizing and working through core issues for self-discovery, growth and returning Home (ego treats core issues as all-or-none, and gets stuck in them as a martyr or victim).

Working Through A Problem, Conflict Or Issue

The core-issues approach to recovery can help us apply a name to particular problems or conflicts. Once we name an issue, we can begin to focus on more of the essentials of our particular struggle. Once focused we are less and less distracted by nonessentials and can thus concentrate on working to resolve the issue.

To do this work of resolving an issue, we can use experiential techniques. Using experiential techniques involves four characteristics: (1) being real, (2) being focused on our inner life, (3) being structured and (4) doing our healing work through them in a safe environment. We can use these four characteristics to assist us in working through each of our core issues[652].

Working It Through

As we name and work through a core issue, it can be most helpful to address it in a series of steps or stages.

1. **Identify** and **name** my specific **upset, problem** or **conflict.**

Table 15.1. Some Steps in Transforming and Integrating Recovery Issues

Recovery Issues	Early	Middle	Advanced	Recovered
1. Grieving	Identifying our losses	Learning to grieve	Grieving	Grieving current losses
2. Being real	Identifying our real self	Risking being real	Practicing being real	Being real
3. Neglecting our own needs	Realizing we have needs	Identifying our needs	Beginning to get our needs met	Getting our needs met
4. Being over-responsible for others, etc.	Identifying boundaries	Clarifying boundaries	Learning to set limits	Being responsible for self, with clear boundaries
5. Low self-esteem	Identifying	Sharing	Affirming	Improved self-esteem
6. Control	Identifying	Beginning to let go	Taking responsibility	Taking responsibility while letting go
7. All-or-none	Recognizing and identifying	Learning both/and choices	Getting free	Freedom from all-or-none choices

8. Trust	Realizing trusting can be helpful	Trusting selectively	Learning to trust safe people	Trusting appropriately
9. Feeling	Recognizing and identifying	Experiencing	Using	Observing and using feelings
10. High tolerance for inappropriate behavior	Questioning what is appropriate and what is not	Learning what is appropriate and what is not	Learning to set limits	Knowing what is appropriate, or if not, asking a safe person
11. Fear of abandonment	Realizing we were abandoned or neglected	Talking about it	Grieving our abandonment	Freedom from fear of abandonment
12. Difficulty handling and resolving conflict	Recognizing and risking	Practicing expressing feelings	Resolving conflicts	Working through current conflicts
13/14. Difficulty giving and receiving love	Defining love	Practicing love	Forgiving and refining	Loving self, others, and Higher Power
15. Dependence	Identifying our dependence needs	Learning about healthy dependence and healthy independence	Practicing healthy dependence and independence	Being healthily dependent and independent

2. **Reflect** upon it from my powerful **inner life.**
3. **Talk about** it with safe people (that is, tell that specific part of my story).
4. Ask for **feedback** from them.
5. **Name** the core issue.
6. **Talk** about it some **more.**
7. Ask for some **more feedback.**
8. Select an appropriate **experiential technique.**
9. **Use** that **to work** on my specific conflict and feelings at a **deeper** level.
10. **Talk** and/or **write some more** about it.
11. **Meditate** or **pray** about it.
12. Consider **how** I might **learn** from it.
13. If I still feel incomplete, **repeat** any of the above.
14. Whenever I am ready, **let it go.**

The Sequence Of Working Through A Core Issue

As we work through a specific core issue, we can do so in an evolutionary sequence, depending on where we might be in our healing around that particular core issue (see Table 15.1). For example:

1. **Early** in our work on a particular issue, we may be most interested in initiating such healing actions as questioning, risking, realizing, recognizing, identifying and defining.
2. In the **middle stage** of our healing around a core issue we may use learning, practicing, clarifying, experiencing and working at a deeper level.
3. During an **advanced stage** we may begin to consolidate our progressively increasing awareness around the core issue, while using that awareness at working through upsets and conflicts without being a martyr or victim.
4. When we are **recovered** we can continue using all of the above with still more awareness, success and enjoyment.

Working through core issues as they come up for us is a key part of the recovery process in healing co-dependence and the adult child syndrome. There is no need to rush when working on any core issues. We can take our time — as much time as we need.

16

What Is Healthy Dependence?

The hyphen in the word co-dependence emphasizes that it is about being in relationships. The ability to be dependent and independent in a healthy way is an important goal in recovery from co-dependence and in relationships.

I have long been interested in this core recovery issue of dependence. Yet at all the conferences and talks I have attended and in all the articles and books I have read in psychology, including those on the topic of co-dependence and the adult child syndrome, not once have I seen or heard anyone seriously address healthy dependence and independence.

Interaction Among Core Issues

Each of the core issues is important in recovery from co-dependence and the adult child syndrome. Each one interrelates with one or more of the others, as shown in Figure 16.1. This illustration shows how the primitive yet powerful core issue of *fear of abandonment* leads to and through all the others, ending in *difficulty being real.* And when we are not real — not our True Self — we cannot heal and thereby experience fulfillment and serenity.

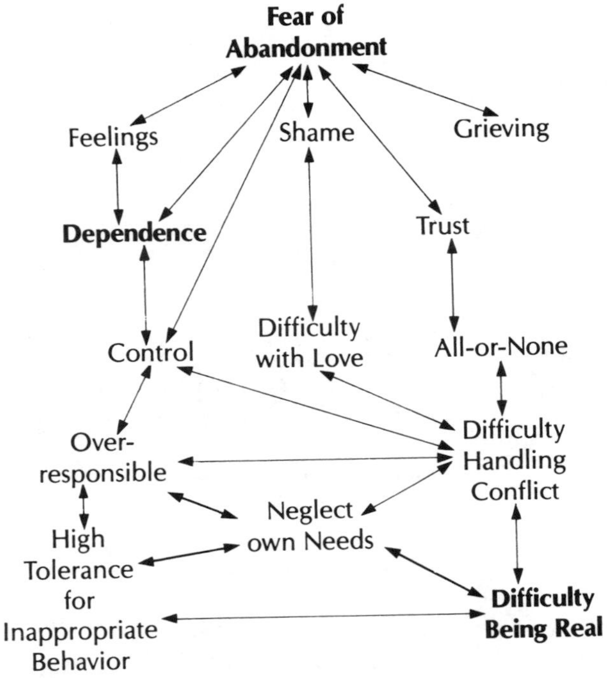

Figure 16.1. Interrelationships among Core Recovery Issues: From the perspective of fear of abandonment, which ultimately may block ability to be Real.

If we are not real, we cannot have healthy and fulfilling relationships. And healthy relationships have as crucial components healthy dependence and independence. We cannot have a successful and enjoyable life without being dependent and vulnerable with selected safe people and with our Higher Power. In this chapter we will begin to differentiate healthy dependence and independence from their unhealthy opposites — unhealthy dependence and unhealthy independence.

Developmental Aspects

In the 1940s Fairbairn emphasized that the evolution of healthy dependence was crucial in healthy child development. He described three stages in this process. He called the first early infantile dependency. In this stage the infant is so dependent upon and identified with the mother (or other parent figure) that it has little sense of itself as being a separate person. At perhaps five or six months of age, the infant enters a transitional period, wherein it begins to deal with and adjust to separations from the mother and changes in their relationship. This phase eventually includes the rapprochement stage as described by Mahler. The final stage is mature dependence, which develops slowly as the child grows older. Here the child learns to accept differences, and learns about exchange and mutuality. This is the stage of healthy interdependence[137].

This dependence interrelates with other developmental tasks and core issues such as trust, control and all-or-none thinking and behaving, and can be damaged by dysfunctional parenting. *In recovery* adult children usually have to *retrace some of these stages in a safe setting* with healthy parent figures and healthy others. These people may include individual and group therapists, sponsors, group members, friends, colleagues and safe others.

Healthy Dependence Versus Unhealthy Dependence

In recovery the goal is progress, not perfection. It is neither necessary nor possible to reach all of these qualities of healthy dependence overnight.

Figure 16.2 illustrates some of the relationships and interactions among the four possible kinds of dependence. Notice that in healthy dependence and independence we are in a harmonious relationship with our self, safe others and our Higher Power. But in the state of unhealthy dependence and unhealthy independence, we are actually co-dependent.

Healthy Dependence

In healthy dependence we ask for and accept help when needed and appropriate. We feel safe and secure in the relationship. We trust. The relationship is an intimate one — each person is real. And each has integrity, which the Second of the Twelve Steps calls "sanity." Each person in the relationship is whole. That means we are aware of and caring for ourself on all levels — physical, mental, emotional and spiritual.

A relationship of healthy dependence includes sharing. This relationship is reciprocal, so each person does an equal amount of sharing. Each supports the other and accepts the other for who they are. The partners share an equality of many characteristics and values, including importance and respect. Healthy dependence also means being flexible and having healthy boundaries[649]. The partners are not manipulative — they do not try to get things from one another indirectly. They are direct in asking for their needs and support.

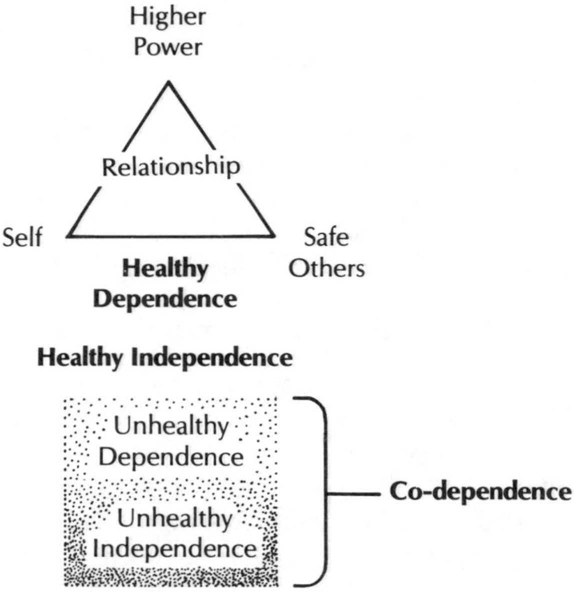

Figure 16.2. Relationship Among Four Forms Of Dependence: with relationships of healthy dependence

Unhealthy Dependence

By contrast, actively co-dependent people have difficulty asking for and accepting help. This may be due to a number of factors. They may have been hurt many times in the past when they reached out, and so they have difficulty trusting. In this unhealed state, they do not experience the full dimensions of their physical, mental, emotional and spiritual health.

The co-dependent relationship is neither equal nor reciprocal. Rather, it is unidirectional, with only one giving to the other or both closed and not giving. And rather than being supportive, one or both people are unsupportive or enabling of the other. Often there are one of two extremes: overaccepting of the other's needs, wants and behavior, or not accepting them at all — or flip-flopping back and forth. They are often inflexible and rigid. They have unhealthy boundaries — blurred, fused, enmeshed or rigid. They often use manipulation — indirect attempts to influence, get or control.

Table 16.1 summarizes each of these characteristics.

Healthy Dependence

Even though they ask for what they want and need, people in a healthy dependent relationship do not try to control or exploit and are not abusive. Being dependent on each other also means that the partners in this relationship are also healthily independent. While each has a healthy narcissism or self-caring, they are compassionate with each other. And they include appropriate amounts of shared and spontaneous contact and activities.

The recovered person, comfortable being in healthy dependent relationships, tends to avoid any attempts at intimate relationships with people who are unrecovered, actively co-dependent and who also may be unhealthily independent. Rather, the person prefers to be in relationships with people who are comfortable being dependent and independent in healthy ways. Finally, the healthy person has an awareness and experience of the spiritual, and a growing and healthy dependent relationship with their Higher Power.

Unhealthy Dependence

By contrast, co-dependent people may try to control, exploit or abuse one another. Rather than being healthily independent, they are either dependent or independent in an unhealthy way. They frequently experience a high tolerance for inappropriate behavior, and are often overindulgent with others. Little is genuinely shared; and when it is, their activities are often planned and not spontaneous.

Table 16.1. Some Characteristics of Healthy Dependence and Healthy Independence in Relationships, in Contrast with Unhealthy Dependence and Independence.

Unhealthy Dependence	Healthy Dependence
• Difficulty asking for or accepting help	• Asks for and accepts help when appropriate
• Unauthentic	• Authentic, real (both parties)
• Not trusting	• Trusting
• Unintegrated	• Integrated: integrity realized
• Withholding or uneven	• Sharing
• Unidirectional, or both closed	• Reciprocal
• Enabling or unsupportive	• Supportive
• Overaccepting or unaccepting	• Accepting
• Unequal	• Equal
• Inflexible	• Flexible
• Boundaries blurred, fused and rigid; enmeshment	• Boundaries clear and flexible
• Manipulative (indirect attempts at influence or control)	• Non-manipulative. Direct asking for needs and support
• Exploitive	• Non-exploitive
• Controlling	• Non-controlling
• May be abusive	• Non-abusive
• Co-dependent or unhealthily independent	• Partners are healthily independent
• Other-indulgent, often with high tolerance for inappropriate behavior	• Self and other-indulgent. Healthy narcissism
• Little genuinely shared. Often planned	• Appropriate amounts of shared and spontaneous contact and activities
• Objective, passionate or numb	• Compassionate with others
• Often with abusing or other co-dependents. Usually martyr/victim. May feel bored with healthy people.	• Tends to avoid relationship with co-dependents and unhealthy independents. Prefers relationships with healthy dependent and independent people.
• Imprisoned and stagnating	• Free and growing
• May exclude Higher Power	• Includes Higher Power

Unhealthy Independence	Healthy Independence
• Difficulty asking for or accepting help	• Asks for and accepts help when appropriate
• Isolated	• Independent
• Unauthentic when in relationship	• Real with self and others
• Not trusting	• Trusts self
• Unintegrated	• Integrated
• Withholding	• Enjoy self/Self
• Denying, closed	• Considering
• No support	• Available to support or be supported
• Rejecting, critical	• Accepting; fulfilling own wants and needs
• Alone, "better than"	• Content in self/Self
• Rigid	• Firm or flexible, as needed
• Boundaries rigid	• Boundaries clear and flexible
• May be manipulative	• Non-manipulative
• May be exploitive	• Non-exploitive
• May be controlling	• Non-controlling
• May be abusive	• Non-abusive
• Unhealthily independent	• Healthily independent
• Self-indulgent only	• Appropriately self-indulgent
• Unhealthy narcissism	• Healthy narcissism
• Little shared	• Appropriate amounts of shared and spontaneous contact and activities
• Often objective or numb	• Compassionate with self/Self
• When in relationship, is often with co-dependent. Often attacking or abusive. Frequently impulsive and compulsive.	• Tends to avoid relationships with co-dependents and unhealthy independents. Usually hero/heroine. Prefers relationship with healthy dependent and independent people.
• Imprisoned and stagnating	• Free and growing
• Usually excludes Higher Power	• Includes Higher Power

Rather than being compassionate, they tend to be either passionate, numb or "objective." They often find themselves in relationships with either active co-dependents or abusers (who are also co-dependent underneath). Rather than leaving such relationships, they tend to stay with them as a martyr or a victim. Due to several factors, including a low self-esteem and that these kinds of mistreatment feel so familiar, they may feel bored being in relationship with a healthy person. And so, rather than feeling free and growing, they often feel imprisoned and stagnating. Finally, they may or may not have a healthy relationship with a Higher Power.

Healthy Independence Versus Unhealthy Independence

The core recovery issue of dependence includes *independence* as an important and indispensable dynamic. In fact, a person *cannot have a healthy* experience of *dependence* in any relationship *without also being independent in a healthy way.*

When people are independent in an *un*healthy way they are co-dependent. This is because they are still focused on others to their own detriment. They are so focused on others that even with safe and appropriate others they cannot have a healthy dependent relationship. They may be afraid of such closeness and intimacy, perhaps because they have been hurt in past close relationships and because in their childhood they never had healthy dependent and independent relationships modeled for them. They have difficulty trusting and *their self-detrimental focus on others* is manifested by their *fear and general avoidance of healthy and close relationships.* This may be carried to such an extent that they cannot generally have relationships where they experience a healthy dependence and a healthy independence. As such, their unhealthy independence is a guise of active co-dependence.

Healthy Independence

The person with healthy independence asks for help when appropriate and accepts it, and thereby is dependent in a healthy way. This help or assistance may be with all sorts of things, from the impersonal to the personal in their life, including help getting their healthy human *needs* met. While at other times they are appropriately independent, they are at almost all times real with themselves and with safe others. They are trusting of their True Self.

They are also aware of the physical, mental and emotional aspects of their being, and are thus whole, sane and fully integrated. Because they have realized their True Self and experientially connected it to their Higher Power, they feel a sense of fulfillment most of the time, and thereby enjoy their life. Being humble, they are also open to many possibilites and consider them as appropriate. They are available and open to support others when needed and to be supported by others. Fulfilling their own wants and needs, they are also accepting of others.

Unhealthy Independence

People with unhealthy independence pretend to be in control, independent and *not* in need of help or assistance from others. But underneath this veneer they have the basic feelings and dynamics of any co-dependent person. They may just manifest their co-dependence differently than the more stereotyped overly dependent co-dependent. Certainly, they have difficulty asking for help and accepting it. So they have difficulty being dependent, and often end up feeling isolated and alone.

Not having realized their True Self, they are unable to be authentic in relationships. Even when they are in a relationship, they have difficulty trusting. They have thus not fully experienced their whole self — their physical, mental, emotional and spiritual dimensions. Rather than extending and sharing themselves, they withhold. They often deny important aspects of their inner life, and are closed to its empowering experiences. They may have difficulty supporting others and may be critical or rejecting. Being so "independent," they often feel "better than" others.

Healthy Independence

People who have healthy independence have clear and healthy boundaries. They can be either firm or flexible, as needed and appropriate. They tend not to control, manipulate, exploit or abuse others. They have a healthy sense of self, and care for themselves by getting their needs met without hurting others. In this sense they have a healthy narcissism.

Because they are also dependent in a healthy way, they engage in shared and spontaneous contact and activities with others — and on multiple levels: physical, mental, emotional and spiritual. They are compassionate with themselves and with others. They prefer relationships with healthy people and avoid relationships with active co-dependents and people who are unhealthily independent. They have a loving and constructive relationship with their Higher Power, and are free and growing.

Unhealthy Independence

By contrast, people with unhealthy independence tend to have personal boundaries that are too loose at times, but are more often rigid. And either knowingly or not, they may try to control, manipulate, exploit or even abuse another. They may be "selfish," that is, show unhealthy narcissism. They may share little in their contact and in spontaneous activities with others. Out of touch with their feelings, they may be "objective" and numb.

When they are in relationships, it is often with other co-dependents. Because they have difficulty being dependent with anyone, they may or may not have an ongoing relationship with their Higher Power. If they do, it tends not to be experiential and fulfilling. They frequently end up feeling a life of imprisonment and stagnation.

Working Through The Core Issues Of Dependence

It is not easy to work through this core issue of dependence. To do so takes great courage, risking, persistence and patience.

A specific recovery plan may include addressing any of the core issues, including dependence. Table 16.2 is an example part of a treatment plan that includes dependence as an issue.

Table 16.2. Treatment Plan with Dependence as an Issue.

Problem	**What I Want to Happen (Goals)**	**How I Plan To Accomplish That (Objectives)**
Difficulty being in a healthy dependent relationship	Be in at least three healthy relationships (e.g., best friend or spouse, therapy group, and sponsor)	Practice these by the following: 1. Attend group therapy weekly long term. 2. Risk asking the group for feedback and assistance on a personal issue at least monthly. 3. Attend a self-help group of my choice at least weekly. 4. Within three months of starting the self-help group, get a sponsor and communicate weekly. 5. Talk to someone else who feels safe at least weekly about my specific issues around dependence.

17

Blocks In Recovery

Recovery from co-dependence and being an adult child of a dysfunctional family is not easy. That uneasiness, discomfort and pain can be a block to completing the healing process. And several other experiences, beliefs and core issues can slow down or even stop recovery.

Being aware of these blocks makes *it easier to recognize* them when they come up in recovery. This awareness can facilitate *working through each block if it occurs* so that recovery can progress more successfully and even enjoyably.

While there are distinct disadvantages to experiencing any of these blocks, there is also *at least one potential advantage* to each. Experientially learning about each block and working through it is an important part of the recovery process. Any of these blocks can occur at any time. For convenience, I have arranged them according to an appropriate time sequence of early, middle and later recovery.

The Earliest Blocks In Recovery

Although early blocks to recovery may keep us from getting started, they can also have the opposite effect: Our very frustration causes us to look deeper. Table 17.1 summarizes these early blocks.

Table 17.1. Some Early Blocks to Healing.

Block	***Disadvantage***	***Advantage***
Active addiction, compulsion or **distracting** co-dependence	Blocks ability to focus, work and experience	Provides frustration to search for deeper answers.
Lack of knowledge of how to do the recovery	Can delay healing and prolong pain.	We heal most completely when we work through, discover and create our own recovery
Fear of the unknown	Any fear can bind other feelings and paralyze us in surrendering into the recovery process.	Part of the recovery process is learning what fear is and is not, how it can be helpful, and most of all how fear is almost completely useless.
Not regularly attending therapy sessions, self-help groups or other helpful aids	Person misses healing opportunities	Allows them to recover at their own pace and in their own way.

Active Addiction And Distracting Co-dependence

My experience assisting people in their recoveries has shown that at least 20 percent of people who seek recovery from co-dependence and the adult child syndrome are actively addicted or have distracting co-dependence — or both. Even though they are sincerely motivated to get free of their pain and confusion, these problems may distract them from their ability to concentrate and focus on important issues. Other conditions that may block recovery include any disabling major psychological or psychiatric disorder.

Each of these can be viewed as being a Stage Zero disorder or condition. Each requires an appropriate Stage One full recovery program to stabilize it for a sufficient duration of time. This stabilization prepares the way for a more efficient use of the process of healing co-dependence and the adult child syndrome, which occurs in Stage Two recovery.

This Stage Zero disorder or condition seriously interferes with our ability to focus and to do the work and authentically experience the recovery process. However, like all such distractions, these blocks can also provide a *positive frustration* that impels us to search for deeper answers to healing our emptiness and pain[646].

Therapists need to make a thorough evaluation to identify these potential disorders or conditions as part of the intake procedure in preparation for beginning recovery for co-dependence and the adult child syndrome.

Lack Of Knowledge

A second block to recovery and healing is a lack of knowledge of how to do the recovery work. This can delay healing and prolong unnecessary pain.

However, a paradox and advantage to this block is that we heal most completely when we work through, discover and create our own recovery. It is a delicate balance of finding and using what might be available from a number of recovery sources that may be more *intellectually oriented* in combination with *experiencing* and *working through* the confusion and pain of the ungrieved grief from the adult child wounding.

Fear Of The Unknown

Because of our lack of knowledge and experience of recovery, we may feel scared about what might happen if we surrender to the healing process. Any fear can bind other feelings, such as shame or hurt, that may be more primary and basic. Fear can thus paralyze and prevent us from risking and surrendering to the recovery process.

At the same time, an important part of recovery is learning just what fear is and is not, how it can be helpful, and most of all how fear is almost completely useless in most aspects of our life[528].

Irregular Attendance Or Participation

Irregular attendance or participation in any committed-to recovery aids such as group therapy, individual therapy sessions or self-help fellowship meetings prevents us from having a strong and effective ongoing recovery program. Each missed session is a missed healing opportunity.

The advantage of not attending or participating is that it allows us to recover at our own pace and in our own way.

Blocks In Middle Recovery

After the first few months of recovery, we may encounter some additional blocks. Although any block can occur at any time, some are common in the middle stage of recovery. Table 17.2 summarizes these blocks in middle recovery.

Table 17.2. Some Blocks in Middle Recovery.

Block	***Disadvantage***	***Advantage***
Fear of **criticism** or **rejection**	Keeps our Child in hiding.	Helps us sort out who is safe.
Core issues get in the way, especially:		
• **Low self-esteem**	Dampens motivation for self healing and self care.	Helps keep us humble, and feel compassion for others with low self-esteem.
• **Difficulty trusting**	Delays our healing.	Teaches us to trust those who earn our trust.
• **Needing to be in control**	Aggravates pain. Prevents surrender to recovery process.	Helped us survive in the past.
• **All-or-none**	Blocks diversity and choice in full recovery program.	Teaches us about all-or-none.

Fear Of Criticism, Rejection Or Abandonment

As we begin to see the need for risking to be real with safe and supportive people, we may fear that we will be criticized or rejected by those with whom we may be sharing. We are afraid that as we risk exposing and being who we are — our True Self — that we will be rejected or abandoned. And so that True Self, our Child Within, stays in hiding — afraid to come out and express itself.

An advantage of this, however, can be that our caution can help us sort out who is safe from who is unsafe. Doing so is crucial in achieving a successful recovery.

Low Self-Esteem And Shame

Underneath these fears of criticism and rejection may be a feeling of shame and low self-esteem, a sense that we are bad, unworthy, defective, imperfect or somehow not good enough. And this hurts. Both of these feelings — the shame and the fear that may be protecting it — tend to dampen our motivation for self-healing and self-care.

In recovery we learn that the way to heal fear and shame is to share both it and our reasons for feeling it with safe people. Some of these safe people may turn out to be our therapist, therapy group, self-help group, sponsor or a best friend. When they accept us as we are and don't try to change us, we can begin to let go of these painful feelings.

The only advantage to feeling this shame, in addition to pointing to our woundedness so that we may heal it, is that it keeps us humble and helps us to feel compassion for others with low self-esteem. Humility is a powerful healing aid. It allows us to remain open to learning new things about our self, others and our Higher Power.

Difficulty Trusting

Another major and related core recovery issue that can block our healing is difficulty trusting. When we risk being real, we are beginning to trust. Ultimately, we learn to trust our True Self, safe others and our Higher Power.

An advantage of not trusting people right away is that doing so teaches us to trust those who earn our trust. And that earning takes time.

Needing To Be In Control

This is a major issue. We may have survived growing up in an unhealthy family or some other unhealthy relationship by being "in control." Yet in recovery the need to be in control can be a crippling block. To get free of its shackles, we begin to risk being real.

All-Or-None

All-or-none thinking and behaving, also known as "splitting," is a core issue that commonly blocks recovery. It may be manifested in one or more ways:

1. Dropping out of group therapy prematurely because "A Twelve-Step program is all I need."
2. Avoiding a Twelve-Step program because "I'm in individual (or group) psychotherapy."
3. Moving from working with one therapist who is encouraging us to go under a Level One *conflict* and examine Level Two to a second therapist who doesn't support that and thus enables us to stay stuck at Level One (explained below).
4. Dropping out of all recovery prematurely for any of a number of reasons, often including the inability to tolerate emotional pain.

A situation like any of these is a perfect opportunity to work through unhealed aspects of this core issue of all-or-none. Getting stuck in this core issue blocks the power of diversity of using several modalities in a full recovery program.

Blocks Later In Recovery

Some blocks are most common in the latter part of recovery. However, as with the above, they may also occur at any time. Table 17.3 summarizes these later blocks.

No Recovery Plan

Not formulating and putting a clear recovery plan in writing is one of the most common blocks to the process of healing from co-dependence and the adult child syndrome. After the first few months — and at least by the end of the first year of recovery — it is helpful to make an individualized, personal recovery plan.

Table 17.3. Some Blocks in Later Recovery.

Block	***Disadvantage***	***Advantage***
No recovery plan	Keeps goals and methods vague or unknown.	None
Difficulty with commitment to recovery	Delays our healing.	Works best when we find and initiate it ourself.
Difficulty going below and beyond **Level One conflict**	Prevents complete healing.	Defends against greater pain.
Blaming or **projecting pain** onto others	Prevents complete healing.	May allow some beginning movement in grieving process.
Inability to tolerate emotional pain	Prevents complete healing.	Prevents being overwhelmed by pain.
Fixating on a time duration for therapy and recovery	Ends recovery prematurely.	May give an approximate time.
Resisting spirituality	One of the strongest ways to block our recovery.	Can help us get free from collective religious co-dependence.
Lack of finances	Can limit our recovery choices.	Teaches us to focus on what might be most productive in recovery.

The idea is simple. On a piece of 8½x11 inch paper, make three columns. Call the first column "Problems, conflicts or concerns." Call the second column "What I want to happen — Goals." Call the third column "How I plan to accomplish the goals." That's the easy part.

Then take a few days or weeks and begin to consider each of these areas, moving from left to right. Make notes on the page. Carry it with you. For more details on how to go deeper into this important undertaking, consult *A Gift To Myself, My Recovery Plan,* or Chapter 13 above.

Making and periodically updating such a recovery plan may be one of the most helpful and practical things we can do to strengthen and facilitate ongoing recovery.

Not making a recovery plan may frustrate us into seeing the helpfulness of making one.

Difficulty Committing To Recovery

Difficulty committing to recovery is related to several of the blocks described above, including low self-esteem. If we feel so bad about ourself that we feel *unworthy* of a successful recovery, then how can we make a commitment to it?

Rather than someone else pushing us, commitment to recovery tends to work best when we find and initiate it ourself. Yet we may become so discouraged and down on ourself that we may benefit by sharing those feelings with safe others, such as our therapy group, therapist, sponsor, or best friend. The paradox here is that we need safe others to assist us in our recovery, yet the only way we can recover is by our own internal motivation and work.

Difficulty Going Below Level One Conflict

Level One is the *conflict* in which we may find ourself in any relationship *that we have now.* In recovery we have the opportunity to learn that this conflict may represent only the surface of an iceberg of unfinished conflicts from our past. This is *Level Two* conflict. We can tell if such a deeper unfinished conflict is in operation when we over-react to a given situation. Here our degree of reaction is not appropriate for the particular Level One conflict, indicating that something else is going on[652].

Level Three conflict is the old tapes that play repeatedly in our minds — "You're not good enough." "You could never do that . . ." These are messages we incorporated internally from Level Two.

The only possible advantage of *not* going deeper is when we feel so unsafe and afraid that we cannot tolerate the pain, and so it helps us defend against greater pain. The way out is to find one or more safe people and tell them about as much of the pain as we can tolerate now. Then when we feel safe enough, perhaps we will be able to go below Level One.

Blaming Or Projecting Onto Others

This one is related to difficulty going below Level One conflict. If we are stuck in the martyr or victim stance, we may have difficulty taking responsibility for creating our own pain. Doing so often results in blaming others or projecting pain onto others to such an extent that over time there is little or no movement for us in the grieving and healing process.

It is appropriate to name the truth about what happened, how we were mistreated and, in a safe setting, to express our anger and our grief at what happened and whomever mistreated us. That, however, is not blaming or projecting. Rather, it is naming, expressing and grieving.

The only advantage to blaming or projecting is that doing so may be helpful to prepare to grieve authentically. If we persist in doing so, it can become a disadvantage and thus a block to recovery.

Intimacy Issues

Intimacy is one of 12 basic dynamics in relationships[649]. An intimate relationship is one where two people are real with one another over time. They dare to be vulnerable and to share their True Self with each other. An intimate relationship works most successfully when both partners have realized or actualized their True Self, that is, they have each healed their Child Within.

An intimate relationship requires risking and commitment, which can frequently be scary. It is this fear, often combined with some shame, that can scare us away from that risking and commitment. And so we run away from intimacy, while at the same time we crave it.

These and other intimacy issues may block our recovery. However, if we share with safe people exactly how we are feeling, we can work through these and other important issues around intimacy.

Inability To Tolerate Emotional Pain

It is difficult to learn to tolerate painful feelings. Yet until we learn how to feel, use and then let go to each of our painful feelings, our recovery will be blocked. This is in part why a full recovery takes such a long time. Learning about and experiencing each of these feelings is a crucial part of the healing process.

What we learn is that we don't have to numb out, that we can experience and work through any painful feeling or issue, and that we can learn to differentiate necessary from unnecessary pain. It is at those times when our emotional pain gets worse, then, if we are with safe people in a full recovery program, we can learn a powerful lesson: how to tolerate and work through the pain and conflict.

Fixating On A Time Duration

The three to five years that it often takes to complete the healing when working a full recovery program is only an estimate. For many people it takes longer. And this is perfectly acceptable. I have assisted several people who chose to remain actively participating in recovery for over eight years.

I and others recommended a minimum of three to five years in active full recovery to give oneself the best chance for making a successful recovery. Some people choose a "trial" of one, two or three years before committing to a longer time. This is perfectly acceptable. Sometimes, however at the end of their committed time they conclude that they are complete in their recovery. I have seen several people terminate their active recovery prematurely due to this fixation on a particular time duration.

A way to avoid this block to a successful recovery is to make and use a personal recovery plan and to ask your therapy group or therapist for their feedback about the completion of your recovery. Take plenty of time to listen to and consider this feedback. Ask your Higher Power for assistance if you choose. Fixating on a specific time duration may involve getting stuck in several core issues, including all-or-none thinking and behaving and difficulty grieving.

A key reason why complete recovery takes this long is that one cannot fully grieve major losses, hurts and traumas quickly.

From the vast research available, healthy grieving takes at least two to four years. And many people who start recovery don't *begin* to *grieve authentically* until they have spent some time learning to trust themself, the group, their therapist and the process. And learning how to grieve in a healthy way can take a long time. Part of healing involves learning about and making healthier choices. We can choose to continue our recovery work for as long as it takes. All that we have to lose is our unnecessary pain and suffering.

Resisting Spirituality

I have seen several people block and delay their recovery by resisting spirituality. I define spirituality as being about our relationship with ourself, others and our Higher Power. To help overcome this block, I suggest using one or more daily spiritual practices, such as meditating, praying and working the Twelve Steps.

The only way to fill our emptiness is to realize our True Self and then experientially connect it to God. When we do that and also complete our unfinished business, we are healed. We are then free to co-create a successful and enjoyable life.

Lack Of Finances

Lack of finances can block recovery in two ways. First, we may really not have enough money to live on if we pay for group or individual therapy. There are at least three ways to handle this, either alone or in combination: (1) ask the therapist for a reduction in fee; (2) go to a therapist or group at a facility such as a community mental health center that offers a sliding-scale fee schedule; and (3) reduce or eliminate some of one's less essential expenses. For example, a man smoked three packs of cigarettes daily. When he stopped smoking he could afford to pay for weekly group therapy and he had more energy to work on his recovery.

We may also use lack of finances as an excuse to stop a particular form of therapy. Rather than deal directly with the conflict in or around the therapy, the person uses this excuse to stop participating. The way to handle this block constructively is to discuss it directly in group or individual therapy or in whichever recovery aid one may be. Here the conflict is not really a lack of finances, but is usually about something else.

A true lack of finances can limit our recovery choices, and from this dilemma we can learn to be creative in healthy caring for ourself. This block may also bring in related blocks, such as low self-esteem. Are we worth the time and money?

Other Blocks

Other blocks may drain so much energy that we are unable to focus on our work of recovery:

1. A recent, ungrieved major loss.
2. A current major conflict that is incomplete.
3. The moderate to heavy use of alcohol or other drugs, including nicotine, caffeine and sugar.

For example, I have seen people who have entered into separation or divorce proceedings, or who were breaking up from a longstanding relationship, or who had just lost a parent, or who were in a major work or legal conflict. This loss or conflict required so much psychological energy from them that they were unable to focus on their recovery as a co-dependent/adult child. As in many of the above blocks, they were distracted.

And I have seen many people with active addictions to nicotine, caffeine, or sugar who likewise used up so much of their energy that they had little left for their recovery. Other people were not actually alcoholic or chemically dependent, but they drank or used drugs enough to block their ability to fully experience their inner life, which is a crucial part of recovery and life. Some treatment/recovery programs even recommend total abstinence from all alcohol and other drugs during recovery, whether or not one has the disease of chemical dependence. And a few recommend abstaining from nicotine, caffeine and sugar during recovery.

Whenever a person feels stuck in their recovery or may want to stop individual or group therapy prematurely, it can be helpful to review these blocks to recovery and to discuss any with which they may identify with their therapist or therapy group. It is most helpful in the healing process to give such consideration and discussion important attention.

18

Evaluating And Recycling

In the last chapter I discussed some blocks to recovery from co-dependence and the adult child syndrome. But once we have removed these blocks and gone deeply into the experience of our recovery, how can we know when we are complete in our healing? If problematical pain and conflict come up later, how can we handle them?

Have I Completed Most Of My Healing?

How can you know if you have completed your healing? There are no sure criteria for making such a determination. Knowing what we do today about recovery, we can begin to consider some factors that may assist us. Table 18.1 lists these.

To achieve these may be quite an accomplishment for anyone to do even in one lifetime, much less in three to five years. Use these guidelines to consider whether you are ready to discontinue the intensity of your full recovery program, including weekly group or individual therapy.

- Review whether you have completed your recovery goals.

- Review whether you have worked through most of a workbook like *A Gift To Myself*.
- Talk all of this over with your therapy group or individual therapist.
- Discuss it with other safe people who are in recovery. (A caution here: Avoid becoming attached to opinions from people who have not *fully completed* the recovery program about which you are asking.)

Table 18.1. Some Factors in Determining When Most of the Healing Process is Complete

1. Completed recovery goals about 90 percent.
2. Getting needs met regularly.
3. Seeing progressively more possibilities and choices.
4. Making healthy choices.
5. Able to set boundaries and limits when appropriate.
6. Transformed martyr/victim stance to Hero/Heroine's Journey.
7. Addictions and repetition compulsions close to zero.
8. Grieving losses healthily, as appropriate.
9. A minimum of unnecessary pain and suffering.
10. Forgiveness and compassion for self and others.
11. Openness to learning (humility) and growth.
12. Able to laugh, play and have fun.
13. Experientially realized spirituality and serenity.
14. Able to love and be loved.

Recycling: Gentle Reminders

Even after we have completed our healing and are feeling good about ourself and our life, we may relapse, recycle or fall back into some of those old self-destructive habits or patterns. These can be painful, but they can also be gentle reminders that we are getting off the healthy track of being real with ourself and safe with others, and off the healthy track of taking responsibility for working through our conflicts and co-creating our life with our Higher Power. Table 18.2 summarizes some of these gentle reminders[652].

As you study these, consider which ones you may have experienced in the *past* (make an X mark next to these) and which ones you might be *most prone* to experience in the *future* (make a check mark next to these). As any of these come up in your life, write them down and make a plan that would be beneficial for your ongoing self-caring and healing. Use the form provided on Figure 18.1 for this purpose.

Table 18.2. Gentle Reminders: Some Relapse Warning Signs of Recycling in Co-dependence

Loss of awareness of presence of True Self (Child Within)	Unhandled stress (distress)
Neglecting needs	Defensiveness
Neglecting self-caring (rest, nutrition, exercise, intimacy)	Blaming others
Overdoing it	Building resentments
Medicating feelings	Need to control people, places and things
Active addictions, compulsions or attachments arise or return	Loss of connection with Higher Power
Self-esteem lowers or grandiosity increases	Stop using support systems
Choicemaking narrows	All-or-none thinking or behaving
Loss of spontaneity and playfulness	People-pleasing
Isolation	Irritability to an inappropriate extent
Loss of healthy boundaries or ability to set limits	Frequent or persistent confusion or inability to make decisions
Unhandled feelings	Frequent or persistent return of original or new symptoms (physical, mental, emotional or spiritual)

When these "reminders" come up, we do not have to beat ourself up over it. As long as we are human, these kinds of things will be happening. To help avoid *unnecessary* pain and suffering, we can recognize them when they come up and use them in our life, in our relationships with our self, others and our Higher Power.

At the same time there may be a loss, hurt or trauma that we *do* need to grieve. Or we may have a conflict that we need to work through. Or someone might be mistreating us. Or we might have lapsed in our crucial self-caring.

Use any of the healing methods in this book or from any other sources that may work for you[652].

Figure 18.1. Relapse Care

"Gentle Reminder" Relapse Warning Sign	Plan for Self-Caring and Healing

Part III

Co-dependence: The New Paradigm

19

A New Paradigm

Parts I and II of this book presented an introduction to some important aspects of co-dependence from a clinical perspective. As the co-dependence and adult child movement evolved over the last few years, we have learned many new things about ourselves and the human condition. We have learned all this information by taking one step back from conventional clinical approaches and looking at our life and its various disorders from a broader perspective.

In Part III we will take yet another step back and view all of this from an even broader perspective. We will see how co-dependence and the adult child syndrome are a major part of an emerging new paradigm in the helping professions and in human well-being.

What Is A Paradigm?

A paradigm is a worldview: a particular way of looking at things (see Figure 19.1). And it tends to be based on a set of assumptions, theories, beliefs or belief systems that are accepted by most people in a population as being true — the way things are. How constructive, useful and creative people may be who hold to a particular paradigm is limited by the actual and potential dimensions of the paradigm itself. That is, we can go only about as far as our beliefs will allow us.

The following story may help illustrate: A man was to interview a famous scientist at the scientist's home. As he approached the house, he noticed a dog frolicking on the lawn. When the scientist opened the door and greeted the man, the dog ran into the house, going from room to room, sniffing the various contents of the house as dogs often do. Later, as they concluded their interview, the scientist remarked to the man that he didn't know that he was going to bring his dog with him. The man replied, "That's not my dog. I thought it was yours." What we believe — our paradigm — can determine not only what we believe is true, but also what happens for us in our life and how we experience it[721].

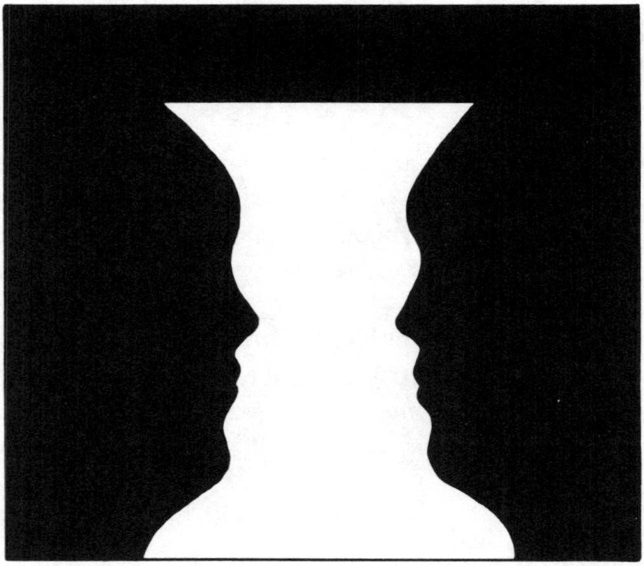

Figure 19.1. Visual Gestalt of Two Simple Paradigms

Before the sixteenth century, the beliefs of the existing worldview or paradigm were that the Earth was the center of the universe, and that everything else revolved around the Earth. This paradigm was supported by governments and organized religion, especially the Catholic church. When Copernicus proved that this belief was not true — that in fact the sun was the center of our universe — the transition to that new paradigm did not come easily for many people. Copernicus and his followers were ridiculed, embarrassed, rejected and punished by those who held most tightly to the old paradigm, and especially by the Catholic church.

Groups tend to hold onto their theories, beliefs and paradigms for as long as they are useful to them. The goals of the paradigm, what its believers want or expect to happen, may be known or unknown to them, or both. These goals usually occur on at least two levels, overt and covert. The *overt* goal may be to help people or to keep them from harm. The *covert* or unconscious goal may be to keep a certain group of people in power while others may be less empowered. Another covert goal may be to avoid facing up to an issue or to avoid a necessary or impending change.

Whatever the reasons for remaining in an old and ineffective paradigm — and there are often many reasons — the group, nation or culture will resist changing. For example, Communists held on to their paradigm of collectivism for nearly a century before they recently became open to the fact that their paradigm and its system wasn't working.

Paradigm Changes

In his landmark book, *The Structure of Scientific Revolutions,* Thomas Kuhn discusses paradigm changes, including what kind of people tend to be instrumental in creating such a new worldview. Two characteristics stand out. One, the person who is instrumental in creating the new paradigm tends not to have been formally trained in the field where the change is made. For example, Albert Einstein, who helped revolutionize modern physics, was never formally trained in physics. He was a mathematician who worked at various jobs, including as a postal clerk. And there are many other similar examples of people who help change paradigms[733].

One possible conclusion from this observation is that it may be unlikely that anyone from a particular discipline or profession will be instrumental in making a major change in their own field. They are wearing the blinders constructed by the already existing beliefs and belief system that they acquired in their formal training. To break out of an old worldview that may not be working, we may need a clear and full vision of what is possible, an imagination so free and creative that it dares to risk venturing beyond the current worldview.

A second characteristic of paradigm changers is that they tend to begin writing or speaking about their new ideas at a relatively young age, usually before age 40 and often before 30. So they did not necessarily wait until the conclusion of a hard-working career to introduce their new and often radical ideas — although they may have continued to work in their dedication to their area of interest throughout their life.

Toward A New Paradigm In The Helping Professions, Recovery And Well-Being

Who might be instrumental in the paradigm change that we are currently undergoing in the helping professions, recovery from illness and in human well-being?

There is no single pioneer. There is no Copernicus or Einstein. This time there are multiple pioneers. And while many were young when they began their work in their particular area, they are of all ages. And they are from diverse backgrounds and professions. Some had training in a helping profession, but not in mental health. Others had formal mental health training. And still others had neither, but were simply recovering in a Twelve-Step or other program and were astute observers and writers.

Another characteristic, not described in Kuhn's or others' observations, is that these pioneers tend to pay serious attention to their own recovery and well-being. Finally, there is an agreement among nearly all of them that spirituality is a major part of the emerging new paradigm.

The Paradigm

So how can we begin to describe this emerging new paradigm? What are some of its aspects and characteristics? Whenever a new paradigm challenges or replaces an old one, the new one will be controversial, as will the way its advocates and practitioners describe the characteristics of the old paradigm. And so, as we begin to explore this area, it may seem controversial, confusing or exciting — or all three. At the least I hope this exploration will stimulate thinking and discussion.

Underlying Belief System

The underlying belief system of the preexisting or old paradigm is that there is a separate dynamic or cause, or combination of causes, of each illness or condition that may befall humankind, and that the cause is usually biological or psychological. A problem with this view is that, with a few exceptions, it is often one-dimensional and reductionistic.

The belief system of the emerging new paradigm is more expansive. It acknowledges multiple dimensions of each illness or condition: multiple factors and dynamics, levels of recovery and wellness, methods of recovery and backgrounds and professions of therapists. These multiple levels include the physical, mental, emotional and spiritual. The co-dependence and adult child movement is a *major dynamic and part of each of these dimensions.* The following are *characteristics* of this new paradigm.

Scope Of Belief System/Paradigm

The scope of the old paradigm is limited to itself alone. It tends to remain stagnant or to retreat and regress into a lower level of being, such as the physical. For example, a major trend in psychiatry over the past decade has been to move away from its former, more multi-dimensional stance (however limited that also may have been) and into diagnostic categories and drug treatment. With increasing emphasis on the biological, it continues to seek physical causes of mental disorders.

While the new paradigm moves away from this direction, it doesn't reject all parts of the old. Rather, it still uses what is useful from the old paradigm. So it includes, supports and nurtures the useful parts of the old, while at the same time transcending the old. One other difference is that except in specific and individualized circumstances, it avoids the use of most psychoactive drugs in recovery, since they usually interfere with our ability to access our crucial inner life, as shown in Figure 1.1.*

(See footnote next page.)

Awareness Of Problem

In the old paradigm, for any specific problem for which a person may present asking for assistance, the helping professional and society gave the person a diagnosis or a label. Even though doing so may have been helpful and the helping professional may not have intend it, if it was in the realm of mental health the label often ended up being pejorative. As a consequence the person and the clinician may have translated the label as implying that somehow the person was "bad," "sick," "crazy" or "stupid" — or even "untreatable."

These labels are further ingrained in our culture by such organizations as health insurance companies and health maintenance organizations, which insist that a fully insured person's health care will not be paid for — as it should be under their contract agreement — unless there is an acceptable diagnosis or label given the person. Currently, the diagnoses of co-dependence and adult child syndrome are not acceptable to insurance companies. Indeed, most of their employees do not even know how to define these terms. Thus clinicians are forced to use another diagnosis that is acceptable, even though doing so may not be clinically relevant or useful. Having to do this may divert energy and attention away from the person's recovery work, and trigger unnecessary feelings of guilt in the person and the helping professional.

In the new paradigm, giving the person such a medical, psychiatric or insurance company-approved label when Stage Two recovery is reached — that is, when the person seeks assistance for co-dependence or the adult child syndrome — is less important than is assessing the presence and dimensions of their woundedness and assisting them in getting free of that woundedness.

---

*In carefully selected situations, such as manic-depressive disorder or a thought disorder (psychosis) or severe depression, the use of lithium, neuroleptics (major tranquilizers), or antidepressant medication as one part of a full recovery program can be helpful when used in the lowest possible effective dose. In my practice about 2 percent of the people that I assist may fit this description and may benefit from using one of these drugs.

Usefulness Of A Label Or Diagnosis

In the old paradigm, the usefulness of a diagnosis or label was mostly for basic management during Stage Zero and Stage One recovery. And this is appropriate and necessary to help an afflicted person recover up to the end of Stage One recovery.

The new paradigm includes and supports this practice from the old one. But it also transcends it by moving beyond any limitations that may be associated with the old. The new paradigm includes the use of a diagnosis (1) for basic management in Stages Zero and One, (2) for insurance reimbursement and (3) for any crucial or otherwise important management issues. Beyond these uses the new paradigm views such diagnoses as being limited. The new thus emphasizes the wholistic management and assistance — physical, mental, emotional and spiritual — of the person in whatever stage of recovery they may be, including Stage Two (co-dependence and the adult child condition) and Stage Three (spirituality).

Awareness Of Inner Life

The old paradigm attends to only limited areas of our crucial inner life, such as insight and understanding, and adds behavior change, symptom relief or improved coping or functioning to these as goals of therapy. These are treated as more important than other areas and dynamics of inner life, such as feelings, experience and transformation. While many psychotherapists with a psychodynamic and experiential approach work toward emotional transformation as goals of therapy, they may limit the total span of recovery to something approaching Stage Two only. And so, while useful, the old paradigm at best assists the person in healing and growing only so far, because that is as far as its imagination can stretch.

The new paradigm adds to the above awareness and use of inner life, especially feelings and experience, thus promoting and facilitating understanding, healing and transformation. Rather than being the goal, symptom relief and behavior change usually follow and are the *result of the process* of the person's working for sufficient duration in a full recovery program.

Responsibility For Healing

In the old paradigm the responsibility for healing is seen to be outside of the afflicted person.* Whether it be a drug (medication), surgery, irradiation or another person (physician or therapist), the person cannot get well without some thing outside of itself. If the person doesn't then get well from thus interacting with the external object or person, they and others may say that "the treatment didn't work." This characteristic of the old paradigm is exemplified in the word "treatment" itself. The person is *treated*. Something is *done to* the person. And that comes from the outside.

A way to differentiate the new from the old paradigm is to contrast the word *recovery* with "treatment." In recovery the responsibility for getting well is inside the afflicted person. And part of that responsibility may be to go outside and seek appropriate assistance. For example, we consult a physician when we have acute chest pain. In the same way, when appropriate we consult a therapist who is knowledgeable and skilled in assisting people in recovery from co-dependence and the adult child syndrome. This appropriate going outside is hinted at in the Second of the Twelve Steps: *Came to believe that a Power greater than ourselves could restore us to sanity.* Ultimately, we have to find that Power within and connect it to the Higher Power that also exists without.

But such *going outside* is only a *catalyst* to change from within. This responsibility, which comes from within, is to change ourself from the inside. We change when we rediscover our Child Within, our True Self, live from and as our True Self and then experientially connect it to God. This allows us to let go of our co-dependent self or ego, and we heal.

Recovery Techniques

In the old paradigm the treatments and recovery techniques for each condition tend to be limited to one or two. And these treatments may be related to the discipline that the individual helping professional practices, such as internal medicine, surgery,

*An exception may be seen with some psychodynamic approaches, although even they may exhibit manifestations of the old paradigm.

cognitive or behavior therapy. While the results of these are often successful in the short term, in the long term they are frequently not successful, or only partially so.

The recovery methods or techniques available in the new paradigm are unlimited. Those that may be selected by the helping professional for a particular person are chosen because they facilitate healing for whichever stage of recovery the person may be in currently. The particular method or approach is appropriate for where the person is now in recovery. The person also participates in making that choice, but now with more awareness and responsibility.

Methods For Determining What Is True

How can we know for sure what is correct or true about something? What methods can we use to help us determine what is true? Gregory Bateson and Ken Wilber describe three levels of methods to do so, according to what realm the "something" is in that we are measuring or testing[745,746].

The first realm is the physical. The most useful and accurate method for determining what is true about one or more physical entities is the scientific method. This involves measurement through one or more of our five senses and applying the appropriate mathematical testing formula.

The next realm is that of the mind, exemplified by the study of psychology. For it the most useful and accurate method for determining what is true about one or more of its aspects is observation (phenomenology) and interpretation (hermeneutics). Using the *scientific method alone* to study the mind will produce erroneous results, what Bateson and Wilber call a *category error.* To determine what is true about the mind requires going beyond the scientific method into observation and interpretation.

The final realm is that of the spiritual. The most useful and accurate method for determining what is correct or true about the spiritual realm of human existence is to apply the approach of ontology, the study of consciousness or being. And the most sophisticated measuring device in the spiritual realm is experience. That experience may be direct or shared.

People who have been in Twelve-Step self-help groups, other support groups or therapy groups are especially familiar with the use of *shared* experience to validate many aspects of their lives. *Direct* experience is what we have every second of every day, in relationship with ourself, with others and with the Universe.

To try to measure the spiritual with either of the two prior methods alone is again to make a category error. Such measurement and testing is not valid and will not work in the spiritual realm of our human existence. Table 19.1 summarizes these principles.

Table 19.1. Methods of Determining What Is True

Area to be tested	Tested by	Brief Description
Physical or Biological	Scientific Method	Measurement through one or more of five senses, with or without control group. Application of appropriate formulae.
Mind	Observation and Interpretation	Phenomenology and Hermeneutics
Spirit	Experience	Direct or shared experience

The old paradigm uses mostly the scientific method, with some observation and interpretation when appropriate. However, feelings and other crucial parts of our inner life are often left out. The new paradigm uses all three methods — whatever may be appropriate for which specific realm of human existence is being looked at and tested.

Awareness Of Spirituality

The old paradigm is mostly unaware of the spiritual and only partially aware of the emotional realms of our existence. Freud, an atheist, viewed the spiritual as fantasy and therefore unreal, or as psychopathology, and therefore unhealthy. His followers, in their own way — dare we call it co-dependent? — continued and froze this belief.

Those in the old paradigm, wedded to the scientific method, also excluded the spiritual and its methods of measurement for the sake of being "objective" and for other reasons. Since Heisenberg postulated the uncertainty principle, we have understood that objectivity is only relative, and that *even the most rigorous scientists influence their results.* There is no such thing as the independent observer who can stand on the sidelines watching nature run its course without influencing it[621,647,686].

While including, supporting and nurturing what is useful in the old, the new paradigm also transcends it by including the spiritual as equally and ultimately potentially more important than the physical and mental realms of our existence. It sees us as spiritual beings and therefore as co-creators with the greater Spirit.

The old paradigm rejected the spiritual because it could not be proven by its methods. The new paradigm experiences the spiritual and uses it constructively throughout all levels of existence. And therefore it needs no further proof of the existence of the spiritual. Einstein said, "Propositions arrived at by purely logical means were completely empty of reality . . . It is very difficult to explain this feeling to anyone who is entirely without it. I maintain that cosmic religious feeling is the strongest and noblest incitement to scientific research . . . all means prove but a blunt instrument if they have not behind them a living spirit."[747]

The spiritual cannot be known without the mental and the emotional, and to some extent the physical. In *A Gift To Myself* I have described how the only way to know the spiritual is through our True Self, our Child Within. The false or co-dependent self is incapable of knowing anything about the spiritual. Christ said, "To get into the Kingdom of Heaven, you have to become like a little child." The emotional is a crucial part of the spiritual. Without experientially knowing each of our feelings, we cannot strip away the layers of our co-dependent self to realize what appears to be our core: creative Unconditional Love.

Cycling between the lower dimensions of the mental and the physical in the old paradigm, we focus mostly outside of ourself. Trying desperately to survive — or numbing out — this lower dimension of the mental comes from our attachment to our co-dependent self, false self or negative ego. It limits its approach to the healing process to "treatment."

The new paradigm cycles *from the Spiritual* through the emotional and mental to the physical, and back through the mental and emotional. Here the mental/emotional is the True Self or Child Within, which through its powerful awareness and consciousness ultimately chooses to cycle back through the Spiritual. The new is synergistic, limitless, and cycles through the Whole of Creation (see Figure 19.2).

In the new paradigm, at any instant the True Self can choose to co-create success and enjoyment in its life with the Spiritual — its Higher Power, or God/Goddess/All-That-Is. Or it can lapse and allow the co-dependent self to attempt to run its life. But the co-dependent self is incapable of connecting to the spiritual, and attached to it, we remain in the old paradigm, unempowered, a martyr or victim, or grandiose.

Training Of Therapists And Other Helping Professionals

While it may be "state of the art" for each particular profession, the training of therapists and other helping professionals is usually "standard" and "conventional" in the old paradigm. And there is usually little or no attention given to anything outside of the limited belief system of the profession. A combined approach that addresses the physical, mental, emotional and spiritual is rare, as is attention to the inner life and to experiential approaches to recovery.

Training in the new paradigm view includes adequate attention to the physical, mental, emotional and spiritual. It emphasizes the inner life of the afflicted person and offers effective experiential approaches and methods for healing and recovery. As exemplified by gestalt therapy, it teaches therapeutic creativity so that the therapist can go appropriately beyond the conventional, but not dangerously or unethically, to help facilitate the person's healing process. Unfortunately, few (if any) training programs use such an approach.

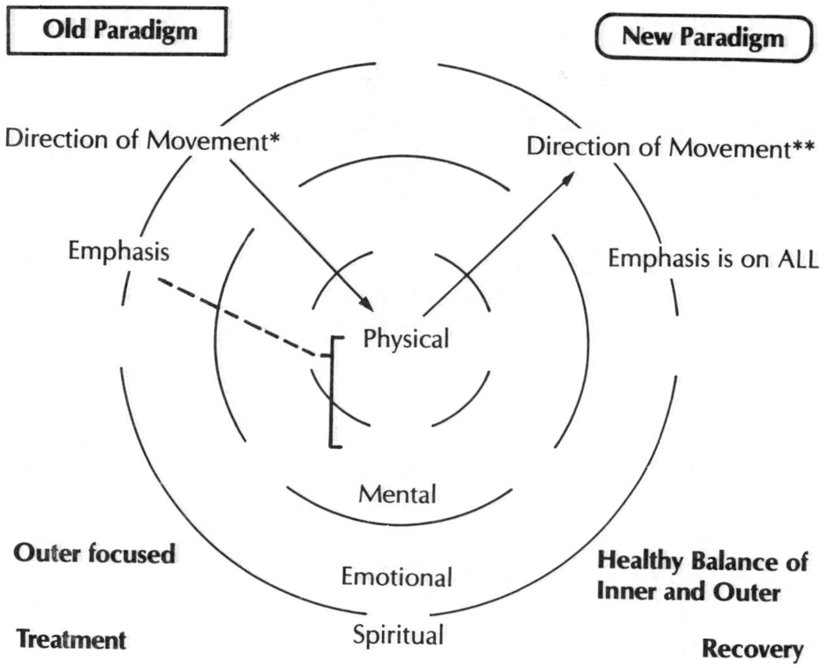

Figure 19.2. Schematic Comparison of the Old and New Paradigms

---

*This movement cycles from the lower dimensions of the mental to the physical and back.
**This movement cycles from the Spiritual back to the emotional, mental, and physical, and returns through the mental and emotional. It is synergistic, limitless and cycles through the Whole of Creation.

Health Of Therapist And Other Helping Professional

The old paradigm pays little or no attention to the physical, mental, emotional and spiritual health of the therapist or other helping professional. Over the past century the only specialty that appears to have recommended that its trainees receive any kind of therapy is psychoanalysis. However, while helpful, and certainly better than nothing, that accepted therapeutic modality has always been only psychoanalysis itself. And that analysis has been contaminated by the politics, including a lack of complete confidentiality, of the "training analysis" that each trainee is required to undergo[736]. In the past some psychiatry training programs have at the most suggested and at the least supported that their trainees receive some personal psychotherapy experience. Today, however, even that has decreased so much that with the regression toward the biological model, diagnostic categories and drug treatments, few suggest that their trainees participate in any therapy for themselves.

The new paradigm puts an increasing emphasis on the total health — physical, mental, emotional and spiritual — of each practitioner, both during training and ongoing afterwards. This is reflected in several areas, including the various "impaired" or troubled professional programs (which are more accurately called *professional assistance programs*) that each state professional association or society may sponsor and maintain. Among therapists who are most skilled and experienced at helping people with co-dependence and the adult child syndrome, the total health and ongoing personal growth of each therapist is encouraged and supported. While it is not a requirement, I and others believe that an important contributor to that growth may be a Twelve-Step program, or at the least using the Twelve Steps in some constructive way.

Sources Of Motivation And Change

Change and growth are difficult and painful. People who are comfortable with the belief systems of the old paradigm may have little motivation to change. However, there may be three potential motivations for both helping professionals in the old paradigm and the people they assist: (1) People may come to the helping professional requesting assistance from the perspective of a co-dependence or adult child syndrome approach. (2) This and the threat or reality of competition may generate a financial incentive that the helping professional acquire knowledge and skills for working with these conditions. (3) The helping professional may realize their own co-dependence or adult child syndrome, and thereby enter into and complete a full recovery program of their own.

In this latter case, however, there is a potential danger: The helping professional who does not participate in full recovery or makes few or no changes from within may be unable to assist patients or clients appropriately in their recoveries as co-dependents and adult children. This is why the ongoing recovery and well-being of the clinician is so important. People in ongoing therapy may be able to grow only about as far as their helping professional has grown, as long as that therapeutic relationship continues.

In the new paradigm helping professionals develop progressive awareness of their own woundedness and take responsibility for their ongoing healing and well-being. And the people they assist learn to take responsibility for being more assertive and speaking up for what they want and need in healing their woundedness.

Table 19.2 summarizes the major characteristics that differentiate the old from this emerging new paradigm among the helping professions and the healing, recovery and well-being of the people they assist.

Who Pays For The Services?

In the old paradigm certain health care services may be neglected if an insurance company or agency will not pay for it. But a problem is that these insurance companies — currently an integral part of the old paradigm — tend to pay easily for the care of physical conditions and with much difficulty for mental, emotional and spiritual ones.

When people heal themselves as described in this book, they tend to have less chronic distress, less acute and chronic illness and require less hospitalization. While many of my colleagues and I have observed this clinically for years, insurance companies will likely have to prove that for themselves by appropriate research. The health insurance companies or agencies of the new paradigm will recognize that payment for new paradigm-oriented services for emotional, mental and spiritual illnesses is just as appropriate and cost effective as it is for physical illness. Insurance companies and agencies that acknowledge that physical illness has its roots deeply buried in the mental, emotional and spiritual will support and perhaps even encourage their customers to receive treatment in those areas. Then we will have real "Health Insurance Programs" instead of the present "Physical Illness Insurance Programs" that we have in the old. When they make these healthy changes, they may realize, as Berkus says, that "Disease is the soul screaming through the body, attempting to get the Truth out once and for all."

Table 19.2. Aspects of a Potential New Paradigm among the Helping Professions

Aspect or Characteristic	*Old Paradigm*	*New Paradigm*
Includes	Physical & Mental	Physical, Mental Emotional and Spiritual
Underlying Belief System	Often unidimensional and reductionistic. Separate cause or dynamic of condition or illness, usually biological or psychological.	Expansive, with multiple dimensions of condition or illness, including: • Factors and dynamics • Methods of recovery • Backgrounds of therapists
Scope of Belief System or Paradigm	Limited to itself. Retreating and regressing into physical.	Includes, supports and nurtures old paradigm, while extends, expands, and transcends it.
Awareness of Problem	Label or diagnosis, often pejorative, which generally translates "Bad, sick, crazy or stupid"	Label less important than dimensions of woundedness and healing — i.e., what happened, and how to get free.
Usefulness of DSM Diagnosis	1. Basic management during Stage Zero or One recovery 2. Insurance reimbursement 3. Crucial management issues	Otherwise limited. Wholistic management during Stages 2 and 3 recovery.

Aspect or Characteristic	***Old Paradigm***	***New Paradigm***
Awareness of Inner Life	Insight, understanding, behavior change, or symptom relief are more important than feelings, experience, and transformation.	Awareness of, release and use of inner life, esp. feelings and experience, promote and facilitate understanding, healing and transformation. Symptoms & behavior change usually follow.
Responsibility for Healing	Outside of me.	Inside me.
Recovery Techniques	Tend to be limited to one or two techniques.	Unlimited. Selected for what facilitates healing.
Methods for Determining What is True	Scientific method; Some description and interpretation	Both of these, plus direct or shared experience (ontology).
Awareness of Spirituality	Little or none.	Present. Facilitates healing on all levels of being.
Training of Therapists & Other Helping Professionals	Conventional, based on limited belief systems.	Expanded. Not locked in to limited belief systems.
Health of Therapists	Not emphasized.	Increased. And increasing importance.
Sources of Motivation & Change of "Patients" & "Helping Professionals"	Few currently. May be changed by new paradigm sources and financial incentive.	"Patients" "clients," and "helping professionals" with increasing awareness, responsibility, and recovery.

20

Two Clinical Examples: The Old And The New Paradigm

Let's explore further how the co-dependence adult child movement represents a major part of the new paradigm. We can begin to look at how a mental health professional working from each paradigm might approach two common clinical complaints: first, sadness and emptiness (called "depression" in the old paradigm) and then fear (called "anxiety" and other names in the old).

The following descriptions are not intended to put down or demean any of the helping professions. Indeed, there are mostly well-trained, dedicated and compassionate people working in all of them. Rather, these descriptions are meant to illustrate how the old contrasts with the new paradigm.

Sadness And Emptiness

The Old Paradigm

Joe comes to Dr. Brown, a helping professional, seeking assistance for dealing with what turns out to be chronic sadness and emptiness. He calls it "depression," as he has been taught by the culture of the old paradigm. Dr. Brown, reinforced by his training, diagnostic code books and health insurance company requirements, calls it a "depressive disorder" and writes a specific diagnosis — dysthymic disorder (300.40) — in Joe's record.

Dr. Brown is otherwise well-trained and experienced, but he does not know that over 90 percent of people who present in this way are unrecoverd adult children from dysfunctional families, and therefore actively co-dependent, or actively chemical dependent, or both.

Dr. Brown may be a psychiatrist or a general physician. He finds that the appropriate treatment of choice is to prescribe a drug that will alter Joe's brain chemistry, hopefully favorably. He may also offer psychotherapy, but it will probably be no more than supportive. The goal of the treatment is mood elevation and improved coping or functioning. If Joe has insomnia, Dr. Brown may also recommend a sedative hypnotic drug. If Joe is still unresponsive, Dr. Brown — if a psychiatrist — will prescribe stronger drugs with more side effects. And if Joe is particularly unresponsive, electroconvulsive shock therapy maybe given. The subsequent loss of memory and motivation from this shock therapy can make it difficult for Joe to get into a successful recovery and the new paradigm.

Some psychologists, social workers or counselors with a belief system based mostly in the old paradigm may use either a behavioral or cognitive approach, with the latter emphasizing "insight." Joe's experience here would be similar. They may also recommend that Joe take a drug for his "depression" and refer him to a physician who will prescribe one. Others may take a psychodynamic approach, which, while helpful, may still have some limitations.

What May Be Underneath

None of these helping professionals is likely to give sufficient attention to Joe's alcohol or other drug intake (including caffeine and nicotine), his diet, his exercise routine or his personal support system.

It may not occur to them that Joe's "depression" may be due to his grieving (or block in grieving) one or more losses, hurts or traumas. They may give little attention to validating Joe's feelings and helping him to release them through a process of healthy grieving.

Joe thus remains stuck in ungrieved grief — using drugs or something else outside himself — to try to feel better and cope. As part of an addicted society, he may go from one quick fix to another. And after each fix he still feels empty, becomes frustrated and blames himself for not being good enough and/or doing it well enough. Or he may blame his helping professional. Or both.

Joe's unfinished adult child and co-dependence issues may not be addressed efficiently, nor will his integrity and full potential. The usefulness and effectiveness of spirituality will likely never be brought up — or it may be ignored or dismissed. Never knowing that he can have more, Joe remains no better or perhaps somewhat better, and still addicted to this old limited system.

Going Within: Encountering The New Paradigm

Joe could encounter the new paradigm in two ways: (1) He hits bottom and is forced back into the old paradigm. Frustrated with the old, he either searches out the new or (2) happens upon it "by accident." If he finds aspects of the new and is interested, he now has the exciting opportunity to make a life transformation: to give up being preoccupied with what is outside of him — being actively co-dependent — and begin to look within. Within is where the new paradigm is. The old was focusing without, a life of unnecessary suffering and active co-dependence. The old paradigm is based on the illusion that the answer is outside — that our "locus of control" or responsibility for our life is outside of our True Self.

Of course, here we encounter the paradox: To get inside ourself — our True Self — we may have to go outside selectively to a person and group skilled in helping people through the process that the new paradigm supports. What we may have *thought* was inside and therefore was us — our co-dependent or false self — is of no help here. Identifying with it and relying on it, we will be still actively co-dependent. Indeed, a crucial part of recovery is learning to differentiate our True from our false self.

Going within, Joe has his first and only chance to feel fulfilled, to fill his emptiness by experientially realizing who he really is and living from and as that. And who Joe really is — his True Self — is the only part that can connect in a healing way with his Higher Power. In this sense the only way "up" is *in*.

Some approaches in the old paradigm may have focused on developing and healing what is inside, but the method was to do it alone — in individual counseling or therapy only. Thus people often become stuck in all-or-none thinking and behaving. The new breaks away from all-or-none, recognizing that healing requires the connectedness of several safe others, as exemplified by the use of group therapy and self-help fellowship groups in the new; if appropriate, these may be in addition to individual counseling or psychotherapy, not instead of.

Working In The New

When Joe consulted Dr. Green, a helping professional working in the new paradigm, he received the same careful attention in the intake evaluation as he got from Dr. Brown. But Dr. Green went further. She asked for details of his family of origin and other relationships, recent and past losses, hurts or traumas, alcohol and other drug intake (including nicotine and caffeine), diet and exercise, and she gently inquired about his spiritual life.

Assessing The Possible Stages Of Recovery: Stages Zero And One

In making an assessment and diagnosis, Dr. Green carefully considered which stage of recovery Joe might be in. She then developed a treatment plan according to that stage and Joe's particular Stage Zero conditions. Joe was still distracted and foundering in a Stage Zero condition, so she gave her attention first in a Stage One full recovery program that was specific for his particular Stage Zero condition. She used her skills to give assistance to Joe for as long as his recovery required.

Dr. Green would give little attention to Stage Two recovery at this time. (If Joe were in the first or second relapse of a Stage Zero condition that had been first adequately treated in Stage One full recovery program, however, treatment would be somewhat different.) And so in Stages Zero and One, using any diagnostic assessment structure — such as is suggested in approaches like DSM-III-R — would be appropriate.

Assessing Stage Two

When Joe is in Stage Two, with *stable* long-term recovery in a Stage One recovery program, Dr. Green will focus therapeutic attention on his adult child syndrome and active co-dependence. However, she would not neglect the first two Stages (Zero and One). Indeed, she would attend to them appropriately, based on Joe's individual needs. This is how the new paradigm builds upon the old, while at the same time transcending it.

While being skilled in assessing and diagnosing someone like Joe for a depressive disorder, the helping professional working from the new paradigm may prefer to help clarify the person's complaint as being sadness and emptiness. These terms tend to be more helpful for a number of reasons. They give more *hope, clarity* and *attention* to inner life — including *feelings* and *self-responsibility* for recovery. They help give a person like Joe a "handle" by which he can better grasp what is really happening in both his inner and outer life. In the evaluation and later these may be expanded to terms like *grieving* and *adult child syndrome.*

Assessing Stage Three

In Stages One and Two recovery, attention to the spiritual will be progressively important as a component of each of their respective full recovery programs. However, as Joe completes his recovery goals in Stage Two recovery, he will have likely realized his True Self more completely and will therefore be more likely to connect experientially with the spiritual, and eventually the healing Unconditional Love of his Higher Power. He will now be in Stage Three recovery: working on issues of being a spiritual being in a human incarnation[579a,646].

Dr. Green, a competent helping professional working in the new paradigm, will be able to assess and assist people in all three stages of recovery. If she does not feel skilled and comfortable assisting with a particular stage, she knows the therapeutic advantages of making a referral to a helping professional who is so skilled and comfortable, and then makes that referral.

A Disorder Of Fear

The Old Paradigm

Jenny consults Dr. Roberts, a biologically oriented helping professional who works from the old paradigm, with a complaint of having some or a lot of fear. Rather than call her symptom "fear," she calls it "anxiety" as she has been taught by her culture. Dr. Roberts reinforces that, calling it an "anxiety disorder" or "panic disorder," based on the worldview she learned from her training, diagnostic codebooks and insurance company requirements.

Dr. Roberts offers Jenny something outside herself for relief, probably a benzodiazepine sedative drug. While usually effective in the short-term relief of fear, these and others drugs have several hidden disadvantages, including that they block healthy grieving and recovery from an adult child perspective, numbing important feelings; and they are generally addictive if taken for longer than a few days.

These drugs may also block Jenny's ability to make full use of individual psychotherapy, group psychotherapy and working a recovery program in a self-help fellowship. Fully aware of these dangers, the new paradigm clinician may choose not to use or recommend a psychoactive drug, preferring to focus more on Jenny's total picture, based on her current stage of recovery.

Other clinicians may not be so biologically oriented, yet may still work from the old paradigm. Their treatment of choice may include a behavioral or cognitive approach, with the latter emphasizing "insight." Or they may also recommend that Jenny take a drug for her "anxiety." Still other clinicians may take a psychodynamic approach, which, while helpful, may have some limitations.

What May Be Underneath

None of these above approaches — biological, behavioral or cognitive — would likely give attention to the principles described above for Joe.

A clinician working in the new paradigm would use a similar, although individualized approach with Jenny as Dr. Green did with Joe.

Using Psychoanalysis

If either Joe or Jenny had consulted a psychoanalyst who worked from the old paradigm, the best potential result might be that if they persisted in the analysis over the course of many years, they would reach some insight, mostly of an intellectual nature, about their own psyche and how they may have been wounded. Doing this is not at all bad and can be useful. But what may be missing from their process is a fully experiential component that allows a more complete healing of their woundedness. And while they may have discovered some parts of their True Self by working through the transference, that may have been at best incomplete or at worst could have compounded their wounds.

Part of the potential danger, as psychoanalyst Alice Miller and others have described, is that an analyst who followed strict Freudian practices, may have shamed Joe or Jenny by invalidating their hurt, implying that their painful childhood or other experience was just a fantasy: "It really didn't happen that way"[410,438,645].

Another disadvantage is that classical analysis, by plan, provides nearly no structure and uses only three experiential techniques: free association (saying "what comes up"), dream analysis and interpretation, and working through transference. There is nothing wrong with this approach. But given today's advances through other parts of the old and all of the new paradigm, it is just limited. At best it can assist a person only into the first, most cognitively oriented steps of Stage Two recovery. And it mostly ignores Stages Zero, One and Three. For complete healing many more experiential approaches and techniques are available, and it is also helpful to assist the person in making a recovery plan.

Patients are not usually allowed eye contact with the analyst, and in other ways may be prevented from seeing the analyst as a real, fallible and vulnerable human being — all useful in assisting the person in their healing. Finally with the recommended several appointments per week at a cost of from $300 to $750 weekly, the financial drain can be overwhelming. At worst the analyst could shame and mistreat patients by exaggerating any of the above disadvantages, including their countertransference from the analyst's own unhealed adult child and co-dependence issues. And they still may not have completed *their* healing process because so much of the experiential and spiritual was missing from their own analysis or therapy.

At the same time, however, we have all learned much from the helpful contributions made by countless analysts. Workers in the new paradigm respect all such helpful offerings and use selected parts of them when appropriate. The new paradigm does not split, it is not all-or-none. Rather, it uses both/and, to the benefit of the person's healing process.

Conclusion

These two brief clinical examples may help to illustrate just a few of the differences between old and new paradigm approaches to assisting people with common complaints. These examples, and the related background information in the previous chapter, are not at all meant to denigrate or demean old paradigm approaches. Rather, they are intended to expand upon them into the new, as well as to show a few selected differences as that expansion evolves.

It is difficult to estimate how many helping professionals work from each paradigm. My guess is that today there are more working from the new paradigm than we might imagine. Most of these people were actually trained from an old paradigm perspective, and overcame that training by expanding their clinical approaches. There are also likely many helping professionals practicing from the old who nonetheless use some principles of the new and there are still others who are curious about the methods, potential and success of the new, and are open to exploring it.

Since we are not yet into the middle of the new paradigm, we still have much to learn. Being open to learning about self, others and our Higher Power is a definition of humility, an important characteristic of the new paradigm clinician and its other workers.

21

Controversy And Caution

Every new discovery, movement and paradigm has its critics, and their criticism may be valuable and useful. There are always people who resist the possibilities and changes of the new and different. And there are always people who simply disagree.

Recently, there have been a few published criticisms of the adult child and co-dependence movement. What are they? How accurate might they be? Is there anything that we can learn from them?

Two Kinds Of Disagreement

There tend to be two kinds of disagreement here. Differentiating the two is the key to learning just what in these criticisms and controversies may be useful and what may not. The first kind tends to come from people who have carefully researched and read all the relevant material and writings on the topic in question. Even if they have done so, however, they may or may not have grasped the full intent and meaning of the topic. Those who grasp and understand it will likely be able to provide the most useful feedback and constructive criticism. Those who do not will likely give mixed and marginal feedback at best.

The second kind of disagreement comes from those who appear *not* to have carefully researched and read all of the relevant material and writing on the topic in question. It is unfortunate that much of the criticism of most new ideas and practices comes from this source. Yet their names, professions, backgrounds or methods of communication may make them appear to be credible and to know what they are talking about. For these and other reasons it is important not to believe any expression or opinion — including anything in this book — until you consider four factors: (1) Does what is expressed (however and by whomever) ring true for you in your own heart? (2) What method of criticism is the critic using? (3) Has the critic thoroughly researched the material and writings? And finally, (4) Have you done any of the above? Have you researched or read the material? And in what degree of detail?

For most people such research and extensive reading is neither practical nor desirable. That is in part why I wrote this book: to offer a synopsis of co-dependence from several perspectives, including the practical and clinical.

With all of the above in mind, we can look at several criticisms that have been made toward the co-dependence and adult child movement.

Too "Popular"

One criticism that is seldom published, though occasionally spoken, has been that the movement is too "popular." That is, it has spread information about psychodynamics, the human condition and how to heal its unnecessary pain beyond qualified psychotherapists and into the awareness of millions of people. This has lead to the use of this information by some unqualified helping professionals and even by some people with no academic training at all.

The Helping Professional

Some of the above criticism comes from *within* the recovery field. The first is that, with all good intentions, untrained or marginally trained people have begun to use this information and approach as "therapy" or "counseling" offered to the public. Their qualifications may vary from none at all (other than having been through some degree of recovery themselves), to having attended a workshop or two, to having trained at a residential treatment facility for a few months.

The point is not that these experiences are bad or not useful. Indeed, they are likely to be helpful and useful for any person, including helping professionals. And some "natural healers" with little formal training can be more helpful to some people in their recovery than are those with more formal training. What is problematic is that the therapist or counselor in question may not have a background that provides the ability to give a *comprehensive intake* and *evaluation*, including the ability to make a diagnosis or assessment of any Stage Zero illness, disorder or condition and the appropriateness of the components of any Stage One recovery program for a particular person and to provide the proper ongoing evaluation, monitoring and referral for any problem or concern that may arise in the course of a person's recovery.

A second problem area may arise when an otherwise appropriately trained helping professional acquires a little information about co-dependence and the adult child syndrome and then claims to be qualified in assisting people in their recovery from these conditions. Motivated by financial or other reasons, they may so advertise themselves or may answer yes when asked, "Do you know about co-dependence or the adult child syndrome? Can you help me with this kind of approach in my recovery?" This concern can usually be remedied by more ongoing reading and training and by obtaining clinical supervision in any questionable or difficult situation.

There is one final caution here, an even more delicate one. Helping professionals may not have done their own healing and may be stuck somewhere in their own personal growth. The truism is still useful: "The person can recover only as far as has their helping professional." As an example, when I had not worked through my own anger about my adult child condition, it was difficult for me to hear and allow the anger of my patients and assist them in healing it. A solution here is to work on our own recovery.

The People

Some people may do a little toward their recovery, such as read a book or attend a few (or even many) psychotherapy or counseling sessions, and believe that they are now "recovered." This is one of several ways that we can defend against working completely through the pain of our own recovery.

There is also the danger of participating in intensive opening experiences in workshops, retreats, television series or the like and not having an ongoing strong support system of recovery, as described throughout Part II of this book. I address this caution further under "Too much, Too Fast" later.

Beyond these cautions, however, I believe that the spread of this information and enthusiasm to the public is positive and useful. It has provided much nourishment for the personal growth of many people, including the following.

- In its ongoing synthesis and clarity, it has *demystified* family and individual psychodynamics so that people can understand them and how this information may apply to their life and potential recovery.
- It gives people the ability to *look within* themselves and to *take responsibility* for their own recovery, with the assistance of selected others over time. For many decades this has been recognized as a strength by most helping professionals.
- It has provided a new and *expanded map* for our understanding of the psyche and for recovery.
- It is an expression of the dependence in our internal healing on some degree of *connectedness* with others. This may span the range of healing potential, for example for something as simple as genuine communion with a pet to as complex as a full program of recovery in group therapy and a self-help fellowship.
- Finally, it has included the healing power of the *spiritual* in the whole recovery process.

As a quiet but powerful grass roots movement and part of a larger new paradigm in the helping professions and human well being, it can be no other than with and for the people.

Too Non-Specific

This criticism says that the terms "co-dependence" and "adult child of a dysfunctional family" are not specific. Critics contend that these terms have no agreed-upon definition, and that some of the available definitions may suggest that most people have it.

While some day we may have one accepted definition, there is nothing wrong with having several definitions. This only enriches our understanding of the processes that the terms address so effectively. Having several definitions is also a characteristic of many disorders and ideas throughout our history. Even with the multiple definitions now available to us today (see Table 1.1), these definitions are more similar than they are different. If you discover a better definition than any of these, you might consider publishing it!

My response to the complaint that if most people are co-dependent, the term loses its usefulness, is that in actuality it does not lose any usefulness or meaning. It just more clearly explains important aspects of the human condition and allows more people to identify their problems, issues and needs so that they can work through them.

Too Blaming

It is interesting how a few people have criticized using the term and concept of co-dependence because it is blaming of the co-dependent person. For example, Kokin argues that terms like "co-dependent" and "enabler" take the focus off the alcoholic or other dysfunctional person and unfairly blame their spouse[697].

But he and others miss the point[708,709]. The purpose of terms like "co-dependent," "enabling behavior" and "adult child" is not about blaming. Rather, it is about *naming* the truth of people's painful experiences and what really happened in their life. The only test for this truth is if it ultimately rings true in the person's experience and heart, and if it ends up being useful in helping them to make a healthy recovery. To me and to millions of others in recovery that is so. When we give something an accurate name, we are empowered.

A problem for people with co-dependence is that they grew up learning to live from the perspective of others so much that they lost their own selfhood. Their measurement for truth was outside of themself. In recovery they learn the power of first going within, into their inner life and then connecting that to safe others; and also, if they choose, connecting to the God of their understanding.

The other criticism is that adult children unfairly or inappropriately blame their parents. Of course, *most* of us adult children have ourselves used that argument over and over to defend against the pain of doing our grieving and healing. So we are well acquainted with that one. And if we hear a critic who "speaks with authority" (whatever that is) and says that this is "unfair blaming," then it gives us all — perhaps including the critic — a reason not to go deeper within.

Don't Take Responsibility For Their Recovery

Some critics say that the term and concept of co-dependence can become a block in itself. This is because the person uses it not to recover. And this can be true. But we can use nearly any such descriptive name in this way. As a martyr or victim, and thus actively co-dependent, we can say "poor me" (victim) or "no problem . . . sigh" (martyr) and not take responsibility for going within and doing our recovery work. Here we learn that the term and concept of co-dependence is not the block, but the anti-life process of active co-dependence itself.

For years mental health professionals have worked with their patients and clients, assisting them to learn responsibility for their recovery and well being. We all may have to learn to adjust to that fact, now that it is actually beginning to happen for progressively more people in this movement. Rather than avoiding responsibility, the co-dependence and adult child approach tends to promote each person's taking responsibility for the success and joy of their own life and well being.

"Just Forgive"

All this recovery work is unnecessary, some argue, if we will simply forgive those who have hurt us[688]. But the problem is that even if we try to forgive, until we work through the hurt and heal our True Self, we cannot forgive. My false or co-dependent self doesn't know what forgiveness is, much less how to do it. So as long as I live from that false self, all I can do is pretend to forgive.

To forgive is to let go authentically. And the only part of me that can be consistently authentic is my True Self. But before I can let go of something, I have to know exactly what it is that I am letting go. I have to know experientially — physically, mentally, emotionally and spiritually — what I am giving up or forgiving. And all this takes time. That is why it takes at least three to five years of commitment to and participation in a full recovery program to do the work of healing our True Self.

Not A Diagnosis

Some critics have said that co-dependence and the adult child syndrome is not really a diagnosis. And others have said that it is not a disease[696,701,702]. While they don't usually say what they think that it *is,* some terms they have used include: "too popular," "fad," "confusing," "vague," "untrue," "unscientific" and "excuse."

In the new paradigm, "disorders" and "diagnoses" are most appropriately used in Stage Zero and One recovery. But the terms "co-dependence" and "adult child" are useful in that they appropriately transcend these first two stages, entering Stage Two and eventually Stage Three recovery, while at the same time being aware of, supporting, and nurturing these earlier stages. Thus in truth co-dependence is — in part — a diagnosis that both underlies and transcends the more ordinary ones that we have been used to.

Unscientific

Some critics say that this approach is too unscientific. While there has been some not so careful research, and while we still have much to learn and do, in the few years of its existence we now have possibly more careful and meaningful research that has been accomplished in this field than was completed in the first half of the twentieth century in most of the fields of psychology and psychiatry. This research includes not only empirical observations, but the creative and expansive theory and practice that are also an integral part of this movement.

A problem here is how to define "meaningful" and "research." While the scientific method is helpful in testing the physical and other lower realms, description, interpretation and direct and shared experience are equally valid research methods for testing the validity of higher realms, in which co-dependence is examined and explored. And something is meaningful if it is helpful or useful to us in some way. The final test of meaning ultimately rests in our *own experience* and not simply in any judgment or pronouncement by another, no matter what their "qualifications" may be. Indeed, such blind reliance on others may be another manifestation of co-dependence.

Also, the truth is simple. Left to its own, the false self or ego complicates things. Truth unifies. Our journey appears to be toward self and Truth. As we evolve and grow we get closer to it. This movement provides a clearer and more supportive framework for that evolution and growth than has any other in the past.

Not Systemic

Some family therapists and theorists — perhaps without being fully aware of the dynamics and dimensions of the co-dependence/adult child approach — have said that it is not "systemic." By this they mean that it does not include and address family or other relationship systems. In truth, the opposite is actually the case. This approach is built upon the most useful concepts that systems theory and practice has to offer. And it takes that information and those skills and expands them in progressively more useful ways to assist more people.

It is true that this new movement does not always use exactly the same terms and language as does family systems, and it naturally uses some different terms and language as well, both of which may cause some discomfort for family systems people. In an editorial in *Family Therapy Networker*[705], Simon suggested that the adult child movement is replacing the family therapy movement. My sense is that it is not replacing it. It is expanding it.

Too Selfish

Some have said that the co-dependence and adult child movement somehow implies that those in recovery are selfish and narcissistic. Of course, the opposite is true. They are seeking to live in and from humility, which is openness to learning about self, others and the Universe. Twelve-Step fellowship programs also encourage and support their members' realizing humility. And several clinicians have described some of the differences between healthy narcissism and unhealthy narcissism[414,438,649], which I have explored in an earlier chapter. Recovery is not about being selfish or unhealthily narcissistic. Rather, it is about learning to be self-caring, which is healthy narcissism.

If I don't know myself intimately, how can I know others? Solomon suggests that our priority in relationship is first to our self, second to God and third to our parents and children. Fourth is to our peers, colleagues and friends; and fifth and final is to our spouse or life partner[588]. He does not mean that we should neglect our spouse. Rather, if I know my self better, I can relate to others in a more healthy way. Before I can find the Divine in others and in my self, I have to have a healthy relationship with my Higher Power. Before I can relate to others in a healthy way, I have to work out my unfinished business with my parents or parent figures and other members of my family of origin so that I can stop projecting my pain onto my children. Once I have done this work — which is much of what the co-dependence/adult child movement is about — then I can relate to colleagues, friends and my spouse or life partner in a more healthy way.

Too Much, Too Fast

Doing too much, too fast is a potential danger, and therefore it is a caution rather than a controversy. It extends beyond the recovery field into the realm of general and even what could be called "commercial" mental health.

When teachers or clinicians push people into healing with such intensity that they do too much cognitive and experiential recovery work too fast, their recovery is endangered. Perhaps the most notorious have been commercially available structured "growth" experiences such as Lifespring, Insight, The Forum (formerly est), New Identity, Scientology, Avatar and others. Some of these approaches and experiences may also come out of personal growth centers and summer institutes, or have been modeled after Esalen in California. A number of private teachers or clinicians may offer similar workshops or "growth experiences." This phenomenon can also be seen on a smaller scale even in some individual or group therapy, where the counselor or therapist is not fully aware of the dangers of this approach.

Any of these can at times take on the flavor of "fast food" — temporarily filling, but with a lot of sugar, fat and other forms of empty calories. These experiences are often dramatic, and led by one or more charismatic speakers. They may feel like a "quick hit," but over time they do not hold. And some may become an addiction in themselves.

These groups have several disadvantages. They are often led or run by non-clinicians — or clinicians who are only partially qualified. They may be expensive, and may have a relatively weak screening procedure for and attention to people's special and individual needs. Worse, they can be narrow in focus, neglect some important areas of the process of healing the True Self and at times tend to promote all-or-none thinking and behaving. This latter can result in unhealthy dependence upon beliefs and techniques taught and upon the teacher, trainer, group or organization. Ongoing monitoring and supervision of the participant's functioning and well-being by the teacher, leader or therapist may be absent, or marginal at best. While it may have started out to help people, it can end up distracting them from realizing their True Self and making a successful ongoing recovery.

I have participated in several of these commercially available, structured experiences, and have assisted several of my patients who spontaneously and voluntarily participated in one or more of them. It is my clinical opinion that these groups can be risky and even dangerous unless they are done in the context of a full recovery program of healing our True Self. Even for people in such a full recovery pogram, a relapse into an unhealthy dependence upon the commercial experience, the teacher or the techniques may result to the degree that they drop out of their full recovery program.

Despite serious reservations, I am not necessarily recommending against any of these experiences. My purpose rather, is to alert anyone whose goal is to heal their Child Within about their potential disadvantages, which can interfere with their healing.

Lasting Recovery Cannot Be Rushed

Complete, healthy and lasting recovery cannot be rushed. We know from the research on grieving that to grieve a major loss completely takes at least two to four years of unencumbered psychological and emotional work. In the recovery process it takes at least a few months (and often one or two years or more) in the beginning stages to identify our losses, hurts and traumas and to learn how to feel so that we can even begin to grieve. That is why it takes at least three to five years in the best full recovery program to heal.

I have seen several people drop out of group or individual therapy prematurely due to a dramatic "hit" or "fix" of experiential recovery work. They often tend to gravitate to other similar therapies or other techniques, which do not offer enough time to process important work. While this kind of work is not necessarily bad, it just may be too much, too fast. The message of "The Tortoise and The Hare" may apply here.

Some Of The Critics

While constructive criticism is useful in the evolution of any endeavor, most critics of this approach appear either not to have researched and read the basic literature on co-dependence and the adult child syndrome or not to understand its basic, pervasive and expanded meanings and implications, or both.

Several critics write from an all-or-none perspective[695,697,699,701,702,706,708,709,712]; some encourage premature forgiveness[688]; many deny the importance of feelings; and most simply do not seem to understand the basic principles. This is not surprising, since most of us come from a dysfunctional family and society that is run by actively co-dependent, dysfunctional politicians who interact with actively co-dependent, dysfunctional educational, vocational, religious, communication and industrial systems[584,653,654]. Even with these reservations, we can still learn from critics when they have a valid or useful criticism.

The Shadow Side

Every person, family group or movement has a shadow side. This shadow is whatever part of us that is uncomfortable and which we disown. This painful side of our unconscious is usually related to our unfinished business. So our shadow is whatever unconscious material we have stored away that we have not yet worked through completely[330a,579a].

Since people naturally make up the co-dependence and adult child recovery movement, we can see in it any and all of the manifestations of the shadow that people in general may have. Every movement, government, religion, every helping profession and every group of people have a shadow. They can deny, ignore or minimize it, but it won't go away. Some healthy ways to handle the shadow include becoming aware of it, working through it, owning it and then letting go of it.

We can find examples of shadow material both inside and outside the movement. Some are: unhealthy competition, greed, tunnel vision, ego (co-dependent self) inflation or grandiosity, unhealthy expressions of anger and projecting out onto others (such as attacking another whose point of view differs from ours), not crediting others for their ideas or quotations, and any other aspect of unfinished business or unhealthy behavior, including that related to any of the core recovery issues.

When one person or group interacts with another and there is any degree of conflict, their shadows are likely to be interacting. For example, when one professional clinical organization's newsletter wrote in a derogatory manner about the co-dependence movement, they concluded by saying how financially advantageous it would be to know as much as possible about it when patients or clients ask about it.

Another example is when the media, which can be seductive and has a giant shadow, interacts with anyone or with any group. Expectations of both can come and go rapidly, and there can be disappointment when the media presents the material in their often naive, sensationalistic, controlling or all-or-none way[405]. Because the media is like a large dysfunctional family with many unaware and unrecovered people, it is hard to find workers there with enough integrity to fully research and report the truth. I know that deadlines and pressures from above are a big problem for them, and I have also met and interviewed with several reporters who are excellent and who work with much integrity.

The media is not the only group with a shadow, of course. And each person has one too. I have experienced my own shadow coming out of the darkness of my co-dependent self when I feel overly envious of colleagues who draw a larger audience or readership than I, or who are more articulate and entertaining. All of this is simply grist for the mill of my own ongoing recovery as a co-dependent and adult child, which I have worked on for many years. Because of that work, when I glimpse my shadow nowadays, I usually work through things more quickly than before. Because I have worked through some of my unfinished business (shadow stuff) with my siblings, other peers and my parents and other authority figures, I try to become aware of these kinds of conflicts as soon as possible. This allows me to experience and work through it, own it, learn, and then let go of it. Spirituality is a great help to me here, and I try to co-create this process with my Higher Power (see Chapter 23).

In spite of all of the above shadow material, I am optimistic about our field for several reasons: (1) we have a serious interest in and awareness of the human unconscious, where the shadow hides; (2) the progress that we have made in our ongoing attention to our psychological and spiritual growth; (3) our serious attention to relationship with our self, others and our Higher Power; and finally, (4) our rich spirituality, supported by such aids as Twelve Step and other fellowships, and by other spiritual paths and practices.

Will The Movement Survive?

Whether or not this movement will continue to be as useful as it has been so far is uncertain. My guess is that it will continue, evolve and grow as we evolve and grow on our journey as human and spiritual beings. Even though this movement and its terms have been in use for only about a decade, they have offered insight, solace and recovery to millions of people.

When terms like *co-dependent* and *adult child* are used so much that they have almost become household words, it means that they have been assimilated into the culture. However, when this happens, they can lose their precision, as for example the term "schizophrenic" has over recent decades. At the same time they can also mature and we can become clearer about them *by* their being so assimilated into the culture.

The momentum of these terms and their new paradigm is in some conflict with the inertia of the old paradigm. For example, the movement in psychiatry back toward the biological model is strong among academic and some other psychiatrists. And most psychologists and many other mental health professionals are still wedded to the methods of the old paradigm, as are most other helping professionals.

But the new paradigm has been generating now for at least several decades, in such areas as Jungian psychology, humanistic and transpersonal psychology, the study of loss and post-traumatic disorders, the study of child mistreatment and abuse, family therapy, Twelve-Step fellowships and the movement toward the spiritual.

Part Of A Larger Paradigm

This movement as the new paradigm is a part of a larger one that has been generating from other disciplines, such as modern physics, the ecology and peace movement and spirituality[724, 727, 730, 743, 745, 747]. For the first time, in and through the new paradigm, each individual can take responsibility for creating a successful and enjoyable life. Because of the emerging and powerful spirituality that is a part of it all, I like to use the term *co-creating* instead. This is the focus of the final chapter.

The new paradigm works through and transcends the all-or-none thinking and behaving of the old one by realizing that recovering and living are not usually limited to either/or, but expand to both/and. It thus builds upon and uses, when and where it may be appropriate, whatever is indicated and whatever works from the old paradigm. The new paradigm clinician is not interested in competing, but in working in harmony with anything from the old that is appropriate.

Part IV

From Co-dependence To Co-creation

22

The Illusion Of The Co-dependent Self

An illusion is something that we think is real but is not. It can take a long time to realize that the false or co-dependent self is not real.

The process of coming to this realization is the human journey and adventure of our spiritual True Self. Throughout time we have repeatedly asked ourself four questions: Who am I? What am I doing here? Where am I going? How can I have any peace?

Who Am I?

In the process of healing co-dependence we do the work of answering this question: Who am I? We then discover and realize who we are experientially: in our soul, our heart, guts, bones — in the deepest fiber of our being: our True Self. In this learning we also may connect with the creative, unconditional love of our Higher Power. And all of this may take a long time.

Part of this experiential learning process of who we are seems to be learning also who we are *not*. When we were wounded as children, the pain and confusion was so great that our True Self, our Child Within, had to go into hiding. To survive we made a false self, came to rely on it to run our life, and thereby developed co-dependence — looking for fulfillment outside ourselves. Even though it was uncomfortable and never felt quite right, we became so familiar with that false self, its dominance over us, and all of its consequences that we thought it *was* our identity, who we really were.

We have called it by many names: false self, ego, negative ego, co-dependent self, fear, shadow and even "the devil." And as we learn throughout recovery, it has caused us all kinds of trouble and pain.

But the false self is not real.

The False Self Is A Belief System

If the false self is not real, then what is it? It is the belief by the mind that it is separated from others and God and that it is completely on its own[165]. From this simple beginning come all the other belief systems and functions of the ego, including being an assistant in screening and sorting, reality testing, logic and intellectual functioning, defending against overwhelming emotional pain and cooperating so that our True Self can experience, create, and evolve. When we stay centered in our True Self and in God, this belief that we call ego (or here more accurately, "positive ego") *is* a *useful assistant*. Even though it is our assistant, it is still not real — it is not the center of our consciousness or being, and it is not lasting. It does not seem to stay with us when we die and move on to another adventure[165,278,279,520,687]. We made our ego by believing in it and perpetuated it by identifying ourself as it and living from it. God did not create it, because God does not create anything that is not real[165].

But if we are not centered in our True Self and in God, and if we let our ego run our life, it then becomes a false or co-dependent self or "negative ego." Yet this is not what it set out to do, and so it is not inherently "bad" or "evil." Rather, it is simply incompetent to run our life with success and joy, and it is unable to connect with God. So when we turn the responsibility for running our life over to it, it is *inherently* unable to do so. Thus the false ego self eventually falters and becomes self-righteous, self-destructive and other-destructive. It becomes the epitome — and at times the caricature — of our co-dependent self at its worst.

But it has no power over us unless we give our power to it.

Letting Go Of Our False Self

So how can we get free of its pain and confusion? We can get to know it, use it efficiently and then let it go. We let it go by staying centered in our True Self and in God, and simply observing it until we lose our attachment to it[175a]. That observation may take on different dimensions over several stages, as follows.

1. I begin to know that I have a True Self and practice being it with safe people.
2. As this proceeds I watch for the false self. (See Table 13.2 on page 151.)
3. As the healing progresses, I notice my false self when it comes up in my life. *I observe it.*
4. I ask myself, "Who is doing the observing?" As I heal I will be able to discern and realize more and more that the one who is observing is my True Self.
5. Know that at any instant I can choose to be my True Self or let my false self run my life.
6. While the True Self is real, creative and powerful, it can ultimately be recognized as Love. And while the false self is no more than a belief system that we made to be our assistant, it can usually be recognized as "logic" or "reason," and as fear.
7. As I live my life, I can be aware of my True Self and its crucial inner life, observe it, and use it.
8. And at any instant in this process I can then choose either my True Self — and its connection to God — or my false self. I can choose either love or fear[165,527,528].
9. While a little false self ("reason" or fear) may always linger, and at times may even bother me, I can let it go.
10. Trying to push the false self away doesn't work. I cannot "control" it. The way I let it go most effectively is by choosing Love.
11. When I choose Love, I experience *Serenity*, which *A Course in Miracles* also calls the Holy Instant.

12. When I am Here, Now, there is nothing more that I need do other than just be.

Daily spiritual practices, especially meditation, as the Eleventh Step suggests, can be helpful in facilitating this entire process of letting go of the false self.

Although our false self is not real, it *is* useful to us as an *assistant*. We learn that we are not human beings having a spiritual experience, but we are spiritual beings having a human experience[579a]. Our false self, as positive ego, assists us most efficiently in this experience. As negative ego it may still assist us, although much less efficiently — and is usually destructive to us and others.

What Am I Doing Here?

Ultimately, our purpose is a Divine Mystery. We may be here on Earth to do a number of things. Some of these may include remembering who we are and experiencing that, and learning to love ourself, others and God.

In this process the false self becomes not only our assistant (positive ego), but also, on another level, a fly in the ointment (negative ego) that produces conflict through which we can work toward remembering and loving. Co-dependence and the adult child syndrome are ways that we can help to understand and work through this conflict and experience. By first trying the false, we can more authentically choose, know and be the True. By forgetting, we learn to remember better[165].

Where Am I Going?

Where are we going? This is also a part of the Divine Mystery. We must each discover and work out the answer in our own way and in our own time.

When we are trying to find our way, it can be useful to have a map. And while many such maps have been proposed, we know that "the map is not the territory"[728,732]. Figure 22.1 shows one map that I have found useful.

This map shows that we come from Spirit, our Higher Power. We are each a Child of God in a healthy dependence with It. This is our Real, True Self or Child Within. And we each have a Divine or Higher Self, which some call our "guardian angel."

We are thus in a healthy relationship with our self, Higher Self and Higher Power or God. Since this relationship is so important and powerful, I like to view it as being *one relationship* — a "Sacred Person." It takes a long time to discover and re-member this relationship, but it seems to be worth the journey.

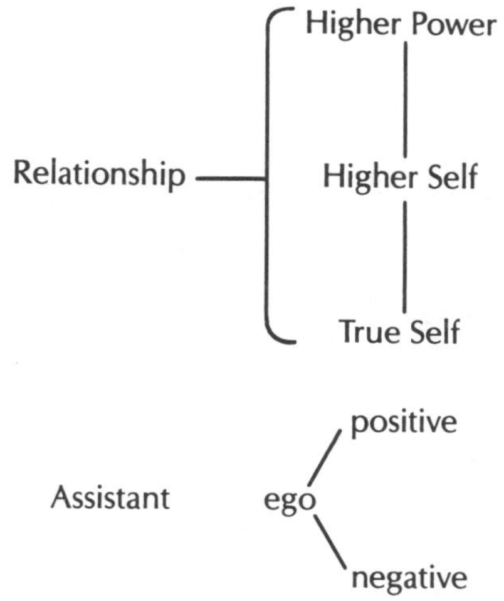

Figure 22.1. Map of Healthy Relationship with Self and Higher Power

And as we journey, our ego can assist us directly, as positive ego, or indirectly (and thus with pain and confusion), as negative ego, false or co-dependent self.

How Can I Have Any Peace?

Peace is possible, and on our path now even likely. As we heal from being an adult child of a dysfunctional family, and *let go* of the state we call co-dependence, it becomes easier to feel peace and serenity. Working this process through is the subject of the final chapter.

23

From Co-dependence To Co-creation

Our journey takes us from co-dependence — living from our attachment to our false self — to co-creation — creating what happens to us and how we feel, in concert with our Higher Power. It is a long, sometimes difficult journey, but one that may be worth taking.

When we let our false self run our life, we are numb or hurting, often afraid, ashamed and empty. If we get stuck in this state, and our True Self remains in hiding, we can become nearly immobilized. No matter what may be happening on the surface or how we may try to handle it, we are actively co-dependent. We feel separated and alienated from our True Self and from our Higher Power, and we cannot create anything. Do we have to stay this way? Is there any way out?

The only way to ease our pain, to fill our emptiness and experience any lasting peace, is to realize our True Self and then experientially connect it to God. That is the essence of the co-creation process.

What Is God's Will For Me?

Have you ever wondered what God's Will is for you? Throughout the ages many people have done so, from the most ordinary person to the most evolved spiritual master. It has to do with those four questions from the last chapter: Who am I? What am I doing here? Where am I going? Can I have any peace?

People in Twelve-Step fellowship programs are also concerned with this question, as addressed in the Second and the Eleventh Steps: *Made a decision to turn our will and our lives over to the care of God as we understood God;* and *Sought through prayer and meditation to improve our conscious contact with God, as we understood God, praying only for the knowledge of God's will for us and the power to carry that out.*

While we each have to discover what God's Will is for us in our own way and in our own time, working a spiritual program helps most people in their recovery. And while it all remains a Divine Mystery, some holy books have discussed God's Will. The clearest discussion that I have found is from *A Course in Miracles.* Most simply, it says that God's Will for us is that we have complete peace and joy, and that we be creative.

I believe that once we have healed our Child Within and thereby realized our True Self, and when we have begun to connect experientially to God, we have already begun the process of co-creation.

The Process Of Co-creation

Figure 23.1 is a map of the process of co-creation. The first half of the process, shown on the left side of the figure, is what we do. It is our work. And the remaining half is what we surrender and let God do.

Name The Feeling, Dynamic Or Issue

It is important to become fully aware of what is coming up for us from moment to moment in our inner life, and then, if useful, to give it an accurate name. When we heal our co-dependence and adult child wounding, we will be "tuned-in" and fully aware of our inner life, and thus able to know what it is that we are experiencing. We can give an accurate name to anything in that inner life: any belief, thought, feeling, want, need, intuition pattern or anything else.

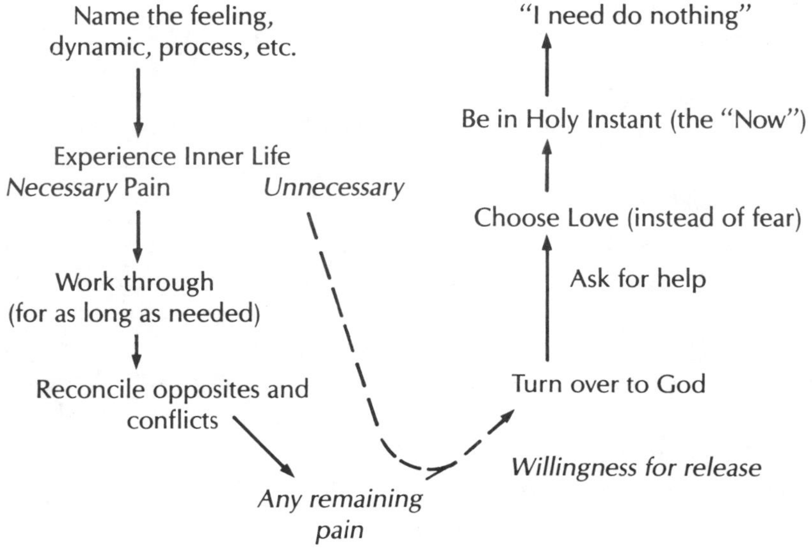

Figure 23.1. Some Steps in the Process of Co-Creation

For example, we can name ourself as an adult child of a dysfunctional family. I remember how enlightening and empowering that was for me when I realized and accepted that I was an adult child. Did anything like that ever happen to you?

Another example is when I feel angry, and fully feel it. Doing so tells me several things — that I may be being mistreated or have lost something important and that I may need to set some healthy boundaries or take some other action[649,652].

Experience My Inner Life

Before we can work through any of our pain, we have to both name it and experience it. To experience something, we open ourself and allow whatever might be in our inner life right now to come up into our awareness. We cannot name something unless we can experience it. And when we name it, that helps us experience it more accurately and completely. These feed one another in a positive reciprocation.

As we experience our inner life, we will learn that some of our pain is necessary — for example when we grieve a loss[576,645]. We also learn that some of our pain is *not* necessary. We don't actually need to experience it. For example, when we "beat ourself up" for getting a parking ticket. In reality, being upset for longer than about five minutes is unnecessary in that kind of situation.

Work Through The Pain

As we experience necessary suffering, we begin to work through it. And as we work through it we experience it more accurately and completely. This shows how the process of experiencing, naming and working through can act together in a healthy way, as we work through the pain or upset. And it *is* work. It takes a lot of energy, grief and time to do this work and to complete it.

We cannot rush our grief work, our necessary pain.

Reconcile Opposites And Conflicts

Part of our work will eventually involve beginning to identify, sort out and reconcile opposites and conflicts on which we are working. For example, do I stay in this relationship, or leave it? Do I stay with this job, or go elsewhere? Should I risk being real, or continue not to be? Yes or no?

Once we have identified the opposites, one of the first core issues that we can work through is *all-or-none.* Remember that in working through any all-or-none conflict, we usually have more choices. So for each conflict, we ask ourself, "What are my choices?" For example, I may not need to choose "all" (stay in this relationship, job or be false) or "none" (leave, work elsewhere or always be real with everyone). In fact, I might be able to do something in between. So I consider what I want to do, share it all with safe others and take plenty of time to work it through.

Any Remaining Pain

Having done "our part" of the co-creation process, we can now more strongly involve our Higher Power. This does not mean that we don't have to stay in conscious contact with the God of our understanding from the beginning of working through our upset, issue or concern. Doing that is certainly appropriate, useful and empowering.

Turn It Over And Let It Go

However, now we are ready to assess how much, if any, pain may be remaining. How much do we still hurt? When we sense that we have done all that we can do for now, we can now take any remaining pain and turn it over to our Higher Power. We let go of it. We let it go.

But to do this, to let go, we must be *willing*. The Big Book of AA and its equivalents in other Twelve-Step fellowships speak of the importance of being willing to let go and to change. *A Course In Miracles* talks repeatedly of the healing power of just "a little willingness." All we need, then, is to be willing to have any remaining pain removed. The *Course*, one of the most sophisticated, detailed and practical writings that I have ever seen on psychological and spiritual recovery, says that taking away our pain is precisely one of the major jobs of the Holy Spirit, which in other faiths may also be called Divine Energy or Spirit, Prana, Chi, or Ki. It *takes* the pain, *outshines it* and it is gone.

And so, being willing to have our pain removed, we ask that the Holy Spirit remove it. And then we let it go.

If we feel stuck in any way, we can assess whether we have done all we can do to work through our conflict. If there is more for us to do, we can do it, and then let go of any remaining pain. And throughout this entire process we can ask our Higher Power for help.

When we have done all our work, and when we let go of any remaining pain, we can actually feel the pain lifted from us. It disappears. It is gone.

Choose Love

Just as we let go of the pain, we can now choose Love. Many holy books describe Unconditional Love as the most powerful, creative and healing energy in the universe[165,582]. And so we choose to experience It, to have It flood our body, mind and spirit. We experience Love in our Total Being.

Thus when we experientially choose Love, we are pure Serenity, complete peace and joy, which is God's Will for us. The *Course* calls it the Holy Instant, others called it Nirvana, and Christ called it the Kingdom of Heaven. It is all the same state of pure, Unconditional Love.

Have you walked into a room that was pitch black, completely dark, and searched for the light switch — and finally turned on the light? When you flipped the switch, what happened to the darkness? It probably completely disappeared. That is what happens when we choose Love over fear or any other pain. The pain simply disappears. The Light outshines the dark.

"I Need Do Nothing"

We are now in complete peace and joy. We are in the Holy Instant. What do we need to do then? The *Course* says that we can remember just four words: "I need do nothing." There is no more for us to do. All we need to do now is just *be.*

In this state of pure joy, we are the most creative and empowered that we can ever be. We have allowed the healing and creative Unconditional Love of our Higher Power to come into and permeate our Being. We have discovered the core of our being: Unconditional Love. (See Figure 23.2.)

The Core of Our Being is Love

In recovery we peel away the co-dependent layers of our false self in a search for our True Self (see page 112, Figure 10.2).

In the early stages of our journey and our recovery — Stages Zero and One — we may feel confused, numb, in pain. We may feel at times like a victim or a martyr. We may sense that there is something wrong, that something is missing, and we seek an answer. And as we search, although it may take a long time, sooner or later we will begin to peel away the first layer. What we discover underneath may be any one or more of a variety of addictions, compulsions, and other physical, mental, emotional and spiritual disorders. These are our Stage Zero conditions.

After working through a Stage One Recovery program for whatever condition or disorder we found, we may be ready to peel that one away also. And what is underneath it? I suggest that it is primary co-dependence, with its two most paralyzing feelings: fear and shame. Not only might it take a long time to recognize this condition and these toxic feelings, it might also take even longer to work through them. We can work through them in a Stage Two full recovery program.

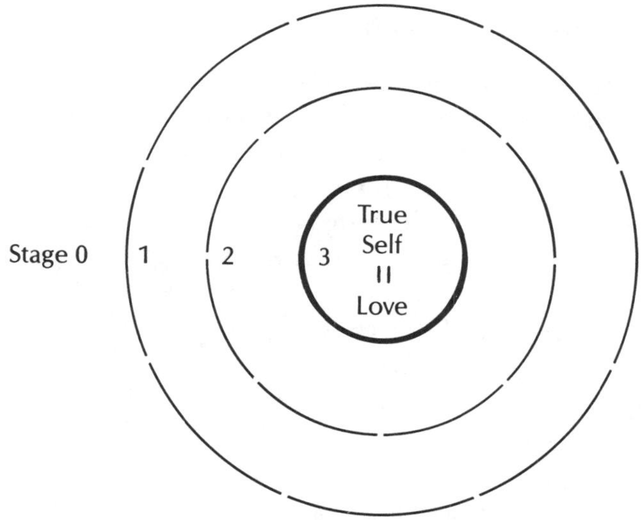

Figure 23.2. The Core of Our Being is Love

As we heal our woundedness at this layer, we can also see that both of the other layers of the onion are also part of (or perhaps more precisely *manifestations of*) that co-dependence and adult child wounding, which are often dominated by fear and shame. The *fear* seems to be mostly of abandonment and of the unknown, and the *shame* is mostly the paralyzing feeling that we are at our core inadequate, bad, not enough, imperfect, flawed and rotten. It can take a long time to work through this stage and discover the startling truth: that at the core of our being we are neither confused, numb, hurting, addicted, compulsive, disordered, co-dependent, scared, ashamed or any other such thing. Although any of them may come up to block our True Self, our Child Within, we learn that we are none of these. What we realize is that we are Love, at the core of our Being.

That Love that I am is connected to, comes from and is empowered by the Unconditonal Love of my Higher Power. When I tap into both of these sources of Love, I am co-creating my life.

As you read this now, how do you feel? Can you sense that Love in your heart? Can you sense its healing power? Can you let yourself "do nothing" and just savor It and be It?

The Fear Of Transcendence And Love

When we feel that Love, we may also feel scared. We may feel that if we let ourself feel good, even joyful, that something bad will happen. And so, by attaching to our false self, we constrict and contract from feeling that Love.

We may do this because in the past when we did feel good, something bad *did* happen to us or to someone else. What we may not have known was that at that time we did not feel authentically good, from our True Self. We were not then consciously connected to our Higher Power. We may have been, rather, *grandiose* or *inflated* in our ego, false or co-dependent self. Our ego may have led us to feel that we were *separated* from others and from God. At times we may have even felt that rather than being a part of God, a Child of God, that we were the *totality* of God.

Ego Inflation

People with co-dependence can feel inflated, and thus inauthentically powerful or good, in several ways. Edinger has described at least eight factors that might bring out ego inflation[191]. These include:

- Acting like an adolescent, which he and others have called the *puer aeternus* (eternal adolescent). This can happen to many people with active co-dependence, addictions, and other disorders.
- Inappropriate outbursts of false pride or attacking others.
- Motivation for power and omnipotence.
- Playing God.

- Playing martyr or victim, and its exaggeration, playing tragic hero or heroine.
- Manipulating, that is, trying to get something indirectly.
- Being narcissistic in an unhealthy way.
- Not paying attention to our unconscious, including any unfinished business that we may have.

I have noticed two more such factors:

- Trying to avoid experiencing and working through necessary pain.
- Basking in self-pity or unnecessary pain.

Caution: Be careful of the trap of seeing everyone else's pain as unnecessary and all of yours as necessary.

One way to guard against becoming inflated is to practice being its opposite: being humble. Humility is that state of being open to experiencing and learning about self, others and God. In this openness we are free not only to avoid any of these above factors when possible, but we are also free to connect with our Higher Power.

In this state of humility and innocence, we can experience whatever comes up for us, which may be joy or pain. And we can then just *be* in that joy or work through the pain, whatever that pain is due to.

When we are not our True Self, innocent and humble, and when we do not experientially include God in our life, we can end up trying to live from our ego or co-dependent self, feeling separated and alienated, feeling empty and without meaning.

To Enjoy Feeling Good

How can we enjoy feeling good? Consider doing the following. When we feel good, excited, happy or expansive, and no factors for ego inflation are present, and we are in conscious, experiential contact with our Higher Power, we can then simply let ourself feel good. And it is likely that nothing "bad" will happen. Daily spiritual practice, such as prayer, meditation and reading spiritual literature, can facilitate this process.

Epilogue

I hope you have profited from and perhaps even enjoyed reading this book.

The concept and movement of co-dependence and the adult child syndrome are wonderful and empowering tools for understanding and working through the recovery process — and for just living life in general.

I wish you the best on your journey.

Charlie Whitfield
Baltimore, 1991

APPENDIX A: THE LITERATURE ON CO-DEPENDENCE

So many articles and books are being published on co-dependence and the adult child syndrome that it is difficult to keep up with them. And if you also try to keep up with related fields, such as practical psychology, psychiatry and counseling, it can feel overwhelming.

What To Read Next?

This book can serve as a synopsis of co-dependence for people who cannot read the already large body of literature, but want a summary or a place to start. But you may want more.

Where should you go after having read this book? Of course, I can't pretend to tell you which may be best for you to read next. But I can share with you my suggestions, based on my experience.

Popular And Academic

To begin to get a handle on the literature, we can start with two broad categories: popular and academic. Neither category is better than the other. I prefer to read some or all of any book or article that interests me, to get a sense of its truth and its usefulness. Both kinds may be concise, clear and accurate — or wordy, unclear and miss the mark in one or more important areas.

Many authors of books on co-dependence give their preferred definition of co-dependence, and most give at least one case history example. Many books, especially the ones in the popular category, give almost too many case history examples for my needs. While I find some carefully selected case histories useful,

I get slowed down by too many or those that are verbose. I prefer meaty, concise and clear writing, without fluff. Surprisingly, I have seen a few books and many articles with "co-dependence" that never define the term.

Clinical And Non-Clinical

Some authors are front-line clinicians who have worked and are continuing to work in assisting co-dependent people and adult children in their recoveries. Their writings make a useful contribution to the clinically oriented literature. Others are not front-line clinicians and don't claim to be, and their writing can also be useful. But I am cautious when I read literature or hear a talk by anyone who has never or is not currently assisting people clinically in their recoveries, yet who substantially address such clinical issues as dynamics, treatment and recovery methods. This field is growing and evolving so rapidly that unless the author stays active clinically, it may be hard to speak with clinical accuracy of that experience.

On what do authors base their information? It is important to have an academic background and present the material with documentation and clarity. However, just because a writing or talk appears to be academic does not mean that all or even part of its contents are true. I have seen several such academic works that come across to me as being naive. Some are also wordy and use a lot of jargon.

Even using these two categories — popular and academic — has some problems. If some academically oriented books sell in large numbers, do we then call them "popular"? And if a book or article written for the general public uses many clear and appropriate documentations and references, might it qualify as being academic? While these categories may at times be useful, they are also arbitrary. Here, the blend of the popular and academic illustrates how this movement continues to demystify individual and family dynamics and helps people in their recoveries and their lives.

Evolution Of The Field

The field of co-dependence and the adult child syndrome has evolved over the last 15 years and is continuing to do so. The literature reflects this evolution to some degree.

In its early stage, perhaps from 1977 to 1985, the literature focused mostly on basic definitions and dynamics. Since 1986 it has focused more on (1) refining these definitions and dynamics; (2) specific methods of treatment and recovery; (3) the various guises, including Stage Zero conditions, through which adult children and co-dependents may present; and it is (4) beginning to explore how all of these relate to other fields, especially mental health and its many subdivisions. Over the coming years we will likely continue to refine all of these and see more research and academically oriented books and articles.

One strength of this field lies in the *diverse* and *rich training*, clinical and recovery *experience* of its workers and authors. And this will likely strengthen even more as its usefulness spreads to more and more helping professionals and people in recovery.

A second and powerful strength is the movement's *grass roots* nature. For the first time, millions of people are taking responsibility for their own recoveries and lives and not relying solely on people, places and things outside of themselves. This is the essence of recovery from co-dependence.

Some Sources Of *References* From The Literature

Because this book is more of a synopsis than a compendium, I must limit the annotated list of references from the literature in the section on Selected Books, below. To obtain a more complete list of references to the many other books, articles, films and tapes, one may consult any or all of several sources, including:

1. Ackerman R and Michaels J: **Recovery Resource Guide. 4th ed.** Health Communications, Deerfield Beach, FL: 1990. Lists many books, articles, research summaries, pamphlets, films, videotapes and audiocassettes on co-dependence, ACoA, family and personal recovery, as well as some helping agencies, that extend into 1989.
2. Johnson JL and Bennett LA: **Adult Children of Alcoholics: Theory and Research.** Rutgers Center of Alcohol Studies pamphlet, Box 969, Piscataway NJ 08855-0969, 201-932-2190, 1989. While skeptical and conservative in tone, this pamphlet cites 55 selected references from the literature that extend partially into 1988. About 21 of these references

address various aspects of the adult child syndrome. Also gives 19 resources of related organizations. For helping professionals.

3. Brown S: **Treating Adult Children of Alcoholics: A developmental perspective.** John Wiley, New York: 1988. Nearly 200 references current to about 1986. A useful reference book for helping professionals written by a pioneer clinician in the field.
4. Vannicelli M: **Group Psychotherapy with Adult Children of Alcoholics.** Guilford Press, New York: 1989. Contains about 152 references current into 1988, over half of which may be useful in addressing the adult child syndrome. For helping professionals.
5. McCann IL, Pearlman LA: **Psychological Trauma and the Adult Survivor.** Brunner/Mazel, New York: 1990. In addition to clinical approach summaries, contains about 500 references on abuse and trauma. For helping professionals.
6. Gil E: **Treatment of Adult Survivors of Child Abuse.** Launch Press, 2nd ed., Walnut Creek, CA: 1990. A compendium of clinical approaches to assisting adult survivors of more severe forms of child abuse that includes nearly 100 references on the topic current into 1990. For helping professionals.
7. National Council on Co-dependence, P.O. Box 40095, Phoenix, AZ 85067-0095, 602-937-4840. Founded and chartered in 1990, this new organization may be an ongoing source of information about co-dependence.

These are only a few potential sources. A health science library computer search of the literature can also be helpful. However, in my opinion some of the scientifically oriented literature misses the mark on the clinical essence and other aspects of co-dependence and the adult child syndrome. A rich source of information can be masters theses and doctoral dissertations, although these are somewhat harder to locate and obtain.

Annotated List Of Selected Books

I consider the following books pivotal, particularly practical in the process of recovery, or a special contribution to the field.

Many more books that are good to excellent are not listed here. Many of these are in the references at the end of this book. There is much in the literature, past and present, that alludes to or enriches our concepts of co-dependence.

For the sake of sequence and continuity, I list these in order of publication date. Unless noted otherwise, each book is suitable for both general readership and helping professionals.

Horney K: **Neurosis and Human Growth.** Norton, NY: 1950. One of the earliest and easiest reading books describing observations of the real self, its disorders and some possible directions to help heal them.

Al-Anon Faces Alcoholism. Al-Anon World Services, NY: 1958. The Big Book of the Twelve-Step fellowship of Al-Anon, one of the first books to address recovery from co-dependence without ever mentioning the term (because it was not yet in existence).

Maslow A: **Toward a Psychology of Being.** Van Nostrand, Princeton, NJ: 1961. Maslow studied and described the state and process of self-actualization, which is closely associated with, if not identical to what we call recovery today.

Cork M: **The Forgotten Children.** Addiction Research Foundation, Toronto, Canada: 1969. First book to focus on problems and issues of children of alcoholics.

Jourard S: **The Undiscovered Self.** (Rev. ed.) Van Nostrand, NY: 1971. Describing differences between the real and false self, Jourard describes physical, mental, emotional and spiritual values, perhaps anticipating and helping us to prepare the way for the co-dependence and adult child movement. One of the first and clearest books on authentic self-disclosure.

Johnson VE: **I'll Quit Tomorrow.** Harper & Row, NY: 1973. A classic on dynamics of the alcoholic and the family.

Anonymous: **A Course In Miracles.** Foundation for Inner Peace, Tiburon, CA: 1975. One of the most useful and detailed holy books — on spiritual psychology — that addresses co-dependence, describing it as a "special relationship." A "Holy Relationship" is one that is from our True Self and includes God. Empowering description of True Self (the Course calls it most closely right mind) and of false self or ego. Reframes sacrifice as being a form of attack. I recommend this book at the end of Stage Two and throughout Stage Three recovery. For those who learn well by hearing, the entire *Course* is available inexpensively on audiotape.

NIAAA Monograph 4: **Treatment Services for Children of Alcoholics.** National Institute of Alcohol and Alcohol Abuse, Rockville, MD, 1980. Position papers and some dialogue from the first national conference on the topic in 1979 in Silver Spring, Maryland.

Miller A: **The Drama of the Gifted Child.** Harper & Row, NY: 1981. The first accurate and clear book on some of the essential principles of psychoanalysis and how some of them have gone awry. This and her subsequent books — *For Your Own Good, Thou Shall Not Be Aware* and *Banished Knowledge* — appropriately minimize or refute some of Freud's least useful theories, such as the oedipal, and speak in favor of the trauma theory (which Freud co-dependently rejected in favor of the less threatening oedipal). Describes "poisonous pedagogy" in detail — one of the most toxic causes in the genesis of co-dependence.

Wegscheider S: **Another Chance: Hope and Health for the Alcoholic Family.** Science and Behavior Books, Palo Alto, CA: 1981. Based on her own pioneering work and that of Virginia Satir and others, this is the first to describe some of the roles in a dysfunctional family.

Black C: **It Will Never Happen To Me!** MAC Publications, Denver, CO: 1981. Description of special issues of children of alcoholics of all ages.

Halpern HM: **How To Break Your Addiction To A Person.** Bantam, NY: 1982. One of many books describing some of the important dynamics of co-dependence and its recovery — without ever mentioning the term. Some other books that do the same include Lerners' *The Dance of Anger* from a family systems perspective and Peck's *The Road Less Traveled* from a psychospiritual perspective.

Woititz JG: **Adult Children Of Alcoholics.** Health Communications, Pompano Beach, FL: 1983. Best-selling book describing some of their issues based on extensive interviews and time limited group discussion and therapy with several Adult Children of Alcoholics.

Masson JM: **The Assault On Truth: Freud's Suppression of the Seduction Theory.** Farrar, Straus and Giroux, NY: 1984. Psychoanalyst and former projects director of the Sigmund Freud Archives, Masson describes Freud's and nearly the entire psychoanalytic community's refutation and coverup of the trauma theory (which they also called the "seduction theory" in sexual abuse) in childhood wounding. Similar to Alice Miller, in his most recent book *Final Analysis* (Addison-Wesley, 1990) he describes his own story and some of the politics and unethical behavior, verified by Anna Freud and others, in the field of psychoanalysis.

Based on this list, 1985 saw perhaps the largest number of pivotal, quality or meaningful books published. That means that the late 1970s and early 1980s is when they were germinating and being written, and this energy and creativity continues today.

Norwood R: **Women Who Love Too Much.** Simon and Schuster, Pocket Books, NY: 1985. Another best-seller that describes practical ways to recognize and recover from co-dependence.

Schaef AW: **Co-dependence: Misunderstood — Mistreated.** Harper & Row, NY: 1985. One of first books to describe co-dependence from a societal as well as an individual perspective. Little information on the recovery process.

Gravitz HL and Bowden JD: **Guide To Recovery: A Book for Adult Children of Alcoholics.** Simon and Schuster, NY: 1985. First practical guide for adult children by two pioneer front-line clinicians.

Kritsberg W: **The ACoA Syndrome: Discovery and Recovery for Adult Children of Alcoholics.** Bantam, NY: 1985. A concise and practical book for adult children by another pioneer and front-line therapist.

Wegscheider-Cruse S: **Choicemaking: For Co-Dependents, Adult Children And Spirituality Seekers.** Health Communications, Pompano Beach, FL: 1985. Describes some dynamics of co-dependence and its recovery. Optimistic approach with a strong family flavor.

Cermak TL: **Diagnosing and Treating Co-dependence.** Johnson Institute, Minneapolis: 1986. Concise and conservative book describing and advocating co-dependence as a personality disorder with DSM-like diagnostic criteria. Some early outline descriptions of treatment. Reference for helping professionals.

Fossum M and Mason M: **Facing Shame: Families in Recovery.** Norton, NY: 1986. Discusses shame from a family systems and transgenerational perspective.

Subby R: **Lost In The Shuffle: The Co-dependent Reality.** Health Communications, Pompano Beach, FL: 1987. A book especially useful for the general public that clearly describes many of the dynamics of co-dependence. Strong AA/NA/Al-Anon flavor.

Whitfield CL: **Healing The Child Within: Discovery and Recovery For Adult Children Of Dysfunctional Families.** Health Communications, Pompano Beach, FL: 1987. Based on numerous sources, including object relations and self-psychology theory and practice. The first and most basic book on the crux of the healing and recovery process: assessing, living from and as the True Self or Child Within. First book to expand ACoA to adult children of dysfunctional families in general.

Wood B: **Adult Children Of Alcoholics: The Struggle for Self and Intimacy in Adult Life.** University Press, NY: 1987. Dynamics of the wounding process of ACoA's from an object relations theory perspective, focusing mostly on the British object relations school, including Guntrip, Fairbairn and Winnicott. Some inclusion of Kohut and self-psychology. Recommended for helping professionals only (see *The Process of Wounding* on page 23 for a summary of this perspective).

Beattie M: **Co-dependent No More.** Harper/Hazelden, NY: 1987. A look at co-dependence in large part from the perspective of the Al-Anon program (not Al-Anon "conference approved" — nor are most books on this topic) by a person who has been through her own recovery. Some readers say her sequel *Beyond Co-dependency* is clearer and more focused.

Masterson JF: **The Search For The Real Self: Unmasking the Personality Disorders of Our Age.** Free Press/MacMillan, NY: 1988. Describes important differences between the real and false self and how they manifest and interact in personality disorders, from a modern psychoanalytic perspective.

"Co-dependence: Issues In Treatment And Recovery." *Alcoholism Treatment Quarterly*, vol. 6, no. 1. Haworth Press, NY: 1989. Compendium of articles by selected clinicians and teachers. Some specialized discussions related to co-dependence include: overview, assessment, system dynamics, treatment, roles, gays and lesbians, couples groups and outpatient treatment. Recommended for helping professionals only.

Snow C and Willard D: **I'm Dying to Take Care of You: Nurses and Co-Dependence — Breaking the Cycles.** Professional Counselor Books, Redmond, WA: 1989. First book to address head-on the consequences of co-dependence in a helping profession. The field is open for equivalent works on other professions.

Abrahms J: **Reclaiming the Inner Child.** Tarcher, Los Angeles: 1990. A concentrated collection of writings on the Child Within by 20th-century authors, addressing a blend of its practical and mythic aspects.

Whitfield CL: **A Gift To Myself: A Personal Workbook And Guide To Healing My Child Within.** Health Communications, Deerfield Beach, FL: 1990. Nuts and bolts, "how to," gentle guide to the process of healing for adult children and co-dependent people. A practical and detailed expansion of *Healing The Child Within.*

Cermak TL: **Evaluating and Treating Adult Children of Alcoholics. Volume Two. Treatment.** Johnson Institute, Minneapolis: 1991. Important contribution to the field for therapists who are more used to using conventional approaches in their practice. Helpful discussion on some clinical approaches to PTSD. Excludes adult children of other dysfunctional families. For professionals only.

Kitchens JA: **Understanding and Treating Co-dependence.** Prentice-Hall, Englewood Cliffs, NJ: 1991. One of the most thorough of all the books on the topic by an experienced clinician and teacher in the field. Many diverse references. For helping professionals only.

Small J: **Awakening In Time: The Journey from Co-dependence to Co-creation.** Bantam, NY: 1991. Transformation from a spiritual perspective, with emphasis on the chakra system of energy centers and levels of consciousness.

Co-Dependents Anonymous: "The CoDA Book". Due from Co-Dependents Anonymous in 1992. Several years in formulation and writing, this book is a rich source of recovery reading. CoDA also has other useful literature, including a folded leaflet for each of its Twelve Steps.

Whitfield CL: **Boundaries And Relationships In Recovery.** Health Communications, Deerfield Beach, FL. In process for late 1992. Theory and practice of how to set healthy boundaries and limits in recovery and life.

Gravitz HL: **Breaking the Spell: Adult Children of Trauma** (ACT). Volume 1 for adult children, volume 2 for professionals. (Working title, available about 1992 from author at 5266 Hollister Ave. #220, Santa Barbara, CA 93111.) An expanded and practical look at trauma and its recovery.

Addictions And Compulsions

To be effective as a helping professional in adult child/co-dependence work it is essential to understand the recognition and the recovery process of addictions, compulsions and other distracting attachments. This includes knowing the importance of both Twelve-Step self-help groups and long-term group therapy in recovery. While there are numerous books available on addictions, two basic ones are Gitlow and Peyser: *Alcoholism — A Practical Treatment Guide.* ad. ed. Grune & Stratton, NY: 1987; and Washton A and Boundy D: *Willpower's Not Enough: Recovery From Addictions of Every Kind.* Harper & Row, NY: 1989. A classic book in Twelve-Step programs is the "Big Book" of AA: *Alcoholics Anonymous: The Story of How Many Thousands of Men and Women Have Recovered from Alcoholism.* 3rd ed. AA World Services, NY: 1976. Many other Twelve-Step programs have their own equivalent to the "Big Book." A comprehensive textbook on addictions is Lowinson et al (eds): **Comprehensive Textbook of Substance Abuse.** Williams & Wilkins, Baltimore, 1992.

APPENDIX B: DIAGNOSTIC AND SURVEY INSTRUMENTS

A person may *identify* with the symptoms, signs and other characteristics of co-dependence given in this book and have no reason to pursue diagnostic or survey instruments. However, if the person's therapist chooses to pursue a more detailed written survey assessment, the following are available. I use the **Recovery Potential Survey** routinely in my practice and use some of the others when needed.

Other similar surveys and checklists are available, including:

- A Co-dependence Test (Kitchens 1990)
- Co-dependent Assessment Inventory (Gossett, cited in Kitchens 1990)
- Co-dependency Assessment Inventory (Friel 1985)
- Acquaintance Description Form (Wright & Wright 1990)
- Co-dependent Relationship Questionnaire (Kritsberg 1988)
- The Original Laundry List: The Problem And The Solution (Tony A. 1990)
- Relationship Addiction (Norwood 1985, reproduced in Black 1990)
- Sexual Addiction (Sexaholics Anonymous 1985, reproduced in Black 1990)
- Family Drinking Survey (Whitfield 1987)
- Checklist from Co-Dependents Anonymous (CoDA 1990)

Recovery Potential Survey

Circle or check the word that most applies to how you *truly* feel.

1. Do you seek approval and affirmation?
   Never Seldom Occasionally Often Usually
2. Do you fail to recognize your accomplishments?
   Never Seldom Occasionally Often Usually
3. Do you fear criticism?
   Never Seldom Occasionally Often Usually
4. Do you overextend yourself?
   Never Seldom Occasionally Often Usually
5. Have you had problems with your own compulsive behavior?
   Never Seldom Occasionally Often Usually
6. Do you have a need for perfection?
   Never Seldom Occasionally Often Usually
7. Are you uneasy when your life is going smoothly? Do you continually anticipate problems?
   Never Seldom Occasionally Often Usually
8. Do you feel more alive in the midst of a crisis?
   Never Seldom Occasionally Often Usually
9. Do you care for others easily, yet find it difficult to care for yourself?
   Never Seldom Occasionally Often Usually
10. Do you isolate yourself from other people?
    Never Seldom Occasionally Often Usually
11. Do you respond with anxiety to authority figures and angry people?
    Never Seldom Occasionally Often Usually
12. Do you feel that individuals and society in general are taking advantage of you?
    Never Seldom Occasionally Often Usually

If you answered "Occasionally," "Often," or "Usually" to any of these questions, you may find it useful to continue reading. (These questions are modified from Al-Anon Family Group, 1984, with permission.[645])

13. Do you have trouble with intimate relationships?
    Never Seldom Occasionally Often Usually
14. Do you attract and seek people who tend to be compulsive?
    Never Seldom Occasionally Often Usually
15. Do you cling to relationships because you are afraid of being alone?
    Never Seldom Occasionally Often Usually
16. Do you mistrust your own feelings and feelings expressed by others?
    Never Seldom Occasionally Often Usually
17. Do you find it difficult to express your emotions?
    Never Seldom Occasionally Often Usually
18. Do you fear any of the following:
    - losing control?

    Never Seldom Occasionally Often Usually
    - your own feelings?

    Never Seldom Occasionally Often Usually
    - conflict and criticism?

    Never Seldom Occasionally Often Usually
    - being rejected or abandoned?

    Never Seldom Occasionally Often Usually
    - being a failure?

    Never Seldom Occasionally Often Usually
19. Is it difficult for you to relax and have fun?
    Never Seldom Occasionally Often Usually
20. Do you find yourself compulsively eating, working, drinking, using drugs or seeking excitement?
    Never Seldom Occasionally Often Usually
21. Have you tried counseling or psychotherapy, yet still feel that "something" is wrong or missing?
    Never Seldom Occasionally Often Usually
22. Do you frequently feel numb, empty or sad?
    Never Seldom Occasionally Often Usually
23. Is it hard for you to trust others?
    Never Seldom Occasionally Often Usually

24. Do you have an over-developed sense of responsibility?
    Never Seldom Occasionally Often Usually
25. Do you feel a lack of fulfillment in life, personally and in your work?
    Never Seldom Occasionally Often Usually
26. Do you have feelings of guilt, inadequacy or low self-esteem?
    Never Seldom Occasionally Often Usually
27. Do you have a tendency toward having chronic fatigue, aches and pains?
    Never Seldom Occasionally Often Usually
28. Do you find that it is difficult to visit your parents for more than a few minutes or a few hours?
    Never Seldom Occasionally Often Usually
29. Are you hesitant to respond when people ask about your feelings?
    Never Seldom Occasionally Often Usually
30. Have you wondered if you were mistreated or neglected as a child?
    Never Seldom Occasionally Often Usually
31. Do you have difficulty asking for what you want from others?
    Never Seldom Occasionally Often Usually

If you answered "Occasionally," "Often," or "Usually" to any of these questions, recovering from co-dependence may be freeing for you. If you answered mostly "Never," you may not be aware of some of your feelings.
Source: Whitfield, 1990.

The Co-dependent Relationship Questionnaire

The C.R.Q. can be used to assess whether or not you are in a co-dependent sexual relationship. If you are not currently in a sexual relationship, you can use the C.R.Q. to determine if in the past you have been in one. If you are currently in a relationship, fill out this questionnaire by yourself. Please check the answer below that most closely describes your feelings or behavior.

Answer all questions yes or no.

YES	NO	
___	___	1. Do you place your partner's needs ahead of yours?
___	___	2. Have you ever hit or been hit by your partner?
___	___	3. Are you afraid to tell your partner when your feelings are hurt?
___	___	4. Does your partner tell you how to dress?
___	___	5. Do you smile when you are angry?
___	___	6. Do you have difficulty establishing personal boundaries and keeping them?
___	___	7. Is it difficult to express your true feelings to your partner?
___	___	8. Do you feel nervous and uncomfortable when alone?
___	___	9. Do you feel rejected when your partner is spending time with friends?
___	___	10. Do you feel shame when your partner makes a mistake?
___	___	11. Do you have sex when you don't want to?
___	___	12. Do you withhold sex to get even with your partner?
___	___	13. Do you think your partner's opinion is more important than your own?
___	___	14. Do you rely on your partner to make most of the decisions in the relationship?
___	___	15. Do you become very upset when your partner does not follow your plan?
___	___	16. Are you afraid to let your partner really know what you are feeling?
___	___	17. Do you keep silent in order to keep the peace?

YES	NO	
___	___	18. Do you feel you give and give and get little or nothing in return?
___	___	19. Do you freeze up when in conflict with your partner?
___	___	20. Are you unhappy with your friendships?
___	___	21. Do you often find yourself saying, "It's not that bad"?
___	___	22. Do you feel you are "stuck" in this relationship?
___	___	23. Do you have to control your emotions most of the time?
___	___	24. Do you lose control of your emotions during times of conflict?
___	___	25. Do you feel that your relationship would fall apart without your constant efforts?

___ Total number of YES answers.

A total score of 5 or more yes answers indicates that you may be in or have been in a co-dependent relationship. The higher the number of yes answers, the more dysfunctional the relationship. From 1 to 7 yes answers indicate a mildly dysfunctional relationship, from 8 to 18 yes answers indicate a moderately dysfunctional relationship, and 19 to 25 yes answers indicate a severely dysfunctional relationship.

Source: Copyright 1988 by Wayne Kritsberg, Family Integration Systems[365].

Family Drinking Survey

	YES	NO
1. Does someone in your family undergo personality changes when he or she drinks to excess?	___	___
2. Do you feel that drinking is more important to this person than you are?	___	___

	YES	NO
3. Do you feel sorry for yourself and frequently indulge in self-pity because of what you feel alcohol is doing to your family?	___	___
4. Has some family member's excessive drinking ruined special occasions?	___	___
5. Do you find yourself covering up for the consequences of someone else's drinking?	___	___
6. Have you ever felt guilty, apologetic or responsible for the drinking of a member of your family?	___	___
7. Does one of your family member's use of alcohol cause fights and arguments?	___	___
8. Have you ever tried to fight the drinker by joining in the drinking?	___	___
9. Do the drinking habits of some family members make you feel depressed or angry?	___	___
10. Is your family having financial difficulties because of drinking?	___	___
11. Did you ever feel as if you had an unhappy home life because of the drinking of some members of your family?	___	___
12. Have you ever tried to control the drinker's behavior by hiding the car keys, pouring liquor down the drain, etc.?	___	___
13. Do you find yourself distracted from your responsibilities because of this person's drinking?	___	___
14. Do you often worry about a family member's drinking?	___	___
15. Are holidays more of a nightmare than a celebration because of a family member's drinking behavior?	___	___
16. Are most of your drinking family member's friends heavy drinkers?	___	___

	YES	NO
17. Do you find it necessary to lie to employers, relatives or friends in order to hide your spouse's drinking?	___	___
18. Do you find yourself responding differently to members of your family when they are using alcohol?	___	___
19. Have you ever been embarrassed or felt the need to apologize for the drinker's actions?	___	___
20. Does some family member's use of alcohol make you fear for your own safety or the safety of other members of your family?	___	___
21. Have you ever thought that one of your family members had a drinking problem?	___	___
22. Have you ever lost sleep because of a family member's drinking?	___	___
23. Have you ever encouraged one of your family members to stop or cut down on his or her drinking?	___	___
24. Have you ever threatened to leave home or to leave a family member because of his or her drinking?	___	___
25. Did a family member ever make promises that he or she did not keep because of drinking?	___	___
26. Did you ever wish that you could talk to someone who could understand and help the alcohol-related problems of a family member?	___	___
27. Have you ever felt sick, cried or had a "knot" in your stomach after worrying about a family member's drinking?	___	___
28. Has a family member ever failed to remember what occurred during a drinking period?	___	___
29. Does your family member avoid social situations where alcoholic beverages will not be served?	___	___

	YES	NO
30. Does your family member have periods of remorse after drinking occasions and apologize for his or her behavior?	___	___

31. Please write any symptoms or medical or nervous problems that you have experienced since you have known your heavy drinker. (Write on back if more space needed.)

If you answered "YES" to any 2 of the above questions, there is a good possibility that someone in your family may have a drinking problem.

If you answered "YES" to 4 or more of the above questions, there is a definite indication that someone in your family *does* have a drinking problem (from Whitfield 1987).

(These survey questions are modified or adapted from the Children of Alcoholics Screening Test (CAST)[327], the Howard Family Questionnaire, and the Family Alcohol Quiz from Al-Anon[19].)

Checklist From Co-Dependents Anonymous

This checklist, created by Co-Dependents Anonymous (CoDA), can help determine the presence of co-dependence. Mark the items that apply to you "always," "usually," "often," "sometimes" or "never." If you can identify with several of these characteristics, you can find help and understanding at CoDA meetings.

CONTROL PATTERNS

___ I must be "needed" in order to have a relationship with others.

___ I value others' approval of my thinking, feelings and behaviors over my own.

___ I agree with others so they will like me.

___ I focus my attention on protecting others.

___ I believe most other people are incapable of taking care of themselves.

____ I keep score of "good deeds and favors," becoming very hurt when they are not repaid.

____ I am very skilled at guessing how other people are feeling.

____ I can anticipate others' needs and desires, meeting them before they are asked to be met.

____ I become resentful when others will not let me help them.

____ I am calm and efficient in other people's crisis situations.

____ I feel good about myself only when I am helping others.

____ I freely offer others advice and directions without being asked.

____ I put aside my own interests and concerns in order to do what others want.

____ I ask for help and nurturing only when I am ill, and then reluctantly.

____ I cannot tolerate seeing others in pain.

____ I lavish gifts and favors on those I care about.

____ I use sex to gain approval and acceptance.

____ I attempt to convince others of how they "truly" think and "should" feel.

____ I perceive myself as completely unselfish and dedicated to the well-being of others.

COMPLIANCE PATTERNS

____ I assume responsibility for others' feelings and behaviors.

____ I feel guilty about others' feelings and behaviors.

____ I have difficulty identifying what I am feeling.

____ I am afraid of my anger, yet sometimes erupt in a rage.

____ I worry how others may respond to my feelings, opinions and behavior.

____ I have difficulty making decisions.

____ I am afraid of being hurt and/or rejected by others.

____ I minimize, alter or deny how I truly feel.

____ I am very sensitive to how others are feeling and feel the same.

___ I am afraid to express differing opinions or feelings.

___ I value others' opinions and feelings more than my own.

___ I put other people's needs and desires before mine.

___ I am embarrassed to receive recognition and praise, or gifts.

___ I judge everything I think, say or do harshly, as never "good enough."

___ I am a perfectionist.

___ I am extremely loyal, remaining in harmful situations too long.

___ I do not ask others to meet my needs or desires.

___ I do not perceive myself as a lovable and worthwhile person.

___ I compromise my own values and integrity to avoid rejection or others' anger.

Source: Reprinted with permission of Co-Dependents Anonymous from the pamphlet What is Co-Dependency? 1989.

Note From The Author

I include the following approximately 750 selected references and 105 resources to illustrate the rich foundation of this approach and to provide an extensive reference source for further study and networking. While I have not read every one of these references, I have read most of them. For comments on the literature of co-dependence, see Appendix A on page 259.

I am open to receiving a review copy of pertinent or related books and articles for consideration for referencing here in the future (see my address in the front of this book and please enclose a SASE if you wish a reply).

References

1. Abbott S: Codependent counselor. *Counselor,* 7(4): 48, 1989.
2. Abbott S: Co-dependency: Final Frontier. *Counselor,* 7(5): 48, 1989.
3. Abrahms J: **Reclaiming the Inner Child.** Tarcher, Los Angeles, 1990.
4. Abramson LY et al: Learned helplessness in humans: Critique and reformulation. *Journal of Abnormal Psychology,* 87: 49-74, 1978.
5. ACA: The ACA program and how it works. Report of the Identity, Purpose and Relationship Committee. Adult Children of Alcoholics Central Service Board, Inc, Los Angeles, CA, 1984.
6. ACA: Finding wholeness through separation: The paradox of independence. Report of the Identity, Purpose and Relationship Committee. Adult Children of Alcoholics Central Service Board, Inc., Los Angeles, CA, 1986.
7. ACA: The importance of service in ACA. Report of the Identity, Purpose and Relationship Committee. Adult Children of Alcoholics Central Service Board, Inc, Los Angeles, CA, 1987.
8. Achterberg J: **Imagery in Healing.** New Science Library, Boston, 1985.
9. Ackerman RJ: **Growing In The Shadows.** Health Communications, Pompano Beach, FL, 1986.
10. Ackerman RJ: **Let Go And Grow.** Health Communications, Deerfield Beach, FL, 1987.
11. Ackerman RJ: **Same House Different Homes.** Health Communications, Pompano Beach, FL 1987.
12. Ackerman RJ: **Perfect Daughters.** Health Communications, Deerfield Beach, FL, 1989.
13. Ackerman RJ, Pickering SE: **Abused No More:** Recovery for women from abusive or co-dependent relationships. Tab Books, Blue Ridge Summit, PA, 1989.
14. Ackerman R, Michaels J: **Recovery Resource Guide,** 4th edition. Health Communications, Deerfield Beach, FL, 1990.
15. Adams C, Fay J: **No More Secrets.** Impact Publishers, San Louis Obispo, CA, 1981.
16. Adams C, Fay J: **Free of the Shadow:** Recovering from sexual violence. New Harbinger, Oakland, 1989.

17. Adult Children 6th ACA Business Conference, Hartford, CT, 20-22, April 1990.

18. Agosta C, Loring M: Understanding and treating the adult retrospective victim of child sexual abuse. In S. Sgroi, Ed., **Vulnerable Populations:** Evaluation Treatment of Sexually Abused Children and Adult Survivors, vol. 1, Lexington, MA, 1988.

19. Al-Anon Family Groups, P.O. Box 182, Madison Square Station, NY 10159. Many helpful publications, including: **Al-Anon Faces Alcoholism, Living with Sobriety,** and **Blueprint for Progress.**

20. Alcoholics Anonymous: "Big Book" and other helpful literature, NY, NY, 212-686-1100.

21. Alexander J: **Recovery Plus:** Freedom From Co-dependency. Health Communications, Deerfield Beach, FL, 1990.

22. Allen C: **Daddy's Girl.** Wyndham Books, NY, 1980.

23. Alloy LB: Attributional style and the generality of learned helplessness. *Journal of Personality and Social Psychology,* 46: 681-687, 1984.

24. American Psychiatric Association DSM-III-R: Diagnostic and Statistical Manual of Mental Disorders (3rd ed.). Washington, DC, 1987.

25. Anderson E, Quast W: Young children in alcoholic families: A mental health needs-assessment and an intervention/prevention strategy. *Journal of Primary Prevention,* 3(3): 174-187, 1983.

26. Anderson GL: **Enabling in the school setting.** (Booklet) Johnston Institute, Minneapolis, 1987.

27. Anderson PK: **Adult Children Of Alcoholics:** Coming Home. Glen Abbey Books, Seattle, 1988.

28. Anderson R: personal communciations on family aspects of addiction, 1983.

29. Ann M: Letting go of the need to control. Hazelden, Center City, MN, 1987.

30. Anonymous: **The URANTIA (Earth) Book,** Urantia Foundation, 533 Diversy Parkway, Chicago, IL 60614 (312)-525-3319, or Fifth Epochal Fellowship, 529 Wrightwood Ave, Chicago, IL 60614, 1955.

31. Anonymous: **Letting Go With Love.** Jeremy P. Tarcher, Los Angeles: 1987.

32. Anonymous: **Family Secrets:** Life stories of ACoA's. Harper & Row, San Francisco, 1987.

33. Ansbacher HL, Ansbacher RR (eds): **The Individual Psychology of Alfred Adler:** A systematic presentation in selections from his writings. Basic Books/Harper Torchbooks, NY, 1956.

34. Anthony EJ: The impact of mental and physical illness on family life. *American Journal of Psychiatry,* 127, 211-225, 1970.

35. Anthony EJ: How children cope in families with a psychotic parent. In E. Rexford, L. Sander & T. Shapiro (Eds.), **Infant Psychiatry.** Yale University Press, New Haven, CT, 1976.

36. Armstrong L et al: **Kiss Daddy Goodnight.** Hawthorn Books, NY, 1978.

37. Arnold RP et al: Medical problems in adults who were sexually abused in childhood. *British Medical Journal* 300: 705-8, 1990.

38. Arnold LJ: Three part article on co-dependence — co-dependency: Part I Origins & characteristics, II: The hospital as a dysfunctional family, III: Strategies for healing. *AORN Journal*, May, 51(5): 1341-8, June, 51(6): 1581-4, July, 52(1): 85-9, 1990.

39. Arteburn S, Felton J: **Toxic Faith:** Understanding and overcoming religious addiction. Oliver Nelson, Nashville, 1991.

40. Asher RM: Ambivalence, moral career and ideology: A sociological analysis of the lives of women married to alcoholics. *Dissertation Abstracts International*, 49(6): 1587-A, 1988.

41. Asher R, Brissett D: Codependency: A view from women married to alcoholics. *International Journal of Addictions*, 23(4): 331-350, 1988.

42. Bach GR, Wyden P: **The Intimate Enemy:** How to fight fair in love and marriage. Avon, NY, 1968.

43. Bachman G et al: Childhood sexual abuse and the consequences in adult women. *Obstetrics & Gynecology* 71: 631-642, 1988.

44. Baldwin C: **One to One:** self understanding through journal writing. M. Evans, NY, 1977.

45. Bank SP, Kahn MD: **The Sibling Bond.** Basic Books, NY, 1982.

46. Barnard CP, Spoentgen PA: Children of alcoholics: Characteristics and treatment, *Alcoholism Treatment Quarterly*, 3(4) 47-65, 1986a.

47. Barnard CP, Spoentgen PA: Are children of alcoholics different? A research report on group process, *Focus on Family and Chemical Dependency*, 9(2), 20-22, 1986.

48. Barnes JL et al: Psychosocial characteristics of women with alcoholic fathers, *Currents in Alcoholism*, 6, 209-222, 1979.

49. Bean-Bayog M: Children of alcoholics. *Advances in Alcohol & Substance Abuse*, 6(4): 1-3, 1987.

50. Beardslee WR et al: Exposure to parental alcoholism during childhood and outcome, Adulthood: A prospective longitudinal study, *British Journal of Psychiatry*, 149, 584-591, 1986.

51. Beattie M: **Co-dependent No More.** Hazelden, Center City, Minnesota, 1987.

52. Beattie M: **Beyond Codependency.** Harper & Row, San Francisco, 1989.

53. Becker JV et al: Level of post-assault sexual functioning in rape and incest victims. *Archives of Sexual Behavior*, 15: 37-49, 1986.

54. Becnel BC: **The Co-Dependent Parent:** Free yourself by freeing your child. Lowell House, Los Angeles, 1991.

55. Begun A, Zweben A: Assessment and treatment implications of adjustment and coping capacities in children living with alcoholic parents. *Alcoholism Treatment Quarterly*, 7(2): 23-40, 1990.

56. Behling DW: Alcohol abuse as encountered in 51 instances of reported child abuse. *Clinical Pediatrics,* 18: 87-91, 1979.

57. Beletsis SG, Brown S: A developmental framework for understanding the adult children of alcoholics, *Journal of Addictions and Health,* 2(4), 187-203, 1981.

58. Bell B, Cohen R: The Bristol Social Adjustment Guide: Comparison between the offspring of alcoholic and nonalcoholic mothers. *British Journal of Clinical Psychology,* 20: 93-95, 1981.

59. Benedek EP: The silent scream: Countertransference reactions to victims. *The American Journal of Social Psychiatry,* 4(3): 49-52, 1984.

60. Bennett LA et al: Cognitive, behavioral, and emotional problems among school-aged children of alcoholic parents. *American Journal of Psychiatry,* 145(2): 185-190, 1988.

61. Bennett LA, Wolin SJ: Family culture and alcoholism transmission. In Collins RL et al (eds): **Alcohol and the Family.** Guilford Press, NY, 1990.

62. Benson CS, Heller K: Factors in the current adjustment of young adult daughters of alcoholic and problem drinking fathers, *Journal of Abnormal Psychology,* 96(4), 305-312, 1987.

63. Bepko C, Krestan JA: **The Responsibility Trap:** A blueprint for training the alcoholic family. The Free Press, NY, 1985.

64. Berenson D: A systemic view of spirituality: God and Twelve-Step programs as resources in family therapy. *Journal for Strategic and Systemic Therapies,* Vol 9, No 1, Spring 1990.

65. Berenson D: A Family Approach to Alcoholism. *Psychiatric Opinion,* Vol 13, No 1, 1976.

66. Berenson D: The Therapist's Relationship with Couples with an Alcohol Problem, chapter in **Family Treatment of Alcohol and Drug Problems,** E Kaufman and P Kaufmann (eds), Gardner Press, NY, 1979.

67. Berenson D: Alcohol and the Family System, chapter in **Family Therapy:** Theory and Practice, P. Guerin (ed), Gardner Press, NY, 1976.

68. Berenson D: Between I and Thou. *Family Therapy Networker,* Sept/Oct, 1990.

69. Berenson D: Personal communication, Sausalito, CA, 10 Nov 1990.

70. Berkowitz A, Perkins HW: Personality characteristics of children of alcoholics, *Journal Consultation Clinical Psychology,* 56, 206-209, 1988.

71. Berkowitz DA: An overview of the psychodynamics of couples. In Nadelson C, Polonsky D (eds): **Marriage and Divorce:** A contemporary perspective. Guilford Press, NY, 1983.

72. Berrick JD, Gilbert N: **With the Best of Intentions:** The child sexual abuse prevention movement. Guilford, NY, 1991.

73. Bierig S: **Transforming The Co-dependent Woman.** Health Communications, Deerfield Beach, FL 1991.

74. Billings AG et al: Marital conflict resolution of alcoholic and nonalcoholic couples during drinking and non-drinking sessions. *Journal of Studies on Alcohol,* 40(3): 183-195, 1979.

75. Birrell RG, Birrell JHW: The maltreatment syndrome in children: A hospital survey. *Medical Journal of Australia,* 2(23): 1023-1029, 1968.

76. Black C et al: The interpersonal and emotional consequences of being an adult child of an alcoholic. *International Journal of Addictions,* 21(2): 213-231, 1986.

77. Black C: **It Will Never Happen To Me!** MAC Publications, Denver, 1981.

78. Black C: **Repeat After Me.** MAC Publications, Denver, 1985.

79. Black C: **Double Duty.** Ballantine, NY, 1990.

80. Blane HT: Prevention issues with children of alcoholics. *British Journal of Addiction,* 83: 793-798, 1988.

81. Blatner A, Blatner A: **The Art of Play:** An adult's guide to reclaiming imagination and spontaneity. Human Sciences Press, NY, 1988.

82. Blume ES: **Secret Survivors:** Uncovering incest and its aftereffects in women. John Wiley & Sons, NY, 1990.

83. Blume SB: Public policy issues relevant to children of alcoholics. *Advances in Alcohol & Substance Abuse,* 6(4): 5-15, 1987.

84. Boaz D: Let's quit the drug war. *NY Times,* 17 Mar 1988.

85. Bolen JS: **Goddesses in Everywoman.** Harper, NY, 1989.

86. Bolen JS: **Gods in Everyman.** Harper, NY, 1984.

87. Bonnington S: Correlations among measures of divorce adjustment, self-esteem, & health of the family of origin. *Psychological Reports* 62(2): 561-562 Apr 1988.

88. Booth L: **Breaking The Chains.**

89. Borysenko J: **Mending The Body, Mending The Mind.** Addison-Wesley, NY, 1987.

90. Bowlby J: **Attachment and Loss:** Vol. I. Attachment, Hogarth, London, 1969.

91. Bowles C: Children of alcoholic parents. *American Journal of Nursing,* 68: 1062-1064, 1968.

92. Bradshaw J: **Bradshaw On: The Family,** Health Communications, Deerfield Beach, FL, 1988.

93. Bradshaw J: **Homecoming.** Bantam, NY, 1990.

94. Bradshaw J: **Healing The Shame That Binds You.** Health Communications, Deerfield Beach, FL, 1989.

95. Brady K: **Father's Days.** Seaview Books, NY, 1979.

96. Bragdon E: **The Call Of Spiritual Emergency:** From personal crisis to personal transformation, Harper & Row, San Francisco, 1990.

97. Branden N: **If You Could Hear What I Cannot Say.** Bantam, NY, 1983.

98. Brant R, Tisza V: The sexually misused child. *American Journal of Orthopsychiatry*, 47: 80-90, 1977.

99. Breiner SJ: **Slaughter of the Innocent Child:** Abuse through the ages and today. Plenum, NY, 1990.

100. Brende JO: The use of hypnosis in post-traumatic conditions. In. W. E. Kelly (Ed.), **Post-Traumatic Stress Disorder and the War Veteran Patient,** Brunner/Mazel, NY, 1985.

101. Broucek F: **Shame and the Self.** Guilford, NY, 1991.

102. Brown FH: **Reweaving the Family Tapestry:** A multigenerational approach to families. Norton, NY, 1991.

103. Brown MY: **The Unfolding Self.** Psychosynthesis Press, Los Angeles, 1983.

104. Brown S: Children with an alcoholic parent, In Estes NJ & Heinemann ME, **Alcoholism:** Development, Consequences, and Interventions, Mosby, 207-220, St. Louis, 1986.

105. Brown S: **Treating Adult Children of Alcoholics:** A developmental perspective. Wiley, NY, 1988.

106. Brown S, Beletsis S: The development of family transference in groups for the adult children of alcoholics. International Journal of Group Psychotherapy, 36(1), 97-114, 1986 (reprinted in **ACoA's in Treatment.** Health Communications, Deerfield Beach, FL, 1989).

107. Brown HP Jr, Peterson JH Jr: Refining the BASIC-ISs: A psychospiritual approach to the comprehensive outpatient treatment of drug dependency. *Alcoholism Treatment Quarterly*, 6(3/4): 27-61, 1989.

108. Brown S, Yalom ID: Interactional group therapy with alcoholics, *Journal of Studies on Alcohol*, 38(3), 426-456, 1977.

109. Buber M: **I and Thou** (second edition). Charles Scribners Sons, NY, 1958.

110. Buchwald D et al: Tips on chronic fatigue syndrome. *Patient Care*, 45-58, 30 May 1991.

111. Bulkley J, Davidson H: Child Sexual Abuse — Legal Issues and Approaches. American Bar Association, Washington, DC, 1980.

112. Bulkley J: Child Sexual Abuse and the Law. National Legal Resource Center for Child Advocacy and Protection, American Bar Association, Washington, DC, 1981.

113. Bulkley J: Innovations in the Prosecution of Child Sexual Abuse Cases. National Legal Resource Center for Child Advocacy and Protection. American Bar Association, Washington, DC, 1982, 2nd edition.

114. Bulkley J: Recommendations for Improving Legal Intervention in Intrafamily Child Sexual Abuse Cases. National Legal Resource Center for Child Advocacy and Protection, American Bar Association, Washington, DC, 1982.

115. Burgess A, Holmstrom L: Sexual trauma of children and adolescents: Pressure, sex and secrecy. *Nursing Clinics of North America* 10: 551-563, 1975.

116. Burgess A et al: **Sexual Assault of Children and Adolescents.** Lexington Books, Lexington, MA, 1978.

117. Burk JP: Labeling the child of an alcoholic: Negative stereotyping by mental health professionals and peers. *Dissertation Abstracts International,* 49(7): 2846-B, 1989.

118. Burk JP, Sher KJ: The "forgotten children" revisited: Neglected areas of COA research, *Clinical Psychology Review.* 8, 285-302, 1988.

119. Butler S: **Conspiracy of Silence.** New Glide Publications, San Francisco, CA, 1978.

120. Calder P, Kostyniuk A: Personality profiles of children of alcoholics. *Professional Psychology: Research and Practice,* 20(6): 417-418, 1989.

121. Campbell J: **The Hero With A Thousand Faces.** Princeton University Press, Princeton, 1968.

122. Campbell S: **The Couple's Journey.** Impact Publishers, San Louis Obispo, CA, 1986.

123. Cantwell D: Psychiatric illness in the families of hyperactive children. *Archives of General Psychiatry,* 27(3): 414-417, 1972.

124. Capacchione L: **The Creative Journal for Children.** Shambhala, Boston, 1989.

125. Capacchione L: **The Power of Your Other Hand.** Newcastle Publication, N Hollywood, CA, 1988.

126. Capacchione L: **The Well-Being — Journal for Children.** Shambhala, Boston, 1989.

127. Capacchione L: **Recovery of Your Inner Child.** Simon & Schuster Fireside, NY, 1991.

128. Carlson EB, Putnam FW: **Dissociative Experiences Scale.** Survey instrument available from the literature and from Putnam FW, National Institute of Mental Health, Washington, DC.

129. Carlson EB, Putnam FW: Further validation of the Dissociative Experiences Scale. Cited in Putnam (#504).

130. Carlson EB, Putnam FW: Integrating research in dissociation and hypnotic susceptibility. Are there two pathways to hypnotizability? *Dissociation* 2(1): 32-38, 1989.

131. Carnes P: **Out Of The Shadows:** Understanding Sexual Addiction. CompCare, Minneapolis, 1983.

132. Carnes P et al: Special issue: Medical aspects of sexual addiction/compulsivity. *American Journal of Preventive Psychiatry and Neurology* 2(3) May 1990.

133. Caron Family Services: Guidelines for re-entry into the world. Wernersville, PA, 1991.

134. Carozza PM, Heirsteiner CL: Young female incest victims in treatment: stages of growth seen with a group art therapy model. *Clinical Social Work Journal,* 10(3): 165-175, 1983.

135. Carter B, McGoldrick M (eds): **The Changing Family Life Cycle:** A framework for family therapy, 2nd ed, 1989.

136. Cartwright JL et al: A cluster analysis of MMPI and CPI profiles of adult children of alcoholics and nonalcoholics. *Alcoholism Treatment Quarterly* 7(4): 57-80, 1990.

137. Cashdan S: **Object Relations Therapy:** Using the relationship. WW Norton, NY, 1988.

138. Castine J: **Recovery From Rescuing.** Health Communications, Deerfield Beach, FL, 1989.

139. Cauthorne-Lindstrom C, Hrabe D: Co-dependent behavior in managers: a script for failure. *Nursing Management* 21(12): 34-5, Feb 1990.

140. Cermak TL: Children of alcoholics and the case for a new diagnostic category of codependency. *Alcohol, Health and Research World,* 8(4), 38-42, 1984.

141. Cermak TL: **A Primer On Adult Children Of Alcoholics.** Health Communications, Pompano Beach, FL, 1985.

142. Cermak TL: **Diagnosing & Treating Co-dependence:** A Guide for Professionals who Work with Chemical Dependents, Their Spouses, and Children. Johnson Institute, Minneapolis, MN 1986.

143. Cermak T: Diagnostic criteria for co-dependency. *Journal of Psychoactive Drugs,* 18: 15-20, 1986.

144. Cermak T: Al-Anon and recovery. In Galanter M (ed) *Recent Developments in Alcoholism,* Vol 7. Plenum Publishing, NY, 1989.

145. Cermak TL: **Evaluating and Treating Adult Children of Alcoholics:** Volume One — Evaluation, Volume Two — Treatment. Johnson Institute, Minneapolis, MN, 1991.

146. Cermak TL, Brown S: Interactional group therapy with the Adult Children of Alcoholics. International Journal of Group Psychotherapy, 32(3), 375-389.

147. Chafetz ME et al: Children of alcoholics: observations in a child guidance clinic. *Quarterly Journal of Studies on Alcohol,* 32: 687-698, 1971.

148. Chafetz ME et al: Alcoholism: A positive view. Chapter in **American Handbook of Psychiatry,** 2nd Edition, Vol 3. Basic Books, NY, 1974.

149. Chandler M: **Late Bloomers:** Weekly Inspirations For Women In Their Prime. Health Communications, Deerfield Beach, FL, 1991.

150. Chandler M: **Gentle Reminders For Co-dependents.** Health Communications, Deerfield Beach, FL, 1989.

151. Christozov C, Toteva S: Abuse and neglect of children brought up in families with an alcoholic father in Bulgaria. Child Abuse and Neglect, 13: 153-155, 1989.

152. The Child (special issue on the child and child archetype). *Parabola,* Vol. 4, No. 3, 1979.

153. The Child Within, The Child Without. Special issue of *Psychological Perspectives.* No. 21, Los Angeles, 1989.

154. Cicirelli VG: Sibling relationships throughout the life cycle. In LL A bate (Ed.), **The Handbook Of Family Psychology And Therapy.** The Dorsey Press, Homewood, IL, 177-214, 1985.

155. Clair D, Genest M: Variables associated with the adjustment of offspring of alcoholic fathers. *J. Stud. Alc.* 48, 345-355, 1987.

156. Clarren S, Smith D: The fetal alcohol syndrome: A review of the world literature. *New England Journal of Medicine,* 298: 1063-1067, 1978.

157. Cleveland M: Treatment of co-dependent women through the use of mental imagery. *Alcoholism Treatment Quarterly,* 4(1): 27-41, 1987.

158. Cloninger CR et al: Inheritance of alcohol abuse. *Archives of General Psychiatry,* 38: 861-868, 1981.

159. **Co-dependency:** Anthology. Health Communications, Deerfield Beach, FL, 1985, 1990.

160. Coleman E: Marital and relationship problems among chemically dependent and co-dependent relationships. *Journal of Chemical Dependency Treatment,* 1(1): 39-59, 1987.

161. Collett L: Step by step (personal story of adult child recovery). *Mother Jones,* July/Aug 1988.

162. Conge JP: **The Body As Shadow.** North Atlantic Books, Berkeley, 1988.

163. Corder BF et al: Brief review of literature on daughters of alcoholic fathers. *N.C.J. Mental Health,* 10 (20), 37-4. 1984.

164. Cork M: **The Forgotten Children.** Addiction Research Foundation, Toronto, Canada, 1969.

165. **A Course in Miracles.** Foundation for Inner Peace, Box 635, Tiburon, CA, 1976.

166. Courtois CA: The incest experience and its aftermath. *Victimology:* An International Journal, 4: 337-347, 1979.

167. Courtois CA: **Healing the Incest Wound:** Adult Survivors in Therapy. W W Norton and Company, NY, 1988.

168. Covington S, Beckett L: **Leaving the Enchanted Forest:** The path from relationship addiction to intimacy. Harper & Row, San Francisco, 1988.

169. Cross S: Study of children of alcoholics: Their identification and their relationship to other selected variables. *Dissertation Abstracts International,* 50(2): 360-A, 1989.

170. Cruse JR: **Painful Affairs:** Looking For Love Through Addiction And Co-dependency. Health Communications, Deerfield Beach, FL, 1989.

171. Cutter C, Cutter H; Experience and change in Al-Anon family groups: Adult Children of Alcoholics. *J. Studies on Alcohol,* 48: 29-32, 1987.

172. Davies WH et al: Parental psychopathology and child-rearing practices in young alcoholic families. Meetings of the Research Society on Alcoholism, 1989.

173. Davis D: The family in alcoholism. In: *Phenomenology and Treatment of Alcoholism,* Spectrum Publications, NY, 1980.

174. Davis D: **Alcoholism Treatment:** An integrative family and individual approach. Gardner Press, NY, 1987.

175. Dean RK: Post-traumatic stress disorder in Adult Children of Alcoholics. *The Counselor,* pp. 11-13, 1988.

175a. Deikman A.: **The Observing Self.** Beacon Press, Boston, MA, 1982.

176. Delson N & Clark M: Group therapy with sexually molested children. *Child Welfare,* LX(3): 175-182, 1981.

177. DeRohan C: **Right Use of Will:** Healing & Evolving the Emotional Body. One World Publications, Sante Fe, NM, 1986.

178. DesRoches B: Working through Conflict; and Faces of Recovery (two booklets). Hazelden, Center City, MN, 1990.

179. DesRoches B: **Reclaiming Your Self** — The co-dependent's recovery plan. Dell, NY, 1990.

180. Diamond J: Series of books on recovery, including: "Love" Addictions — for women, Fatal Attractions, Healing Male Co-Dependency, Looking for Love in All the Wrong Places (sex addiction), and the Warrior's Journey Home. Available from Fifth Wave Press, Box 9355, San Rafael, CA, 94912.

181. Diamond J: **Love It, Don't Label It** (and other books, available from above address).

182. Dinicola VF: The child's predicament in families with a mood disorder. *Psychiatric clinics of North America,* 12(4): 933-49, Dec 1989.

183. Doi T: **The Anatomy of Dependence.** Kodansha Intl/Harper, distributor, 1973.

184. Dossey L: **Beyond Illness:** Discovering the Experience of Health. Shambhala. Boulder, CO, 1985.

185. Dossey L: **Recovering the Soul:** A scientific and spiritual search. Bantam, NY, 1989.

185a. Dossey L: **The Wounded Healer.** In Church D & Sherr A (eds): The Heart of The Healer. Aslan Publishing, Box 496, NY, NY, 10032, 1987.

186. Drake RE, Vaillant GE: Predicting alcoholism and personality disorder in a 33-year longitudinal study of children of alcoholics. *British Journal of Addiction,* 83: 799-807, 1988.

187. Drossman DA et al: Sexual and physical abuse in women with functional or organic gastrointestinal disorders. *Annals Internal Med,* 113: 828-833, 1990.

188. Dulfano C: **Families, Alcoholism & Recovery:** Ten Stories. Hazelden, Center City, MN, 1982.

189. Dura JR, Beck SJ: A comparison of family functioning when mothers have chronic pain. *Pain* 35(1): 79-89, Oct, 1988.

190. Earle et al: **Lonely All The Time:** Recognizing, understanding and overcoming sex addiction. Simon & Schuster, NY, 1989.

191. Edinger E: **Ego & Archetype.** Penguin, NY, 1973.

192. Edwards P et al: Wives of alcoholics: A critical review and analysis. *Quarterly Journal of Studies on Alcohol,* 34: 112-132, 1973.

193. Elkin M: **Families Under The Influence.** W.W. Norton & Co, NY, 1984.

194. Ellenson GS: Detecting a history of incest: A predictive syndrome. *Social Casework,* 66: 525-532, 1985.

195. Ells A: **One-way Relationships:** When you love them more than they love you. Nelson, Nashville, 1990.

196. Ellsworth BA: **Living in Love with Yourself.** Breakthrough Publications, Salt Lake City, 1988.

197. El-Quebaly N: The offspring of alcoholics: Outcome predictors. *Journal of Children in Contemporary Society,* 15: 3-12, 1982.

198. El-Quebaly N, Offord DR: The offspring of alcoholics: A critical review. *The American Journal of Psychiatry,* 134(4): 357-365.

199. Engel B: **The Emotionally Abused Woman.** Lowell House, Los Angeles, 1990.

200. English ES: The Emotional stress of psychotherapeutic practice. *Journal of American Academy of Psychoanalysis,* 4: 191-201, 1976.

201. Erikson EH: **Childhood and Society** (2nd ed.). Norton, NY, 1963.

202. Ervin CS et al: Alcoholic from birth to age 18. *Journal of Studies on Alcohol,* 47(1): 34-40, 1986.

203. Faltz BG , Madover S: Codependency in AIDS: Clinical perspective. *EAP Digest,* 8(4): 56, 1988.

204. Farmer S: **Adult Children as Husbands, Wives and Lovers:** A solutions book. Lowell House, Los Angeles, 1990.

205. Farmer S: **Adult Children of Abusive Parents.** Lowell House, Los Angeles, 1989.

206. Ferrucci P: **What We May Be.** JP Tarcher, Inc, Los Angeles, 1980.

207. Filstead WJ et al: Comparing the family environments of alcoholic and normal families. *Journal of Alcohol and Drug Education,* 26(2): 24-31, 1981.

208. Fine EW et al: Behavioral disorders in children with parental alcoholism. *Annals of the New York Academy of Sciences,* 273: 507-517.

209. Finkelhor D: **Sexually Victimized Children.** Free Press, NY, 1979.

210. Fischer JL et al: Measuring codependency. *Alcoholism Treatment Quarterly,* 8(1): 87-99, 1991.

211. Finkelhor D: Risk factors in the sexual victimization of children. *Child Abuse and Neglect,* 4: 265-273, 1980.

212. Fishel R: **Healing Energy.** Health Communications, Deerfield Beach, FL, 1991.

213. Fleury TM: Child-rearing practices of alcoholic mothers and their children's behavior. *Dissertation Abstracts International,* 49(8): 3436-B, 1989.

214. Forward S, Buck C: **Betrayal Of Innocence:** Incest and its devastation. JP Tarcher, Inc, Los Angeles, 1972.

215. Forward S, Buck C: **Obsessive Love: When Passion Holds You Prisoner.** Bantam, NY, 1991.

216. Forward S, Torres J: **Men Who Hate Women and the Women Who Love Them.** Bantam, NY, 1986.

21, . Fossum M, Mason M: **Facing Shame:** Families in recovery. WW Norton, NY, 1986.

218. Fossum M: **Catching Fire:** Men's renewal and recovery through crisis. Hazelden, Center City, MN, 1989.

219. Fox M: Is the Catholic church today a dysfunctional family? *Creation* Nov/ Dec, pp 23-37, 1988.

220. Fraser S: **My Father's House:** A Memoir of Incest and of Healing. Ticknor & Fields, NY, 1988.

221. Freud S: The aetiology of hysteria. In Strachey J (ed): **The Standard Edition of the Complete Psychological Works of Sigmund Freud.** Hogarth Press, London, 1953-1974.

222. Friedman E: **Generation to Generation:** Family process in church & synagogue. Guilford Press, NY, 1985.

223. Friel JC: Co-dependency assessment inventory: A preliminary research tool. *Focus on Family and Chemical Dependency,* 8: 20-21, 1985.

224. Friel JC, Friel LD: The iceberg model of co-dependency. *Focus,* Nov/Dec, 1987.

225. Friel JC, Friel LD: **Adult Children: The Secrets Of Dysfunctional Families.** Health Communications, Deerfield Beach, FL, 1988.

226. Friel JC, Friel LD: Excellent word, lousy diagnosis? Clarifying the concept of co-dependency. *Focus on Chemically Dependent Families,* 11(6): 30-31, 1988-89.

227. Friesen VL, Casella NT: The rescuing therapist: A duplication of the pathogenic family system. *The American Journal of Family Therapy,* 10: 57-61, 1982.

228. Fuhlrodt RL (ed): **Psychodrama:** Its application to ACoA and substance abuse treatment. Thomas W. Perrin, E. Rutherford, NJ, (800-321-7912), 1990.

229. Gabe J: Adolescent co-dependency. *Counselor,* Mar/Apr: 20-23, 1990.

230. Gabrielli WF Jr, Mednick SA: Intellectual performance in children of alcoholics. *Journal of Nervous and Mental Disease,* 171(7): 444-447, 1983.

231. Galanter M et al (eds): Recent Developments in Alcoholism. Vol. 9. **Children of Alcoholics.** Grune & Stratton, NY, 1991.

232. Gardano AC: Revised scoring method of kinetic family drawings and its application to children from alcoholic families. *Dissertation Abstracts International,* 49(4): 1385-B, 1988.

233. Garmezy N: Children at Risk: The search for the antecedents of schizophrenia. Part II: Ongoing research programs, issues, and intervention. *Schizophrenia Bulletin,* 9: 55-125, 1974.

234. Garmezy N: Stressors of childhood. In N Garmezy & M Rutter (Eds), **Stress, coping and development in children.** McGraw-Hill, NY, 1983.

235. Garmezy N: Stress-resistant children: The search for protective factors. In JE Stevenson (Ed), **Recent research in developmental psychopathology.** Pergamon Press, Oxford, 1985.

236. Gawain S: **Creative Visualization.** Bantam Books, NY, 1982.

237. Geiser R: **Hidden Victims.** Beacon, Boston, 1978.

238. Gelinas DJ: The persisting negative effects of incest. *Psychiatry,* 46: 312-332, 1983.

239. Gelles RJ, Cornell CP: **Intimate Violence in Families.** Sage, Beverly Hills, CA, 1985.

240. Gelles RJ, Straus MA: Is violence toward children increasing? *Journal of Interpersonal Violence,* 2: 212-222, 1987.

241. Gendlen E: **Focusing.** Bantam Books, NY, 1981.

242. Gil J: **Unless You Become Like a Little Child:** Seeking the inner child in our spiritual journey. Paulist Press, NY, 1985.

243. Gil E: **Treatment of Adult Survivors of Childhood Abuse.** Launch Press, Box 491, Walnut Creek, CA, 94598, 1989. (415-943-7603).

244. Gil E: **The Healing Power of Play:** Working with abused children. Guilford, NY, 1991.

245. Gil E: Multiple Personality Disorder, (Booklet for Recovering People). Launch Press, Walnut Creek, CA, 1990.

246. Gilbert RM: Caffeine as a drug of abuse. In Israel Y et al, (eds), *Research Advances in Alcohol and Drug Problems.* Wiley, NY, 1976.

247. Giles R: PTSD: the relationship between co-dependence and sexual abuse trauma. 1st Co-dependency Conference, Scottsdale, AZ, Sept 1989.

248. Gioretto H: Humanistic treatment of father daughter incest. *Journal of Humanistic Psychology,* 18(4): 59-76, 1978.

249. Glatt MM-chart cited in: Royce J: **Alcohol Problems and Alcoholism.** Macmillan/Free Press, NY, 1981.

250. Goodman LM: Support for the family of the person with alcohol-related problems. In: *The Community Health Nurse and Alcohol Related Problems,* National Institute on Alcohol Abuse and Alcoholism, Rockville, MD, 1978.

251. Goodwin DW et al: Alcohol problems in adoptees raised apart from alcoholic biological parents. *Archives of General Psychiatry,* 28: 238-243, 1973.

252. Goodwin DW et al: Drinking problems in adopted and nonadopted sons of alcoholics. *Archives of General Psychiatry,* 31: 164-169, 1974.

253. Goodwin DW et al: Alcoholism and the hyperactive child syndrome. *Journal of Nervous and Mental Diseases,* 160: 349-353, 1975.

254. Goodwin DW: Genetic determinants of alcoholism. In: **The Diagnosis and Treatment of Alcoholism.** McGraw-Hill, NY, 1979.

255. Goodwin R: Adult Children of Alcoholics. *Journal of Counseling and Development,* 66: 162-16, 1987.

256. Gordon LH: **Love Knots.** Dell, NY, 1990.

257. Gravitz HL, Bowden JD: Therapeutic issues of Adult Children of Alcoholics, *Alcohol Health and Research World,* 8(4), 25-36, 1984.

258. Gravitz HL, Bowden JD: **Guide to Recovery:** a book for Adult Children of Alcoholics. Simon & Schuster, NY, 1985.

259. Gravitz HL: Is the honeymoon over or the marriage just begun: stirrings of an anti-recovery backlash. *Changes,* Sept/Oct 1991.

260. Gravitz HL: Breaking the Spell: Adult Children of Trauma (ACT), Vol. 1 for adult children, Vol. 2 for professionals. 5266 Hollister Ave., #220, Santa Barbara, CA 93111 (working title, available from author, for 1992).

261. Greenleaf J: Co-alcoholic, para-alcoholic: Who's who and what's the difference? (Booklet), MAC Publications, Denver, 1981.

262. Greenspan S: on *Nova,* program on emotions, PBS, 1987.

263. Griner ME, Griner PF: **Alcoholism and the family.** In: M Lipkin Jr et al, (eds), Alcoholism: A guide for the primary care physician, Springer-Verlag, NY, NY, 1988.

264. Groth AN, Burgess AW: Male rape: Offenders and victims. *American Journal of Psychiatry,* 137: 806-810, 1980.

265. Guerin PJ: Family Therapy: The first 25 years in Guerin PJ (ed): **Family Therapy:** theory & practice. Gardner Press, NY, 1976.

266. Guntrip H: **Psychoanalytical Theory, Therapy and the Self:** A basic guide to the human personality in Freud, Erickson, Klein, Sullivan, Fairbairn, Hartman, Jacobsen and Winnicott. Basic Books, Harper Torchbooks, NY, NY, 1973.

267. Haber JD, Roos C: Effects of spouse abuse and sexual abuse in the development and maintenance of chronic pain in women. *Advances in Pain Research & Therapy,* 9: 889-895, 1985.

268. Haberman P: Childhood symptoms in children of alcoholics and comparison group parents. *Journal of Marriage and the Family,* 28: 152-154, 1966.

269. Hall JCL: Exploration of self-esteem in children of alcoholic parents. *Dissertation Abstracts International,* 48(12): 3679-B, 1988.

270. Hall SF, Wray LM: Co-dependency: nurses who give too much. American Journal of Nursing pp. 1456-60, November 1989.

271. Halliday L: **The Silent Scream:** The reality of sexual abuse. Sexual Abuse Victims Anonymous, R R No 1, Campbell River, BC, Canada V9W 3S4, 1981.

272. Halpern HM: **How to Break Your Addiction to a Person.** Bantam, NY, 1982.

273. Hanson JW: Fetal alcohol syndrome: Experience with 41 patients. *Journal of the American Medical Association,* 235: 1458-1460, 1976.

274. Harbula PJ: Reframing the family: an interview with Sheldon Z. Karmer. *Meditation*, Spring pp 44-46, 1991.

275. Harman WW: Redefining the possible: the need for a restructuring of science. *The Quest*, Autumn 1989.

276. Harman W, Hormann J: **Creative Work:** The constructive role of business in transforming society. Knowledge Systems, Indianapolis, 1990.

277. Harper JM, Hoopes MH: **Uncovering Shame:** An approach integrating individuals and their family systems. WW Norton, NY, 1990.

278. Harris B: **Full Circle.** Pocket Books/Simon & Schuster, NY, 1990.

279. Harris B: **Spiritual Awakening: Healing into Unconditional Love:** When the Twelfth Step happens first. (Working title) Health Communications, Deerfield Beach, FL, 1992.

280. Harrop-Griffiths J et al: The association between chronic pelvic pain, psychiatric diagnoses, and childhood sexual abuse. *Obstetrics & Gynecology*, 71: 589-594, 1988.

281. Harwood MK, Leonard KE: Family history of alcoholism, youthful antisocial behavior and problem drinking among DWI offenders. *J Studies on Alcohol*, 50(3): 210-216, May 1989.

282. Hayes J: **Smart Love.** Tarcher, Los Angeles, 1989.

283. Hazelden: Series of pamphlets and booklets on recovery. Center City, MN, 1991, (1-800-328-9000).

284. Hecht M: Children of alcoholics are children at risk. *American Journal of Nursing*, 73: 1764-1767, 1973.

285. Heiney SP: Assessing & intervening with dysfunctional families. *Oncology Nursing Forum*, 15(5): 585-590, Sept/Oct 1988.

286. Hellemans A, Bunch B: **The Timetables of History.** Touchstone/Simon & Schuster, NY, 1985.

287. Hellemans A, Bunch B: **The Timetables of Science.** Touchstone/Simon & Schuster, NY, 1991.

288. Hendricks G, Hendricks K: **Conscious Loving:** The journey to co-commitment. Bantam, NY, 1990.

289. Hendrix H: **Getting the Love You Want.** Harper & Row, 1988.

290. Heraty V: Personal communication. Chicago, 1985.

291. Herman JL: **Father-Daughter Incest.** Harvard University Press, Cambridge, MA, 1981.

292. Hetherington SE: Children of alcoholics: An emerging mental health issue. *Archives of Psychiatric Nursing*, 2(4): 251-255, 1988.

293. Hibbard S: The diagnosis and treatment of Adult Children of Alcoholics as a specialized therapeutic population. *Psychotherapy*, 24(4), 779-785, 1987.

294. Hill S: **New Clothes from Old Threads:** Daily reflections for recovering adults. Recovery Publications, San Diego, 1991.

295. Hill SY et al: Event-related potential characteristics in children of alcoholics from high density families. *Alcoholism:* Clinical and Experimental Research, 14(1): 6-16, 1990.

296. Hindman M: Children of alcoholic parents. *Alcohol Health and Research World,* pp 2-6, Winter 1975-1976.

297. Hindman M: Child abuse and neglect: The alcohol connection. *Alcohol Health and Research World,* pp 2-7, Spring 1977.

298. Hobe P: **Lovebound:** Recovery from an alcoholic family. NAL/Penguin, NY, 1990.

299. Hodgson H W: **Parents recover too:** When your child comes home from treatment. Hazelden, Minneapolis, MN 1988.

300. Hoffman E: **The Right to be Human** — A Biography of Abraham Maslow. Tarcher, LA, 1988.

301. Hoffman B: **No One Is to Blame:** Freedom from compulsive self-defeating behavior. Science and Behavior Books, Palo Alto, 1979.

302. Hofford CW: Adult Children of Alcoholics as public high school teachers: comparable risks for occupational burnout. *Dissertation Abstracts International,* 51(3): 749-A, 1990.

303. Holmes GP et al: Chronic fatigue syndrome: A working case definition. *Annals of Internal Medicine,* 108: 387-389, 1988.

304. Horney K: **Neurosis and Human Growth.** Norton, NY, 1950.

305. Horney K: **The Neurotic Personality of Our Time.** Norton, NY, 1952.

306. Hornik EL: **You and Your Alcoholic Parent.** A Young Person's Guide to Understanding and Coping. Association Press, NY, 1974.

307. Horowitz MJ: Psychological response to serious life events. In Hamilton V, Warburton DM (eds.), **Human Stress and Cognition:** An Informational Processing Approach. Eiley, Chichester, 1979.

308. Horowitz M: **Stress Response Syndromes.** (2nd ed.), Aronson, NY, 1986.

309. Houston J: **The Search for the Beloved.** JP Tarcher, Inc, Los Angeles, 1987.

310. Hunter M: **Abused Boys:** The neglected victims of child abuse. Lexington Books, NY, 1990.

311. Imhof JE: Countertransference issues in alcoholism and drug addiction. *Psychiatric Annals,* 21(5): 292-306, 1991.

312. Institute of Noetic Sciences: The Altruistic Spirit, 1987-1990. Sausilito, CA, 1990.

313. Jackson J: The adjustment of the family to the crisis of alcoholism, National Council on Alcoholism, NY, 1954.

314. Jacob T: An introduction to the alcoholic's family. In Galanter, M. (ed), *Currents in Alcoholism,* Vol 7, Grune and Stratton, NY, 1980.

315. Jacob T & Leonard K: Psychosocial functioning in children of alcoholic fathers, depressed fathers and control fathers. *Journal of Studies on Alcohol,* 47(5), 373-380, 1986.

316. Janzen C: Family treatment for alcoholism: A review. *Social Work,* 23(2): 135-141, 1978.

317. Jellinek EM: The Disease Concept of Alcoholism. Hillhouse Press, Highland Park, NJ, (*J Studies Alc,* Rutgers, New Brunswick NJ distributor), 1960.

318. Jesse RC: **Children in Recovery:** Healing the parent-child relationship in alcoholic/addictive families. WW Norton, NY, 1989.

319. Jesse RC: **Healing the Hurt:** Rebuilding relationships with your children. Johnson Institute, MN, 1991.

320. Johnson JL, Bennett LA: School-Aged Children of Alcoholics: Theory and Research. Rutgers University Center of Alcohol Studies Pamphlet Series, New Brunswick, NJ, 1988.

321. Johnson JL, Bennett LA: Adult Children of Alcoholics: Theory and Research. Rutgers University Center of Alcohol Studies Pamphlet Series, New Brunswick, NJ, 1989.

322. Johnson JL, Rolf JE: Cognitive functioning in children from alcoholic and non-alcoholic families. *British Journal of Addiction,* 83(7): 849-857, 1988.

323. Johnson JL, Rolf JE: When children change: Research perspectives on children of alcoholics. In R. L. Collins et al: **Alcohol and the Family:** Research and Clinical Perspectives, Guilford, NY, 1990.

324. Johnson S et al: Drinking, drinking styles and drug use in children of alcoholics, depressives and controls. *Journal of Studies on Alcohol,* 50(5): 427-431, 1989.

325. Johnson VE: **I'll Quit Tomorrow.** Harper & Row, NY, 1973.

326. Johnson RA: **Inner work.** Harper & Row, San Francisco, 1986.

327. Jones JF et al: Evidence for active Epstein-Barr virus infection in patients with persistent, unexplained illnesses. *Annals of Internal Medicine,* 102: 1-7, 1985.

328. Jones JW, Pilat S: Children of Alcoholics Screening Test (CAST), in the Children of Alcoholics Research Series, Camelot Unlimited, Chicago, 1983.

329. Jordan JV: Empathy and Self Boundaries (Work in Progress No 16) Stone Center for Developmental Services and Studies, Wellesley College, Massachusetts, 1984.

330. Jourard S: **The Undiscovered Self,** revised edition. Van Nostrand, NY, 1971.

331. Joy B: **Joy's Way.** JP Tarcher, Inc, Los Angeles, 1979.

331a Jung CG: **Memories, Dreams and Reflections,** ed. Winston R, Winston C, Pantheon, NY, 1963.

332. Justice B, Justice R: **The Broken Taboo.** Human Sciences Press, NY, 1979.

333. Justice B, Justice R: **The Abusing Family.** (Revised ed.), Insight/Plenum, NY, 1990.

334. Kaij L: Alcoholism in Twins. **Studies on the Etiology and Sequels of Abuse of Alcohol,** Almqvist & Wiksell Publishers, Stockholm, 1984.

335. Kane E: **Recovering from Incest:** Imagination and the healing process. Sigo Press, 1989.

336. Kasl CD: **Women, Sex, and Addiction:** A search for love and power. Harper & Row, NY, 1990.

337. Kasl CD: **Many Roads, One Journey:** Moving beyond the Twelve Steps. Harper & Row, NY, 1992.

338. Kauffmann C et al: Superkids: Competent children of psychotic mothers. *American Journal of Psychiatry,* 136: 1398-1402, 1979.

339. Kaufman A et al: Male rape victims: Noninstitutionalized assault. *American Journal of Psychiatry,* 137: 221-223, 1980.

340. Kaufman E, Kaufman P: **Family Therapy of Drug and Alcohol Abuse.** Halsted Press, NY, 1978.

341. Kaufman E, Kaufman P (eds): **Family Treatment of Alcohol and Drug Problems.** Gardner Press, NY, 1979.

342. Kaufman E: Will the ACoA movement include the psychiatrist? Newsletter, American Academy of Psychiatrists in Alcoholism and Addictions. Vol III, No 1, Spring 1988.

343. Kaufman G, Raphael L: **Stick Up For Yourself:** Every kid's guide to personal power and positive self-esteem. Free Spirits Press, Minneapolis, 1990.

344. Kaufman G: **The Psychology of Shame.** Springer, NY, 1989.

345. Kaye Y: **Credit, Cash And Co-dependency:** The money connection. Health Communications, Deerfield Beach, FL, 1991.

346. Kaye Y: **The Child That Never Was:** Grieving Your Past To Grow Into Your Future. Health Communications, Deerfield Beach, FL, 1990.

347. Keirsey D, Bates M: **Please Understand Me:** character & temperament types. Promethous Nemosis Book Company, Del Mar, CA, 1978.

348. Keleman S: **Patterns of Distress:** Emotional insults and human form. Center Press, Berkeley, 1989.

349. Kellerman J: **Grief:** A basic reaction to alcoholism. Hazelden, Minneapolis, MN, 1977.

350. Kellogg T: Series of tapes on co-dependence & intimacy. 20300 Excelsior Boulevard, Minneapolis, MN 55331.

351. Kellogg T, with Harrison M: **Broken Toys Broken Dreams:** Understanding Co-dependency, compulsive behavior & family. BRAT, Amherst, MA, 1990.

352. Kellogg T, Harrison M: **Finding Balance:** 12 Priorities For Interdependence And Joyful Living. Health Communications, Deerfield Beach, FL, 1991.

353. Kern JC: Management of children of alcoholics. In Zimberg S, Wallace J & Blume S B, **Practical approaches to alcoholism psychotherapy** (2nd ed) New York, Plenum, 1985.

354. Kerr ME, Bowen M: **Family Evaluation:** An approach based on Bowen theory. Norton, NY, 1988.

355. Kijek JC: Co-dependency — what is it? *Florida Nurse,* 37(2): 11, Feb 1989.

356. Kitchens JA: **Pathways to Recovery:** new life for the diminished person. ADS-CO, Dallas, TX, 1990.

357. Kitchens JA: **Beyond the Shame:** understanding and treating the child molester: ADS-CO, Dallas, TX, 1990.

358. Kitchens JA: **Understanding and Treating Co-dependence.** Prentice-Hall, Englewood Cliffs, NJ, 1991.

359. Kleeman KM: Families in crisis due to multiple trauma. *Critical Care Nursing Clinics of North America,* 1(1): 23-31, Mar 1989.

360. Knittle B, Tuana S: Group therapy as primary treatment for adolescent victims of intrafamilial sexual abuse. *Clinical Social Work Journal,* 8(4): 237-242, 1980.

361. Knop J et al: A prospective study of young men at high risk for alcoholism: School behavior and achievement. *Journal of Studies on Alcohol,* 46(4): 273-278, 1985.

362. Knowleton JM, Chaitin RD: **Enabling.** Perrin & Tregett, Rutherford, NJ, (800-321-7912), 1985.

363. Kogan KL et al: Personality disturbance in wives of alcoholics. *Quarterly Journal of Studies on Alcoholism,* 1963.

364. Kohut H: **The Analysis of the Self.** International Univ. Press, NY, 1971.

365. Kritsberg W: **The Adult Children Of Alcoholics Syndrome:** From Discovery To Recovery. Health Communications, Pompano Beach, FL, 1985.

366. Kritsberg W: **Healing Together.** Health Communications, Deerfield Beach, FL, 1990.

367. Kritsberg W: **The Invisible Wound:** Healing childhood sexual trauma. Bantam, NY, in process for 1992.

368. Kunzman KA: **The Healing Way:** Adult recovery from childhood sexual abuse. Hazelden, MN, 1990.

369. Kurtz E: **Not-God:** A history of Alcoholics Anonymous. Hazelden, Center City, MN, 1979.

370. Laing R: **The Politics of the Family and Other Essays.** Vintage Books, NY, 1972.

371. Lamb ME: Sibling relationships across the lifespan: An overview and introduction. In M.E. Lamb & B. Sutton-Smith (Eds.), **Sibling relationships:** Their nature and significance across the lifespan, Lawrence Erlbaum, Hillsdale, NJ, 1982.

372. Larsen E: **Stage II Recovery:** Life beyond addiction. Harper & Row, San Francisco, 1985.

373. Lash J: **The Seeker's Handbook:** The complete guide to spiritual pathfinding. Harmony/Crown, NY, 1990.

374. Lasson MA: **New Thought or a Modern Religious Approach:** The philosophy of health, happiness, and prosperity. Philosophical Library, NY, 1985.

375. Latimer JE: **Living Binge-Free:** A personal guide to victory over compulsive eating. Living Quest, Boulder, CO, 1990.

376. Lazare A: Shame and humiliation in the medical encounter. *Archives of Internal Medicine,* 147: 1653-1658, Sept 1987.

377. Lazaris: Series of Spiritual-Psychological Teachings. Available from Concept Synergy, 302 S. County Rd, Ste 109, Palm Beach, FL 33480 (407-588-9599).

378. Lazaris: The crisis of martyrhood. Tape from above source, 1985.

379. LeBlanc D: **You Can't Quit Until You Know What's Eating You.** Health Communications, Deerfield Beach, FL, 1990.

380. Lee J: **The Flying Boy:** Healing the Wounded Man. Health Communications, Deerfield Beach, FL, 1988.

381. Lee J: **The Flying Boy, Book II — The Journey Continues.** Health Communications, Deerfield Beach, FL, 1990.

382. Leichtman RR, Japiske C: **Active Meditation:** The Western Tradition. Ariel Press, Columbus, 1982.

383. Leite E: How it feels to be chemically dependent (booklet). Johnson Institute, Minneapolis, 1987.

384. Leventhal JM: Have there been changes in the epidemiology of sexual abuse of children during the 20th century? *Pediatrics,* 82: 766-773, 1988.

385. Levin P: **Becoming the Way We Are:** An introduction to personal development in recovery and in life. Health Communications, Deerfield Beach, FL, 1988.

386. Levin P: **Cycles of Power:** A user's guide to the seven seasons of life. Health Communications, Deerfield Beach, FL, 1988.

387. Levine R: The pain of co-dependence (editorial) Rn 53(2): 7, Feb 1990.

388. Levine S, Ram Dass: **Grist for the Mill,** Celestial Arts, Berekely, CA, 1987.

389. Levinson DJ et al: **The Season's of a Man's Life.** Ballantine, NY, 1978.

390. Lew M: **Victims No Longer.** Perennial Library, NY, 1990.

391. Lewis DC, Williams CN: **Providing Care For Children Of Alcoholics:** Clinical And Research Perspectives. Health Communications, Pompano Beach, FL, 1986.

392. Liepman MR et al: The use of Family Behavior Loop Mapping for substance abuse. *Family Relations,* 38:282-287, 1989.

393. Lincoln R, Janze E: Process of recovery: Its impact on adult children and grandchildren of alcoholics. *Alcoholism Treatment Quarterly,* 5(1/2): 249-259, 1988.

394. Lipman AJ: Causal attributions in offspring of alcoholics. *Alcoholism Treatment Quarterly,* 7(4): 31-46, 1990.

395. Lloyd R, Fossum M: **True Selves:** Twelve-Step recovery from co-dependency. Hazelden/Harper Collins, San Francisco, 1992.

396. Lord DB: Parental alcoholism and the mental health of children: A bibliography and brief observations. *Journal of Alcohol and Drug Education*, 29: 1-11, 1983.

397. Love P, with Robinson J: **The Emotional Incest Syndrome.** Bantam, NY, 1990.

398. Maeder T: **Wounded Healers.** The Atlantic, Jan, pp 37-47, 1989.

399. MacDonald DI, Blume SB: Children of alcoholics: Editorial review. *American Journal of Diseases of Children*, 140, 750-754, 1986.

400. MacFarlane K et al: **Sexual Abuse of Children:** Selected Readings. National Center on Child Abuse and Neglect, Office of Human Development Services, U.S. Department of Health and Human Services, Washington, DC, 1980.

401. Malin A, Grotstein JS: Projective identification in the therapeutic process. *International Journal of Psychoanalysis*, 47(1), 26-31, 1966.

402. Mannariono AP, Cohen JA: A clinical-demographic study of sexually abused children. *Child Abuse and Neglect*, 10: 17-23, 1986.

403. Manning DT et al: The prevalence of Type A personality in the children of alcoholics. *Alcoholism: Clinical and Experimental Research*, 10(2): 184-189, 1986.

404. Marcus AM: Academic achievement in elementary school children of alcoholic mothers. *Journal of Clinical Psychology*, 42(2): 372-376.

405. Markowitz L M: Trial by newspaper. *Family Therapy Networker*, March/April 1990.

406. Marlin E: **Hope:** New Choices and Recovery Strategies for Adult Children of Alcoholics. Harper & Row, New York, 1987.

407. Martin D: Review of the popular literature on co-dependency. *Contemporary Drug Problems*, 15(3): 383-398, 1988.

408. Maslow A: **Motivation and Personality.** Harper & Row, NY, 1954.

409. Maslow A: **Toward a Psychology of Being.** Van Nostrand, Princeton, 1961.

410. Masson JM: **The Assault on Truth:** Freud's suppression of the seduction theory. Farrar, Straus, and Giroux, NY, 1984.

411. Masson JM: **Against Therapy:** Emotional tyranny and the myth of psychological healing. MacMillian, NY, 1988.

412. Masson JM: **The Complete Letters of Sigmund Freud to Wilhelm Fliess, 1887-1904.** Harvard University Press, Cambridge, MA, 1986.

413. Masson JM: **Final Analysis:** the making and unmaking of a psychoanalyst. Addison-Wesley, NY, 1990.

414. Masterson JF: **The Search for the Real Self:** Unmasking the personality disorders of our age. Free Press/MacMillan, NY, 1988.

415. Matthews-Simonton S, in Simonton, Matthews-Simonton Creighton: **Getting Well Again.** Bantam Books, NY, 1978.

416. Matousek M: America's Darkest Secret. *Common Boundary*, March/April 1991.

417. May D, Maniacek MA: Effects of co-dependency on Adult Children of Alcoholics. *Alcoholism*, 23(1-2): 51-55, 1987.

418. Mayer J, Black R: The relationship between alcoholism and child abuse and neglect. In Seixas F (Ed.), **Currents in Alcoholism.** Grune & Stratton, Vol II, 429-444, New York, 1977.

419. McCabe J: Children in need. *Alcohol Health and Research World*, 2: 2-12, 1977.

420. McCann IL, Pearlman LA: **Psychological Trauma and the Adult Survivor:** Theory, Therapy, Transformation. Brunner/Mazel, NY, 1991.

421. McCann E, Shannon D: **The Two Step:** The Dance Toward Intimacy. Grove Press, NY, 1985.

422. McCann IL, Pearlman LA: Vicarious Traumatization: A contextual model for understanding the effects of trauma on helpers. *Journal of Traumatic Stress*, 3(1): 131-149, 1990.

423. McCarthy B, McCarthy E: **Sexual Awareness:** Enhancing Sexual Pleasure. Carroll & Graf, NY, 1984.

424. McConnell P: **A Workbook For Healing:** Adult Children of Alcoholics. Harper & Row, NY, 1986.

425. McCubbin HI, et al: Family stress and coping: A decade review. *Journal of Marriage and the Family*, 42: 855-871, 1980.

426. McDonnell R, Callahan R: **Hope for healing:** Good news for Adult Children of Alcoholics. New York, Paulist Press, 1987.

427. McElfrish O: Supportive groups for teenagers of the alcoholic parent: A preliminary report. *Med Ecol Clin Res*, 3: 26-29, 1970.

428. Meacham A: Co-dependency: The struggle to find a workable definition. *Focus*, 12(1): 16-17, 1989.

429. Meiselman K: **Incest.** Jossey-Bass, San Francisco, CA, 1978.

430. Mellander DH: Children of alcoholics: High-risk students in the classroom. *Dissertation Abstracts International*, 50(10): 3123A-3124A, 1990.

431. Mellody P, Miller, AW: **Breaking free:** Recovery Workbook for Facing Co-dependence. Harper & Row, New York, NY: 1989.

432. Mellody P, Miller AW & Miller JK: **Facing codependence:** What It Is, Where It Comes From, How It Sabotages Our Lives. San Francisco, CA: Harper & Row, 1989.

433. Mendenhall W: course on co-dependence. Rutgers Summer School of Alcohol Studies, New Brunswick, NJ, June 1987-present.

434. Merikangas KR et al: Depressives with secondary alcoholism: Psychiatric disorders in offspring. *Journal of Studies on Alcohol*, 46(3): 199-204, 1985.

435. Metzner R: **Opening To Inner Light:** The transformation of human nature and consciousness. JP Tarcher, Inc, Los Angeles, 1986.

436. Middelton-Moz J, Dwinell L: **After The Tears:** Reclaiming The Personal Losses Of Childhood. Health Communications, Pompano Beach, FL, 1986.

437. Miller A: **The Drama of the Gifted Child.** Basic Books/Harper Colophon, NY, 1981.

438. Miller A: **For Your Own Good:** Hidden cruelty in childrearing and the roots of violence. Farrar, Straus, Giroux, NY, 1983.

439. Miller A: **Thou Shall Not Be Aware:** Society's betrayal of the child. Farrar, Straus, Giroux, NY, 1984.

440. Miller A: **Banished Knowledge:** Facing childhood injuries. Doubleday, NY, 1990.

441. Miller A: **The Untouched Key:** Tracing childhood trauma in creativity and destructiveness. Doubleday, NY, 1991.

442. Miller A: **The Enabler:** When Helping Harms The One You Love. Hunter House, Claremont, CA/Ballantine, NY, 1988.

443. Miller D, Jang M: Children Of Alcoholics: From alcoholic and non-alcoholic families. *British Journal of Addiction*, 13: 23-29, 1977.

444. Miller EE, Shearer DR: Blossoming: Growing beyond the limits of your family, a program for Adult Children of Alcoholics. (Four guided imagery tapes). Source Cassette Learning Systems, Box W, Stanford, CA 94305, (415-328-7171), 1980-85.

445. Miller M, Gorski T: **Family Recovery:** Growing Beyond Addiction, Independence Press, Missouri, 1982.

446. Miller JE, Ripper ML: **Following The Yellow Brick Road:** The Adult Child's Personal Journey Through Oz. Health Communications, Pompano Beach, FL, 1987.

447. Miller NS: The disease concept of alcoholism and drug addiction, parts 1 & 2. *Psychiatric Annals*, 21 (4 & 5), April & May 1991.

448. Miller SI, Tuchfeld BS: Adult Children of Alcoholics. *Hospital & Community Psychiatry*, 37, 235-236, 1986.

449. Millon T, Everly GS: **Personality and Its Disorders:** a biosocial learning approach. J Wiley, NY, 1985.

450. Mills M et al: What is it about depressed mothers that influences their children's functioning? In Stevenson JE (ed), **Recent Research in Developmental Psychopathology.** Pergamon Press, Oxford, 11-17, 1985.

451. Mitchell J: **The Selected Melanie Klein.** Free Press, NY, 1987.

452. Monti PM et al: Communication skills training, communication skills training with family and cognitive behavioral mood management training with alcoholics. *Journal of Studies on Alcohol*, 15(3): 263-270, 1990.

453. Moos RH, Billings AG: Children of alcoholics during the recovery process: Alcoholic and matched control families. *Addictive Behaviors*, 7, 155-163, 1982.

454. Moos RH, Billings AG: The process of recovery from alcoholism: III. Comparing functioning in families of alcoholics and matched control families. *Journal of Studies on Alcohol*, 45(2): 111-118, 1984.

455. Moos RH, Moos BS: The process of recovery from alcoholism: Comparing functioning in families of alcoholics and control families. *Journal of Studies on Alcohol*, 45: 111-118, 1984.

456. Morehouse ER: Working in the schools with children of alcoholic parents. *Health and Social Work*, 4: 145-161, 1979.

457. Mooney B: Co-dependency in the workplace: Symptoms and solutions. *Counselor*, Jul/Aug 1990.

458. Morris M: **If I Should Die Before I Wake.** JP Tarcher, Inc, Los Angeles, 1982.

459. Morrison AP: **Shame:** The Underside Of Narcissism. Analytic Press, Hillsdale, NJ, 1989.

460. Morrison C, Schuckit MS: Locus of control in young men with alcoholic relatives and controls. *Journal Clinical Psychiatry*, 44, 306-307, 1983.

461. Morrison J, Stewart MA: A family study of the hyperactive child syndrome. *Biological Psychiatry*, 3: 189-195, 1971.

462. Moss R: **Black Butterfly.** Celestial Arts Publishing Co, Berkeley, 1986.

463. Mrazek PB, Kempe CH: **Sexually Abused Children and Their Families.** Pergamon, Oxford, 1981.

464. Muldoon L: **Incest:** Confronting the Silent Crime. Minnesota Program for Victims of Sexual Assault, Saint Paul, MN, 1979.

465. Mumey J: **Loving An Alcoholic:** Help and hope for Co-dependents. Bantam Books, NY, 1988.

466. Murck ME: Co-dependence in the educational setting. *Student Assistance Journal*, 1(1): 37-40, 1988.

467. Murray JB: Psychologists and children of alcoholic parents. *Psychological Reports*, 64(3-Part 1): 859-879, 1989.

468. Naiditch B: Rekindled spirit of a child: Intervention strategies for shame with elementary age children of alcoholics. *Alcoholism Treatment Quarterly*, 4(2): 57-69, 1987.

469. Namka L: **The Doormat Syndrome.** Health Communications, Deerfield Beach, FL, 1989.

470. National Institute on Alcohol Abuse and Alcoholism (NIAAA): **Services for Children of Alcoholics.** Research Monograph, No 4, DHHS Pub No (ADM) 81-1007, Wash, DC, Supt of Docs, US Govt Print Office, 1981.

471. Neumann E: **Amor and Psyche:** The psychic development of the feminine. Princeton University Press, Bolingen Series, NY, 1971.

472. Newlin DB: Offspring of alcoholics have enhanced antagonistic placebo response. *J Stud Alc*, 46, 490-494, 1985.

473. Newton M: personal communication, Atlanta, 1980.

474. NIAAA: A Growing Concern: How to provide services for children from alcoholic families. DHHS publication (ADM) #85-1257, 1985.

475. NIAAA: Children of Alcoholics: are they different? *Alcohol Alert,* 9: PH 288, July 1990.

476. Nigolian DH: Pastoral counseling strategies for helping the co-dependent. *Dissertation Abstracts International,* 49(8): 2115-A, 1989.

477. Norwood R: **Women Who Love Too Much.** Tarcher, Los Angeles, CA, 1985.

478. Nouwen: **The Wounded Healer.** Doubleday, NY, 1973.

479. Nuckols CC: Co-dependency: Performance data can help EAPs. *Employee Assistance:* 2(8): 29-30, 35, 1990.

480. Nylander I: Children of alcoholic fathers. *Quarterly Journal of Studies on Alcohol,* 24: 170-172, 1963.

481. O'Connor G: Co-dependency in the Healer. Talk given at American Society on Addiction Medicine review course, San Francisco, 9 Nov 1990.

482. Ogden G: **Sexual Recovery:** Everywoman's Guide Through Sexual Co-dependency. Health Communications, Deerfield Beach, FL, 1990.

483. O'Gorman P: Developmental aspects of Co-dependency. *Counselor,* Mar/Apr: 14-16, 1990.

484. OJala CA: Prosocial and antisocial interactions between parents and children in alcoholic families. *Dissertation Abstracts International,* 49(8): 2160-A, 1989.

485. Operation Cork: "Soft is the Heart of a Child." (30 min movie) Washington, DC: Croc Foundation Modern Talking Picture Service, 1979.

486. Paine-Gernee K, Hunt T: Emotional Healing: a program for emotional sobriety. Warner, NY, 1990.

487. Pearce JC: **Magical Child.** Bantam Books, NY, 1980.

488. Peabody S: **Addiction to Love:** overcoming obsession and dependency in relationships. Ten Speed Press, Berkeley, CA, 1988.

489. Pennebaker JW et al: The psychophysiology of confession: Linking inhibitory and psychosomatic processes. *Journal of Personality and Social Psychology,* 52: 781-793, 1987.

490. Pennebaker JW et al: Disclosure of traumas and immune function: Health implications for psychotherapy. *Journal of Consulting and Clinical Psychology,* 56: 239-245, 1988.

491. Pennebaker JW: **Opening Up:** The healing power of confiding in others. Morrow Publishers, 1990.

492. Perrin TW: **I am an Adult Who Grew Up in an Alcoholic Family.** Continuum, NY, 1991.

493. Phillip Z: **A Skeptic's Guide to the Twelve Steps.** Hazelden, Center City, MN, 1990.

494. Piaget J: **The Language and Thought of the Child.** Harcourt, Brace, NY, 1926.

495. Picard FL: **Family Intervention Ending The Cycle Of Addiction And Co-dependency.** Beyond Words Publishing, Inc, Hillsboro, OR, 1989.

496. Pollock VE et al: J. Subjective and objective measures of response to alcohol among young men at risk for alcoholism. *J Stud. Alc*, 47, 297-304, 1986.

497. Potter-Efron R, Potter-Efron P: **Letting Go of Shame:** Understanding how shame affects your life. Hazelden, Center City, MN, 1989.

498. Potter-Efron RT: **Anger, Alcoholism and Addiction.** Norton, NY, 1992.

499. Power C, Estaugh V: The role of family formation & dissolution in shaping drinking behavior in early adulthood. *British J Addiction*, 85(4): 521-30, Apr 1990.

500. Prest LA, Storm C: The co-dependent relationships of compulsive eaters and drinkers: Drawing parallels. *The American Journal of Family Therapy*, 13: 339-274, 1988.

501. Prest LA, Storm C: Co-dependent relationships of compulsive eaters and drinkers: Drawing parallels. *American Journal of Family Therapy*, 16(4): 339-350, 1988.

502. Prewett MJ et al: Attribution of causality by children with alcoholic parents. *International Journal of the Addictions*, 16(2): 367-370, 1981.

503. Progoff I: **At a Journal Workshop:** The basic text and guide for using the intensive journal process. Dialogue House Library, NY, 1975.

504. Putnam FW: Diagnosis and Treatment of Multiple Personality Disorder. Guilford, NY, 1989.

505. Ram Dass, Gorman P: **How Can I Help?** Stories and reflections on service. AA Knopf, Inc, NY, 1985.

506. Rama S, Ajaya S & Ballantine R: **Yoga and Psychotherapy:** The evolution of consciousness. Himalayan Publishers, Honesdale, PA, 1976.

507. Raper JE, Morgan LK: Children of alcoholics. *Advances in Alcohol & Substance Abuse*, 6(4): 119-128, 1987.

508. Ratner E: **The Other Side Of The Family.** Health Communications, Deerfield Beach, FL 1990.

509. Ray V: **Striking a Balance:** How to care without caretaking. Hazelden, Center City, MN, 1989.

510. Ray V: **Communicating With Love.** Hazelden, Center City, MN, 1989.

511. Reedy B, McElfresh O: **Detachment:** Recovery for family members. Parkside Medical Services Corp, Park Ridge, Ill, 1987.

512. Reich W et al: Comparison of the home and social environments of children of alcoholic and non-alcoholic parents. *British Journal of Addiction*, 83(7): 831-839, 1988.

513. Restak RM: **The Mind.** Bantam, NY, 1988.

514. Richards TM: Alcohol education for young children of alcoholic parents. *Addictions*, 5: 18-21, 1977.

515. Richards TM: Working with children of an alcoholic mother. *Alcohol, Health & Research World*, Spring 1979.

516. Richards TM: Splitting as a defense mechanism in children of alcoholic parents. In: *Currents in Alcoholism,* Vol 7, Grune & Stratton, NY, 1980.

517. Richardson M, Richardson K, Munroe B, Munroe C: Life Experience Workshop: An intimate journey into recovery from Co-dependency. American Audio & Tape Library, Phoenix, AZ, (602-230-9858), 1990.

518. Rimmer J: The children of alcoholics: An exploratory study. *Children and Youth Services Review,* 4: 365-373, 1982.

519. Rimza ME et al: Sexual abuse: somatic and emotional reactions. *Child Abuse & Neglect,* 12: 201-8, 1988.

520. Ring K: **Heading Toward Omega:** In Search of the Meaning of the Near Death Experience. William Morrow, NY, 1985.

521. Ring K, Rosing CJ: The Omega Project: An empirical study of the NDE-prone personality. *Journal of Near Death Studies,* Vol 8, No 4, Summer 1990.

522. Ring K: **The Omega Project:** Human evolution in an ecological age. William Morrow, NY, 1992.

523. Rivers-Bulkeley NT: Co-dependence. *Insight,* 2: 16-18, 1988.

524. Robinson BE: **Working with Children of Alcoholics:** The practitioner's handbook. Lexington, MA: Lexington Books, 1989.

525. Robinson BE et al: Test-retest reliability of the Children of Alcoholics. *Test Perceptual and Motor Skills,* 70(3): 858, 1990.

526. Robinson B: **Work Addiction.** Health Communications, Deerfield Beach, FL, 1989.

527. Rodegast P, Stanton J: **Emmanuel's Book:** A Manual For Living Comfortably In The Cosmos. Bantam, NY, 1986.

528. Rodegast P, Stanton J: **Emmanuel's Book II:** The Choice for Love. Bantam, NY, 1989.

529. Rolf JE et al: Depressive affect in school-aged children of alcoholics. *British Journal of Addiction,* 83(7): 841-848, 1988.

530. Roosa MW et al: Children of alcoholics life-events schedule: A stress scale for children of alcohol-abusing parents. *Journal of Studies on Alcohol,* 49(5): 422-429, 1988.

531. Roosa MW et al: Preventive intervention for children in alcoholic families: Results of a pilot study. *Family Relations,* 38(3): 295-300, 1989.

532. Rose B: In defense of children. *Vogue,* Nov 1984.

533. Rosett H: Effects of maternal drinking on child development: An introductory review. *Annals of the New York Academy of Science,* 273: 115-117, 1976.

534. Rush F: **The Freudian Cover-up.** *Chrysalis* 1: 31-45, 1977.

535. Rush F: **The Best Kept Secret.** Prentice Hall, NY, 1980.

536. Russell DH: The incidence and prevalence of intrafamilial and extrafamilial sexual abuse of female children. *Child Abuse and Neglect,* 7, 1983.

537. Russell DH: **The Secret Trauma:** Incest in the Lives of Girls and Women. Basic Books, NY, 1986.

538. Russell M et al: Children of alcoholics: A review of the literature. Children of Alcoholics Foundation, New York, 1985.

539. Rutter M: Maternal deprivation, 1972-1978: New findings, new concepts, new approaches. *Child Development*, 50: 283-305.

540. St. Anne J: Co-dependence and the reaction syndrome. *EAP Digest*, 9(5): 37-42, 1989.

541. Salzman L: Chapter 3 — Commitment, sex, and marriage. In **Treatment of the Obsessive Personality.** Jason Aronson, NY, 1985.

542. Sameroff AJ et al: Effects of parental emotional handicap on early child development. In S. K. Thurman (Ed.), **Children of handicapped parents:** Research and clinical perspectives. Academic Press, NY, 47-68, 1985.

543. Sanders CM: **Grief — The Mourning After:** Dealing With Adult Bereavement. John Wiley & Sons, NY, 1989.

544. Sanders SR: Under the influence. *Family Therapy Networker,* Jan/Feb 1990.

545. Sanford LT: **The Silent Children,** A Parent's Guide to the Prevention of Child Sexual Abuse. Anchor Press/Doubleday, NY, 1980.

546. Sanford LT: **Strong At The Broken Places:** Overcoming The Trauma of Childhood Abuse. Prentice Hall, NY, 1990.

547. Satir V: **Conjoint Family Therapy.** Science & Behavior Books, Palo Alto, CA, 1967.

548. Satir V: **The New Peoplemaking.** Science & Behavior Books, Mt. View, CA, 1988.

549. Saulnier C: Intervention with visually impaired children of alcoholics. *Alcohol Health and Research World,* 13(2): 133-137, 1989.

550. Scarf M: **Unfinished Business.** Random House, NY, 1980.

551. Scarf M: **Intimate Partners.** Random House, NY, 1987.

552. Scavnicky-Mylant ML: Process of coping and emotional development of young adult children of alcoholics: A nursing study. *Dissertation Abstracts International,* 49(6): 2133-B, 1988.

553. Schaef AW: **Co-dependence: Misunderstood — Mistreated.** Harper/Winston, San Francisco, 1986.

554. Schaef AW: **When Society Becomes an Addict.** Harper & Row, NY, 1987.

555. Schaeffer B: **Is It Love or Is It Addiction?** Hazelden, Center City, MN, 1987.

556. Schuckit MA: Family history and half-sibling research in alcoholism. *Annals of New York Academy of Sciences,* 1977: 121-125, 1972.

557. Schuckit M, Chiles JA: Family history as a diagnostic aid in two samples of adolescents. *Journal of Nervous and Mental Disease,* 166(3): 165-176, 1978.

558. Schuckit M et al: Differences in intensity of reaction to ethanol in children of alcoholics and controls. In K. Kuriyama et al (Eds), **Biomedical and Social Aspects of Alcohol and Alcoholism.** Elsevier Science Publishers BV, Amsterdam, Netherlands, 1989.

559. Schultz L: **The Sexual Victimology of Youth.** Charles C Thomas, Springfield, IL, 1979.

560. Schwarz JC, Zuroff DC: Family structure and depression in female college students: effects of parental conflict, decision-making power, and inconsistency of love. *Journal of Abnormal Psychology,* 88: 398-404, 1979.

561. Scott EM, Moore L: Suggested alliances and the alcoholic patient: a psychotherapy focus. *Alcoholism Treatment Quarterly* 7(4): 47-56, 1990.

562. Sedney MA, Brooks B: Factors associated with a history of childhood sexual experience in a nonclinical female population. *J Am Acad Child Adolescent Psychiatry,* 23: 215-218, 1984.

563. Segal H: **Introduction to the Work of Melanie Klein.** Basic Books, NY, 1964.

564. Seilhamer RA: Patterns of consumption and parent-child relationships in families of alcoholics. *Dissertation Abstracts International,* 49(9): 4023-B, 1989.

565. Seixas JS: **Living With a Parent Who Drinks Too Much.** Greenwillow Books, NY, 1979.

566. Seixas JS: Children from alcoholic homes. In Estes N J & Heinemann M E (eds): **Alcoholism: Development, Consequences, and Interventions** (2nd ed), CV Mosby, St. Louis, 1982.

567. Seixas JS, Levitan ML: A supportive counseling group for Adult Children of Alcoholics. *Alcoholism Treatment Quarterly,* 1(4), 123-132, 1984.

568. Seixas JS, Youcha G: **Children of Alcoholism:** A survivor's manual. Harper & Row, NY, 1985.

569. Sellitto LA: Comparison of stress and coping by spouses of alcoholics and spouses of opiate addicts. *Dissertation Abstracts International,* 49(4), 1988.

570. Shapiro DH, Walsh RN: **Meditation:** Classic and Contemporary Perspectives. Aldine, NY, 1984.

571. Shengold L: Child abuse and deprivation: Soul murder. *Journal of American Psychoanalytic Association, 27:* 533-599, 1979.

572. Siegel BS: **Love, Medicine and Miracles:** Lessons Learned About Self-Healing from a Surgeon's Experience with Exceptional Patients. Harper & Row, NY, 1986.

573. Sikorsky II: **AA's Godparents:** Three early influences on AA & its foundation — Carl Jung, Emmett Fox, Jack Alexander. Compcare, Minneapolis, 1990.

574. Simons G: **Keeping Your Personal Journal.** Paulist Press, NY, 1978.

575. Simon J: Love: Addiction or road to self-realization, a second look. *Amer J Psychoanalysis, 42:* 252-262, 1982.

576. Simos, BG: **A Time to Grieve:** Loss as a Universal Human Experience. Family Services Association of America, NY, 1979.

577. Sloat DE: **Growing up Holy and Wholly:** Understanding and hope for adult children of evangelicals. Wolgemuth & Hyatt, Brentwood, TN, 1990.

578. Sloboda S: Children of alcoholics: A neglected problem. *Hospital and Community Psychiatry*, 25: 605-606, 1974.

579. Small J: **Transformers:** The therapists of the future, DeVorss & Co, Marina Del Rey, CA, 1982.

579a. Small J: **Awakening in Time:** The journey from Co-dependence to Co-creation. Bantam, NY, 1991.

580. Small J: **Becoming naturally therapeutic:** A return to the true essence of helping. Bantam Books, NY, 1989.

581. Smalley S & Coleman E: Treating intimacy dysfunctions in dyadic relationships among chemically dependent and co-dependent clients. *Journal of Chemical Dependency Treatment*, 1(1): 229-243, 1987.

582. Smart N, Hecht RD: **Sacred Texts of the World:** A universal anthology. Crossroad, NY, 1982.

583. Smith AW: **Grandchildren Of Alcoholics:** Another Generation Of Co-dependency. Health Communications, Deerfield Beach, FL, 1988. Also **Overcoming Perfectionism:** The Key To A Balanced Recovery. Health Communications, Deerfield Beach, FL, 1990.

584. Smith MR: Obedience to insanity: social collusion in the creation and maintenance of dissociative states. Presented at the Sixth International Conference on Multiple Personality and Dissociative States, Chicago, 1989.

585. Marty S: An ACA History. Personal Communication, Los Angeles, 1990.

586. Smith S et al: Parents of battered babies, a controlled study. *British Medical Journal*, 4: 388-391, 1973.

587. Snow C & Willard D:. **I'm Dying to Take Care of You:** Nurses and Co-dependence — breaking the cycles. Professional Counselor Books, Redmond, WA, 1989.

588. Solomon P: Talk on Relationships and spirituality. Richmond, VA, 1982.

589. Spann L, Fischer JL: Identifying co-dependency. *The Counselor*, 8(27), 1990.

590. Spitz RA, Wolf KM: Anaclitic depression. *The Psychoanalytic Study of the Child*, 2: 331-342, 1946.

591. Springle P: **Co-dependency:** A Christian perspective. Word Publishing, Dallas, 1990.

592. Stamas DR: Signs and symptoms of ACoA. *Counselor* 4(5), 22-23, 1986.

593. Stanton MD, Todd TC, et al: **The Family Therapy of Drug Abuse and Addiction.** Guilford Press, NY, 1982.

594. Starr RH, Wolfe DA: **The Effects of Child Abuse and Neglect:** Issues and research. Guildford, NY, 1991.

595. Steinglass P: The alcoholic family in the interaction laboratory. *Journal of Nervous and Mental Disease*, 167(7), 428-436, 1979.

596. Steinglass P: The impact of alcoholism on the family: Relationship between degree of alcoholism and psychiatric symptomatology. *Journal of Studies on Alcohol*, 42: 822-903, 1981.

597. Steinglass P: Research in family behavior related to alcoholism. *Substance Abuse*, 6, 16-26, 1985.

598. Steinglass P et al: **The Alcoholic Family.** Basic Books, New York, 1987.

599. Steinglass P et al: Observations of conjointly hospitalized "alcoholic couples" during sobriety and intoxication: Implications for theory and therapy. *Family Process*, 16, 1-16, 1977.

600. Steinhausen HC et al: Psychopathology in the offspring of alcoholic parents. *Journal of the American Academy of Child Psychiatry*, 23(4): 465-471, 1984.

601. Stevens CM: Career women and Adult Children of Alcoholics. *Dissertation Abstracts International*, 50(1): 269-A, 1989.

602. Stewart MA et al: Alcoholism and hyperactivity revisited: A preliminary report. In Galanter M (ed), **Currents in Alcoholism,** Vol V, Grune & Stratton, NY, 1979.

603. Straus SE et al: Persisting illness and fatigue in adults with evidence of Epstein-Barr virus infection. *Annals of Internal Medicine*, 102: 7-16, 1985.

604. Stuart M: **In Sickness And In Health:** The Co-dependent Marriage. Health Communications, Deerfield Beach, FL, 1988.

605. Subby R: **Lost in the Shuffle:** The Co-dependent Reality. Health Communications, Deerfield Beach, FL, 1987.

606. Subby R, Friel J, Wegsheider-Cruse S, Whitfield CL, Cappel-Sowder K et al. (Series of reprints of articles on Co-dependence) in **Co-dependency: An Emerging Issue.** Health Communications, Pompano Beach, FL, 1984.

607. Summit RC: The child sexual abuse accommodation syndrome. *Child Abuse and Neglect*, 7: 177-193, 1983.

608. Summit RC, Kryso J: Sexual abuse of children: A clinical spectrum. *American Journal of Orthopsychiatry*, 48: 237-251, 1978.

609. Svikis DS, Pickens RW: Children of alcoholics: A target for prevention efforts in: Wright C (Ed), **Alcoholism and Chemical Dependency in the Workplace.** Hanley and Belfus, Philadelphia, 1989.

610. Thompson C et al: An Outline of Psychoanalysis (revised edition). Modern Library, NY, 1955.

611. Thompson K: On the new myth of addiction. Paper presented at the Spiritual Quest, Attachment, and Addiction — The Eleventh International Transpersonal Conference, Eugene, OR, Sept 8-15, 1990.

612. Thornton EM: **Freud and Cocaine:** The Freudian fallacy. Blond & Briggs, London, 1983.

613. Thurman SK: **Children of Handicapped Parents:** Research and clinical perspectives. Academic Press, NY, 1985.

614. Tiebout HM: The act of surrender in the therapeutic process. *Quarterly Journal of Studies on Alcohol*, 1949.

615. Tony A, Dan F: **The Laundry List:** The ACoA Experience. Health Communications, Deerfield Beach, FL 1990.

615a. Travis JW, Ryan RS: Wellness Workbook, second edition. Ten Speed Press, Berkeley, 1988.

616. Treadway DC: **Before It's Too Late:** Working with substance abuse in the family. Norton, NY, 1989.

617. Triplett JL, Arneson SW: Children of alcoholic parents: A neglected issue. *The Journal of School Health,* Dec 1978.

618. Trube-Becker E: Death of children following negligence: Social aspects. *Forensic Secience,* 9: 111-115, 1977.

619. van der Kolk BA: **Psychological Trauma.** American Psychiatric Press, Washington DC, 1987.

620. van der Kolk BA: The trauma spectrum: The interaction of biological and social events in the genesis of the trauma response. *Journal of Traumatic Stress, 1:* 273-290, 1988.

621. Vannicelli M: Group psychotherapy with Adult Children of Alcoholics. In Seligman M & Marshall L A: **Group Psychotherapy:** Interventions with special populations. Grune & Stratton, NY, 1990.

622. Vaughan F, Walsh R (eds): **Beyond Ego:** Transpersonal Dimensions in Psychology. JP Tarcher, Inc, Los Angeles, 1980.

623. Volkan VD: **Linking Objects and Linking Phenomena:** A study of the forms, symptoms, metapsychology, and therapy of complicated mourning. International University Press, NY, 1981.

624. Walker E et al: Relationship of chronic pelvic pain to psychiatric diagnosis and childhood sexual abuse. *Amer J Psychiatry,* 145: 75-79, 1988.

625. Wallace J: Alcoholism from the inside out: A phenomenological analysis. In Estes and Heinemann, eds. **Alcoholism:** Development, Consequences and Interventions, Mosby, St. Louis, 1977.

626. Wamboldt FS, Wolin SJ: **Reality and myth in family life:** Changes across generations in Family Myths: Psychotherapy Implications. Haworth Press, NY, 1989.

627. Wapnick K: Christian Psychology in "A Course in Miracles." Foundation for Inner Peace, Box 635, Tiburon, CA 94920.

628. Washton A, Boundy D: **Willpower's Not Enough:** Recovering from addictions of every kind. Harper & Row, NY, 1989.

629. Watters T, Theimer W: Children of alcoholics — A critical review of some literature. *Contemporary Drug Problems,* 7(2): 195-201, 1978.

630. Wegscheider S: The Family Trap, Nurturing Networks, Crystal, MN, 1976.

631. Wegscheider S: **Another Chance:** Hope and Health for the Alcoholic Family. Science and Behavior Books, Palo Alto, CA, 1981.

632. Wegscheider-Cruse S: **Choicemaking:** For Co-dependents, Adult Children And Spirituality Seekers. Health Communications, Pompano Beach, FL, 1985.

633. Wegscheider-Cruse S: Co-dependency and dysfunctional family systems. In R. C. Engs, Ed, **Women: Alcohol and other drugs.** Kendall/Hunt Publishing Company, Dubuque, IA, 1990

634. Weil A: **Natural Health, Natural Medicine.** Houghton Mifflin, NY, 1990.

634a. Weinhold BK, Weinhold JB: **Breaking Free of the Co-dependency Trap.** Stillpoint, Walpole, NH, 1989.

635. Weir WR: Counseling youth whose parents are alcoholic: A means to an end as well as an end itself. *Journal of Alcohol Education,* 16(1): 13-19, 1970.

636. Weiss J, Weiss L: **Recovery From Co-dependency.** Health Communications, Deerfield Beach, FL, 1988.

637. Weiss J, Weiss L: Guidelines for Co-dependency recovery: Reclaiming the inner child is more than a matter of chance. *Focus,* 12(1): 18-19, 30, 1989.

638. Wellwood J: **Journey of the Heart:** Intimate relationships and the path of love. Harper & Row, San Francisco, CA, 1990.

639. Werner E: Resilient offspring of alcoholics: A longitudinal study from birth to age 18. *Journal of Studies on Alcohol,* 34-40, 1986.

640. West MO, Prinz RJ: Parental alcoholism and childhood psychopathology. *Psychological Bulletin,* 102(2): 204-218, 1987.

641. Whitfield CL: Children of alcoholics: Treatment issues. *Maryland State Medical Journal,* pp 86-91, June 1980.

642. Whitfield CL: Children of Alcoholics: Treatment issues. In Research Monograph No 4 on Services for Children of Alcoholics. Proceeding from the Symposium in Silver Spring, MD, Sept 1979 (reprinted 1981, DHHS publ ADM 81-1007).

643. Whitfield CL: Co-alcoholism: recognizing a treatable illness. *Family & Community Health,* Vol 7, (Summer) 1984.

644. Whitfield CL: Co-dependency: An Emerging Problem Among Professionals. In **Co-dependency: An Emerging Issue.** Health Communications, Deerfield Beach, FL, 1984.

645. Whitfield CL: **Healing The Child Within:** Discovery And Recovery For Adult Children Of Dysfunctional Families. Health Communications, Deerfield Beach, FL, 1987.

646. Whitfield CL: **Spirituality in Recovery** (formerly Alcoholism and Spirituality). Perrin & Treggett E. Rutherford, NJ, 1985 (800-321-7912).

647. Whitfield CL: Advances in alcoholism and chemical dependence (editorial). *American Journal of Medicine,* 85: 465, 1988.

648. Whitfield CL: Co-alcoholism, addictions and related disorders. In Lowinson JH, Ruiz P, Millman RB (eds): **Comprehensive Textbook of Substance Abuse.** Williams & Wilkins, Baltimore, 1992.

649. Whitfield CL: **Boundaries And Relationships In Recovery.** Health Communications, Deerfield Beach, FL, in process for 1992.

650. Whitfield CL: **Wisdom to Know the Difference:** Transforming Co-dependence into Healthy Relationships (working title of manuscript in process) for 1993 or 1994.

651. Whitfield CL: Stress management & spirituality during recovery: a transpersonal approach. Three part article in *Alcoholism Treatment Quarterly*, Vol 1, No 1, 1984 (an early draft of Spirituality in Recovery).

652. Whitfield CL: **A Gift To Myself: A Personal Workbook And Guide To Healing My Child Within.** Health Communications, Deerfield Beach, FL, 1990.

653. Whitfield CL: Early detection and management of chemical dependence. In Practical Clinical Management — Drug Abuse Education of the Primary Care Physician. Monograph of conference Proceedings, Oct 21 & 22, Medical Faculty of Maryland, Baltimore, 1990.

654. Whitfield CL: Series of taped talks on core issues and other topics, available from Perrin & Treggett, E Rutherford, NJ (800-321-7912); and American Audio & Tape Library, Phoenix, (602-230-9858); Conference Recording Services 800-345-2010; and Sounds True.

655. Wilber K: **No Boundary.** Shambhala, Boulder, 1978.

656. Wilber K: In the Eye of the Artist: art and the perennial philosphy. In Grey A: **Sacred Mirrors.** Inner Traditions. International, Rochester, VA, 1990.

657. Wills-Brandon C: **Learning To Say No:** Establishing Healthy Boundaries. Health Communications, Deerfield Beach, FL, 1990.

658. Wills-Brandon C: **Where Do I Draw The Line?** Health Communications, Deerfield Beach, FL, 1991.

659. Wilson C, Orford J: Children of alcoholics: Report of a preliminary study and comments on the literature. *Journal of Studies on Alcohol*, 39(1), 121-142, 1978.

660. Windle M: **Children of alcoholics:** A comprehensive bibliography. New York State Division of Alcoholism and Alcohol Abuse, Buffalo, NY, 1989.

661. Windle M, Searles JS: **Children of Alcoholics:** Critical Perspectives. Guilford, NY: 1990.

662. Winnicott DW: The capacity to be alone. *International Journal of Psychiatry*, 39: 416-440, 1958.

663. Woititz JG: A study of self-esteem in children of alcoholics. *Dissertation Abstracts International*, 37, 7554, 1977.

664. Woititz JG: **Marriage on the Rocks.** Delacorte Press, NY, 1979.

665. Woititz JG: **Adult Children Of Alcoholics.** Health Communications, Pompano Beach, FL, 1983.

666. Woititz JG: **Struggle For Intimacy.** Health Communications, Pompano Beach, FL, 1985.

667. Woititz JG, Garner A: **Lifeskills For Adult Children.** Health Communications, Deerfield Beach, FL, 1991.

668. Wolin S et al: Family rituals and the recurrence of alcoholism over generations. *American Journal of Psychiatry*, 136(4B), 589-593, 1979.

669. Wolin SJ, Bennett LA: Family rituals. *Family Process*, 23: 401-420, 1984.

670. Wolin SJ et al: Chapter 9, Assessing Family rituals in alcoholic families. In **Rituals in Families & Family Therapy.** WW Norton, NY, 1988.

671. Wolin SJ (ed): Proceedings of National Working Conference on Co-dependence and the Adult Child Syndrome (working title). To be published, 1992.

672. Wood BL: **Children of Alcoholism:** The struggle for self and intimacy in adult life, University Press, New York, 1987.

673. Woodman M: **The Pregnant Virgin:** A process of psychological transformation. Inner City Books, Toronto, 1985.

674. Woodside M: Children of alcoholic parents: Inherited and psycho-social influences. *Journal of Psychiatric Treatment Evaluation,* 5(6): 531-53, 1983.

675. Woodside M: Research on children of alcoholics: past and future. *British Journal of Addiction,* 83: 785-792, 1988.

676. Worden M: The children of alcoholics movement: Early frontiers, *The US Journal,* 8(9), 12-13, 1984.

677. Wright PH: Self-referent motivation and the intrinsic quality of friendship. *Journal of Social and Personal Relationships,* 1: 115-130, 1984.

678. Wright PH, Wright KD: Measuring Co-dependents' close relationships: A preliminary study. *Journal of Substance Abuse,* 2: 335-344, 1990.

679. Wylie MS: Around the Network: Murray Bowen. *Family Therapy Networker,* Jan/Feb 1991.

680. Wylie MS: Family therapy's neglected prophet. *Family Therapy Networker,* March/April 1991.

681. Yalom ID: **The theory and practice of group psychotherapy.** (2d ed) Basic Books, New York, 1975.

682. Yoder B: **The Recovery Resource Book.** Simon & Schuster/Fireside, NY, 1990.

683. Young E: Co-alcoholism as a disease: Implications for psychotherapy. *Journal of Psychoactive Drugs,* 19(3): 257-268, 1987.

684. Young EB: Role of incest issues in relapse. *Journal of Psychoactive Drugs,* 22(2): 249-258, 1990.

685. Zimberg et al: **Practical approaches to alcoholism psychotherapy.** 2nd ed, Plenum Press, NY, 1985.

685a. Zinner J: Working with projective identification in object relations family therapy. Talk given at Sheppard Platt Hospital, Baltimore, 10 July 1991.

686. Zukov G: **The Dancing WuLi Masters:** An overview of the new physics. William Morrow, NY, 1979.

687. Zweig P (ed): **Selected Essays of Muktananda.** Harper & Row, NY, 1976.

Critical References: Some References That Criticize Or Discuss Criticisms Of The Co-dependence And Adult Child Approach

688. Blau M: Adult children tied to the past. *American Health,* (pp 57-65), August 1990.

689. Collet L: After the anger, what then? *Family Therapy Networker,* Jan/Feb 1990.

690. Dan D: Recovery: A modern initiation rite. *Family Therapy Networker,* Sept/Oct 1990.

691. Gierymski T, Williams T: Co-dependency. *Journal of Psychoactive Drugs,* 18(1): 7-13, 1986.

692. Gomberg ESL: On terms used and abused: Concept of "Co-dependency." 3(3/4): 113-132, 1989.

693. Haaken J: A critical analysis of the Co-dependence construct. *Psychiatry,* 53: 396-406, 1990.

694. Hillman J: Dedication ceremony address. *Newsletter* Pacifica Graduate Institute, Carpenteria, CA 1:1, 1990.

695. Kaminer W: Chances are you're Co-dependent too. *NY Times Book Review,* Feb 11, 1990.

696. Katz SJ, Liv AE: **The Co-dependency Conspiracy:** How to break the recovery habit and take charge of your life. Warner, NY, 1991.

697. Kokin M, Walker I: **Women Married to Alcoholics.** Wm Morrow, NY, 1989.

698. Lawton M: Co-dependency: Too vague a diagnosis? (editorial comment). *The Addiction Letter,* 3:10:8, Oct 1987.

699. Letters to editor: *Family Therapy Networker,* Vol 14, No 3, May/June 1990 and Nov/Dec 1990.

700. Miller W: Adult cousins of alcoholics. *Psychology of Addictive Behaviors,* 1(1): 74-76, 1987.

701. Nace EP: The concept of Co-dependency, (editorial). Newsletter, American Academy of Psychiatrists in Alcoholism and Addictions. Vol III, No 1, Spring 1988.

701. Peele S: **The Diseasing of America.** New American Library, NY, 1987.

702. Peele S, Brodsky A: **The Truth About Addiction and Recovery.** Simon & Schuster, NY, 1991.

703. Rubin JB: Is transpersonal psychology dangerous? *Common Boundary,* Jan/Feb 1990.

704. Schulman G: Co-dependency: An endangered concept. *Focus on chemically dependent families,* Vol 11, No 4, (pp 22-33), Aug/Sept 1988.

705. Simon R: From the editor, (editorial on the family therapy and adult child movements). *Family Therapy Networker,* Jan/Feb 1990.

706. Special Report on Co-dependency. University of California, *Berkeley Wellness Letter.* Vol 7, 1 Oct 1990.

707. Special Report from Health Communications: *Co-dependency* — An Evolution In Consciousness. Health Communications, Deerfield Beach, FL, 1990.

708. Tavris C: Co-dependency: A guilt trip for women. *Denver Post,* 11 March 1990.

709. Tavris C: The Politics of Co-dependency. *Family Therapy Networker,* Jan/Feb 1990.

710. Travis JW: From Co-dependence to comm-unity: bridging the treatment model to the wellness model. In Travis JW & Callander MG (eds): *Wellness for Helping Professionals.* Wellness Associates Publications, Mill Valley, CA, 1990.

711. Treadway D: Co-dependency: Disease, metaphor, or fad? *Family Therapy Networker,* Jan/Feb 1990.

712. Walters M: The Co-dependent cinderella who loves too much... fights back. *Family Therapy Networker,* July/August 1990.

713. Weiss JB, Weiss L: Co-dependency model: criticized and defended. *Empowerment Systems Newsletter,* Vol 5, No 3, July 1990.

714. Weiss JB, Weiss L: Calling Co-dependency a disease can allow dealing effectively with it. *Denver Post,* 24 March 1990.

715. Williams KF, Robbins SB: New study casts doubt on "roles" of Adult Children of Alcoholics. *The Addiction Letter,* 3:10:8, Oct 1987.

References on Paradigms

716. Assagioli R: **Psychosynthesis,** a Manual of principles and techniques. Viking Press, NY, 1971.

717. Baker C: About wounded healers. In Travis JW & Callander MG (eds): *Wellness for Helping Professionals,* Wellness Associates Publications, Mill Valley, CA, 1990.

718. Briggs J, Peat D: **The Looking Glass Universe.** Comerstone Library, NY, 1984.

719. Buss AR: **A Dialectical Psychology.** Irvington, NY, 1979.

720. Capra F: **The Turning Point.** Bantam Books, NY, 1987.

721. Casti JL: **Paradigms Lost:** Images of man in the mirror of science. William Morrow, NY, 1989.

722. Chopra D: **Quantum Healing.** Bantam Books, NY, 1989.

723. Dossey L: **Space, Time and Medicine.** Shambhala Publications, Boulder, 1982.

724. Ferguson M: **The Aquarian Conspiracy:** Personal and social transformation in the 1980s. St Martins, NY, 1980.

725. Grof S: **Beyond the Brain:** Birth, death and transcendence in psychotherapy. State Univ NY Press, Albany, 1985.

726. Grof S, Grof C: **Spiritual Emergency:** When personal transformation becomes a crisis. Tarcher, LA, 1989.

727. Grof S: **The Adventure of Self-Discovery.** State Univ NY Press, Albany, 1987.

728. Hampten-Turner C: **Maps of the Mind:** Charts and concepts of the mind and its labyrinths. MacMillan, NY, 1981.

729. Harman W: **Toward an extended science.** Institute of Noetic Sciences, Sauslito, CA, 1985.

730. Harman W, Hormann J: **Creative Work:** The role of business in a transforming society. Knowledge Systems, Indianapolis, 1990.

731. Hayakawa, Samuel I, et al: **Language In Thought & Action.** 4th ed. Harcourt Brace, NY, 1989.

732. Korzybski A: **Science and Sanity.** Country Life Press, Garden City, NY, 1948.

733. Kuhn TS: **The Structure of Scientific Revolutions.** 2nd Ed, University Chicago Press, 1970.

734. Kung H, Tracy D (eds): **Paradigm Change in Theology.** Crossroad, NY, 1989.

735. Lifton RJ: **The Life of the Self:** Toward a new psychology. Basic Books/ Harper Colaphon, NY, 1983.

•736. Masson JM: **Final Analysis:** The making and unmaking of a psychoanalyst. Addison-Wesley, NY, 1990 (see Masson's others in general references).

737. Perry JW: **The Far Side of Madness.** Prentice-Hall, Englewood Cliffs, NJ, 1974.

738. Perry JW: **Roots of Renewal in Myth and Madness.** Jossey-Bass, San Francisco, 1976.

739. Regis E: **Who Got Einstein's Office?** Addison-Wesley, Reading, MA, 1987.

740. Sahtouris E: Language and worldview. Noetic Sciences Review No 15, Summer 1990.

741. Serdahely WJ: Thomas Kuhn revisited: near-death studies and paradigm shifts. *Journal of Near-Death Studies,* 9(1): 5-10 Fall 1990.

742. Travis JW, Callander MG: **Wellness for Helping Professionals:** Creating compassionate cultures. Wellness Associates Publications, Box 5433, Mill Valley, CA 94942, 1990.

743. White J: **The Meeting of Science and Spirit.** Paragon House, NY, 1990.

744. Whitfield CL: Toward a New Paradigm in the Helping Professions. Talk given at a Regional Conference, Resource Applications, Baltimore, March 1989 and at 3rd National Conference on Co-dependency, Scottsdale, AZ, US Journal Training, September 1991.

745. Wilber K: **Eye to Eye: The quest for the new paradigm.** Anchor/Doubleday, NY, 1983.

746. Wilber K: **The Holographic Paradigm and Other Paradoxes:** Exploring the leading edge of science. Shambhala, Boulder, 1982.

747. Wilber K (ed): **Quantum Questions:** Mystical writings of the world's great physicists. Shambhala New Science Library, Boston, 1985.

Magazines and Newsletters

Brain/Mind Bulletin
Box 4211
Los Angeles, CA 90042

Changes (for Adult Children), and *Focus:* Educating Professionals in Family Recovery
Health Communications
3201 S.W. 15th Street
Deerfield Bch., FL 33442-8190
1-800-851-9100

Common Boundary
7005 Florida Street
Chevy Chase, MD 20815

COA Review
Thomas W. Perrin, Inc.
P.O. Box 423
Rutherford, NJ 07070
1-800-321-7912

Creation Magazine
(spirituality and expanded Catholicism)
Box 19216
Oakland, CA 94619

Man! A Journal of the Austin Men's Center
1611 W. Sixth Street
Austin, TX 78703
(512) 477-9595

Families in Recovery:
A Parenting Magazine
3232 San Mateo N.E.,
Suite 200
Albuquerque, NM 87110

Family Therapy Networker
8528 Bradsford Road
Silver Spring, MD 20901

Beyond Survival Magazine
1278 Glenneyre Street #3
Laguna Beach, CA 92651

Gnosis Magazine
P.O. Box 14217
San Francisco, CA 94114

Many Voices
(bi-monthly self-help for persons with multiple personalities or dissociation)
P.O. Box 2639
Cincinnati, OH 45201-2639

Medical Self-Care
Box 1000
Point Reyes, CA 94956

MPD Reaching Out
A Newsletter about Multiple Personality Disorder
c/o Public Relations Dept.
Royal Ottawa Hospital
1145 Carling Avenue
Ottawa, Ontario
Canada K12 7K4

New Realities: Oneness of self, mind & body, and revision (both cover new paradigm related material)
4000 Albemarle Street N.W.
Washington, DC 20077-5010

Whole Earth Review
27 Gate 5 Road
Sausalito, CA 94965

Yoga Journal
(new paradigm from various healing perspectives)
Box 6076
Syracuse, NY 13217

Resources for Further Information

ACoA Intergroup of
Greater New York
P.O. Box 363
Murray Hill Station
New York, NY 10016-0363
(212) 582-0840

Academy for Guided Imagery
Box 2070
Mill Valley, CA 94942
(415) 726-2070/289-9324

Adult Children of Alcoholics
(ACoA)
2225 Sepulveda Blvd., #200
Torrance, CA 90505
(213) 534-1815

Adult Children of Alcoholics
Central Service Board
P.O. Box 35623
Los Angeles, CA 90035
(213) 464-4423

Adults Molested as
Children United
P.O. Box 952
San Jose, CA 95108
(408) 453-7616
crisis line (408) 453-0727

Al-Anon Family Service Group
Headquarters, plus Alateen
P.O. Box 862
Midtown Station
New York, NY 10018-0862
(212) 302-7240

Alcoholics Anonymous
World Services, Inc.
768 Park Avenue, South
New York, NY 10016
(212) 686-1100

Al-Anon Family Groups
P.O. Box 862
Midtown Station
New York, NY 10018-0862
(212) 302-7240

American Association for
Marriage and Family Therapy
1717 K Street, N.W.
Washington, DC 20006
(202) 429-1825

American Holistic Medical
Association
2002 Eastlake Ave. E.
Seattle, WA 98102
(206) 322-6842

American Professional
Society on the Abuse of
Children
332 South Michigan Ave.,
Suite 1600
Chicago, IL 60604
(312) 554-0166

American Anorexia/Bulimia
Association, Inc.
133 Cedar Lane
Teaneck, NJ 07666
(201) 836-1800

Anorexics/Bulimia
Anonymous (ABA)
P.O. Box 112214
San Diego, CA 92111
(619) 273-3108

American Society of Addiction
Medicine (ASAM)
12 West 21st Street
New York, NY 10010
(212) 206-6770

Anorexia Nervosa and Related
Eating Disorder (ANRED)
P.O. Box 5102
Eugene, OR 97405
(503) 344-1144

Association for Humanistic
Psychology
1772 Vallejo, Street #3
San Francisco, CA 94123
(415) 346-7929

Association for Transpersonal
Psychology
345 California Ave., Suite 1
Palo Alto, CA 94306

Batterers Anonymous (BA)
BA Press
1269 N.E. Street
San Bernardino, CA 92405
(714) 884-6809

California Consortium of
Child Abuse Councils
1401 Third Street, Suite 13
Sacramento, CA 95814
(916) 448-9135

Chemically Dependent
Anonymous
P.O. Box 4425
Annapolis, MD 21403

Children of Alcoholics
Foundation (CAF)
200 Park Avenue, 31st Floor
New York, NY 10166
(212) 351-2680

Co-Anon (for families &
friends of cocaine addicts)
P.O. Box 64742-66
Los Angeles, CA 90064
(213) 859-2206

Cocaine Anonymous
3740 Overland Avenue
Suite G
Los Angeles, CA 90034
800-347-8998

Co-Counseling
Rational Island Publishers
Box 2081 Main Office Station
Seattle, WA 98111

Co-Dependents Anonymous
P.O. Box 33577
Phoenix, AZ 85067-3577
(602) 277-7991

Co-dependents of Sex Addicts
Minnesota CoSA
P.O. Box 14537
Minneapolis, MN 55414
(612) 537-6904

C. Henry Kempe National
Center for the Prevention and
Treatment of Child Abuse
and Neglect
1205 Oneida Street
Denver, CO 80220
(303) 321-3963

A Course in Miracles
(Information & books):
N.W. Center for ACIM
Box 1362
Hanalei, HI 96714

Foundation for Inner Peace
Box 635
Tiburon, CA 94920

Debtors Anonymous
General Service Board
P.O. Box 20322
New York, NY 10025-9992
(212) 969-0710

Drugs Anonymous
P.O. Box 473
Ansonia Station
New York, NY 10023
(212) 874-0700

Elmwood Institute
(new paradigm from a
non-clinical perspective)
Box 5805
Berkeley, CA 94705
(415) 845-4595

Emotions Anonymous
International Services
P.O. Box 4245
St. Paul, MN 55104
(612) 647-9712

Families Anonymous, Inc.
P.O. Box 528
Van Nuys, CA 91408
(818) 989-7841

Families in Action
3845 North Druid Hills Road
Suite 300
Decatur, GA 30033

Food Addicts Anonymous
P.O. Box 057394
West Palm Beach, FL
33405-7394

Fundamentalists Anonymous
P.O. Box 20304
Greeley Square Station
New York, NY 10001
(212) 696-0420

Gam-Anon International
Service Office, Inc.
P.O. Box 157
Whitestone, NY 11357
(718) 352-1671

Gamblers Anonymous (GA)
National Service Office
P.O. Box 17173
Los Angeles, CA 90017
(213) 386-8789

Incest Recovery Association
6200 N. Central Expressway
Suite 209
Dallas, TX 75206
(214) 373-6607

Incest Survivors Anonymous (ISA)
World Service Office
P.O. Box 5613
Long Beach, CA 90805
(213) 422-1632

Incest Survivor Information Exchange
P.O. Box 3399
New Haven, CT 06515
(203) 389-5166

Incest Survivors Resource Network, International, Inc.
P.O. Box 911
Hicksville, NY 11802
(516) 935-3031

Institute of Noetic Sciences
475 Gate 5 Road S-300
Sausalito, CA 94965
(415) 331-5650

Institute on Black Chemical Abuse (IBCA)
2614 Nicollet Avenue South
Minneapolis, MN 55408
(612) 871-7878

Marijuana Anonymous
1527 North Washington Ave.
Scranton, PA 18509

Nar-Anon (Family Groups)
P.O. Box 2562
Palos Verdes, CA 90274
(213) 547-5800

Narcotics Anonymous (NA)
World Services Office
16155 Wyandotte Street
Van Nuys, CA 91406
(818) 780-3951

National Asian Pacific Families Against Substance Abuse (NAPFASA)
6303 Friendship Court
Bethesda, MD 20817
(301) 530-0945

National Association of Anorexia Nervosa and Associated Disorders (ANAD)
P.O. Box 7
Highland Park, IL 60611
(708) 831-3438

National Association of Adult Children of Dysfunctional Families
Box 463
Fond du Lac, WI 54935

National Association of Lesbian and Gay Alcoholism Professionals (NALGAP)
204 West 20th Street
New York, NY 10011
(212) 713-5074

National Association for
Children of Alcoholics
31582 Coast Highway, No. 201
South Laguna, CA 92677
(714) 499-3889

National Black Alcoholism
Council (NBAC)
417 South Dearborn Street,
Suite 1000
Chicago, IL 60605
(312) 663-5780

National Child Rights Alliance
P.O. Box 422
Ellenville, NY 12428
(914) 647-3670

National Child Abuse Hotline
P.O. Box 630
Hollywood, CA 90028
(800) 422-4453

National Clearinghouse for
Alcohol and Drug Information
P.O. Box 2345
Rockville, MD 20852

National Clearinghouse for
Drug Information
P.O. Box 416
Kensington, MD 20895

National Coalition Against
Domestic Violence
1500 Massachusetts Ave., N.W.,
Suite 35
Washington, DC 20005
(202) 638-6388

National Coalition of Hispanic
Health and Human Services
Organization
1030 15th Street N.W., Street
1053
Washington, DC 20005
(202) 371-2100

National Committee for
Prevention of Child Abuse
332 South Michigan Avenue,
Suite 950
Chicago, IL 60604
(312) 663-3520

National Council on
Alcoholism
12 West 21st Street, 8th Floor
New York, NY 10010
(212) 206-6770

National Council on Child
Abuse and Family Violence
1050 Connecticut Ave., N.W.,
Suite 300
Washington, DC 20036
(202) 429-6695 or
1-800-222-2000

National Council on
Co-dependence
P.O. Box 40095
Phoenix, AZ 85067-0095
(602) 937-4840

National Council on
Compulsive Gambling, Inc.
445 West 59th Street
New York, NY 10019
(212) 765-3833

National Council for
Self-Esteem
Box 277877
Sacramento, CA 95827-7877

National Hispanic Family
Against Drug Abuse
1511 K Street, Suite 1029
Washington, DC 20005
(202) 393-5136

National Organization for
Victim Assistance
1757 Park Road, N.W.
Washington, DC 20010
(202) 232-6682

National Resource Center
on Child Sexual Abuse
11141 Georgia Ave., Suite 310
Wheaton, MD 20902
(301) 949-5000;
(800) KIDS-006

Native American Association
for Children of Alcoholics
P.O. Box 18736
Seattle, WA 98118

National Center on
Child Abuse and Neglect
U.S. Dept. of Health and
Human Services
P.O. Box 1182
Washington, DC 20013
(202) 245-2840

National Chronic Fatigue
Syndrome Association
3521 Broadway, Suite 222
Kansas City, MO 64111
(816) 931-4777

National Coalition Against
Sexual Assault
8787 State Street
East St. Louis, IL 62203
(618) 398-7764

National Self-Help
Clearinghouse
33 W. 42nd Street, Room 1227
New York, NY 10036
(212) 642-2944

National Wellness Institute
(& Association)
South Hall
1319 Fremont Street
Stevens PT, WI 54481

Network Against Psychiatric
Assault (NAPA)
2054 University Avenue,
Room 405
Berkeley, CA 94704

Obsessive Compulsive
Anonymous
P.O. Box 215
New Hyde Park, NY 11040
(516) 741-4901

O-Anon (for families & friends
of compulsive overeaters)
P.O. Box 4350
San Pedro, CA 90731

Overeaters Anonymous
4025 Spencer Street, Suite 203
Torrance, CA 90503
(213) 542-8363

Parents Anonymous
22330 Hawthorne
Torrance, CA 90505